Arabella

A Civil War Romance
Historic Fiction

By Durwood White

ARABELLA

Prologue

Charleston, South Carolina
1855

A rabella Rhett was not the most attractive young woman in Charleston, yet even the older men she knew were trapped by her cunning charm. Men had flattered her, but she told herself she'd choose the man that she wanted—if there was such a creature. She was extremely stunning when robed in the traditional southern hoop dress with all the crinolines and muslin, and she had an enviable waistline. Her eyes were pale blue, the alluring type with natural long lashes that curled at the ends, and shone a mystical radiance in the morning southern light. She had a pixy nose slightly upturned. She was blessed with olive skin that glowed with the mellow patina of bronze inherited from her mother's Spanish/French progenies.

Her slim frame stood five feet seven inches, an inch, or two taller than most other southern women. She wore flat heels so that the shorter boys could dance with her; the poor little things had no dates. Her chestnut hair was bundled on her head by her mother but she never liked it that way, and let it fall around her shoulders. Not satisfied with the length, she cut it shorter with her mother's sewing scissors.

Her mother, a descendant from a prominent family of Charleston, who married into the Rhett family, insisted that she let her hair grow longer; after all, she was a young woman of the South. Arabella's descendants were an aristocratic class; her grandfather was a judge of the superior court of South Carolina, now deceased. Her uncle was a lawyer who still practiced in the Washington capital city.

As Arabella matured, her mother worried incessantly that she'd marry some unknown bloke from the wrong side of the tracks. Arabella had a mind of her own, and cared nothing about her heritage, yet she had no idea what she wanted to be, but she'd find out on her own. She had thought a great deal about her future, was it here on this plantation, or in Nashville or Atlanta, or maybe Memphis, or Chattanooga? Where? When? And who was that man she'd dreamed of so many nights alone in her featherbed. She often lay with her arms clasped behind her neck staring at the chandelier sparkling in a shaft of moonlight across her legs.

The day her father died, the day he was buried beside her mother, the same day she inherited the plantation, and her uncle in Washington had sold most of the land that kept her in funds for the plantation. She retained Hattie, her maid and Danny Boy, the supervisor of the plantation.

Hattie was the daughter of her mother's African maid who was born and raised on the plantation. She had nursed Arabella from infancy and there was a congenial attachment between them from her youth. Hattie was energetic, impulsive, and strong-minded with a few finer traits; stubbornly trustworthy and faithful to Arabella. Hattie's daily attendance was the source of Arabella's independent attitude. She was a vital part of the Rhett family, and had learned from her mother in her childhood the lesson of implicit obedience. Hattie was eternally devoted to Arabella.

Danny Boy was an ornery ole Irishman, with gleaming red hair, a full red beard, a mustache that twirled slightly upward, and sky-blue eyes that demanded attention when one conversed with him. He had muscles to spare, and he could out-drink any farm boy in Mr. Perkin's tavern. He said his ancestors came over on the Mayflower, but it couldn't be proven. Arabella's father had hired him from a family in North Carolina—Raleigh, she thought. She was only age ten, when she cut her finger, and Danny Boy bandaged it with his handkerchief. As she remembered, that was the beginning of his medical treatment; splinters, bee stings, falls, and even the whooping cough. Arabella remembered he'd taken her into Charleston to the local doctor when she had the whooping cough at age twelve. Throughout the years Danny Boy had transformed the plantation into a profitable business. There were about a hundred prime acres left, most of it in cotton, and she expected him to make it profitable.

Arabella sat on a window seat, her head propped on bended knee, hoping she'd enjoy the colors of fall before they drifted into colder days. The lava-red leaves clung to its drying branches like an omen of cool weather ahead. The autumn clouds sailed like heavenly hoods across a misty sky, reminding her of slurping blackberries under a crescent moon. The nights were noticeable arriving earlier and the temperature was inconveniently cooling. The falling leaves of red and gold now blanketed the earth following a warmer than usual summer, paving the way for new growth in the coming spring. Autumn was the languid season in her teenage years. Oh how she missed the spring, the buds of yellow jonquils peeping out of the moist earth, energized by the plentiful rains. Only in these idle moments had she considered her future. She hated the loneliness and knew the exact hour the excitement had gone out of her life. She'd known it each morning she rolled out of bed—the day her father died. She had seen little of him in her teen years while he was away in Washington discussing the plantation with his brother, Uncle Rhett.

    She adored her father.

Finally, she went out on the porch with a shawl draped over her sloping shoulders, cautious of the cool breeze of September. She sat in the swing where she had often relaxed through her teenage years. How she had missed the sweet fragrance of magnolia blossoms that once drifted into her nostrils last spring. It was in the winter that her father died. She always remembered his death when winter arrived. Now that she was alone on the plantation, what was she to do without her father there to guide her?

Autumn grew alien. It was a portal to a time of dread, when winter's suffocating skies throttled the land. At its most glorious moment, autumn was indeed spectacular, the world ablaze in its fiery cloak of colors. But then the dying embers faded into memories. Oh the memories of her father. The wishful thought lingered for only a blissful moment.

She closed her eyes as tears soaked the eyelashes like dewdrops. The daydream vanished into the lifeless smell of winter invading the air. But the whispers of her remembrance called out to the delicate clouds drifting in the heavens. Oh, if only father would come before winter. The reverie of years gone by would not release her mind.

She recalled how her father had trained his only child as a boy living by his side on the plantation. Contrastingly, her mother thought more of her as a lady dressed in a hoop skirt, and carefully impressed her with the ideals of marriage. Arabella turned out somewhere between the two ideals. And now she was alone. Hattie was her only link to the past, yet she yearned for the future. Danny Boy was the only man around, an older man, nothing that marriage might improve. She wanted someone of her own age, perhaps a bit older—what did she care. Finally she admitted to herself that she wanted a beau; might even need a lover; the inhibitions of culture, her mind screamed. She was no lady; more of a tomboy, she thought, yet she wasn't sure. Certainly she was all action now looking to the future. Suddenly the dream of finding that one man she'd often dreamed of entered her lively mind.

The dream strengthened her resolve.

She gripped both chains of the swing, and hauled her maturing body in a swinging loop of exhilarating excitement. She felt that she could fly! The world awaited Arabella. She was ready—was the world? But unknown to Arabella, her world was destined for change, and those who would not adapt where trapped in the jaws of secession.

Winds of Secession
1860

The South went about its agrarian duties, women pounding rice with a handheld pedestal in a hand-hewn rock basin, cultivating cotton in the heat of the day, and planting sweet potatoes in the cool of the morning. The sandy, loamy soil of the South was the secret of the nation's agriculture. Cotton was the king money crop planted in the early spring, but tobacco was a favorite crop—smoking was a major vice, second only to whiskey and rum.

Slavery was not limited to the South; for the northern states used slave labor in their factories, too. In fact, slavery emanated out of Boston. But still slavery was a gnawing nemesis, as violent speech exchanged between opposing legislators declaring that the North was not buying the South's goods made with cheaper labor. Land owners in the north who had relatives in the south often lost their land to devious politicians in a growing bureaucracy in Washington. The arrogance and jaundice of the North against the South most assuredly had played a part in the secession fever festering in the Southern state courthouses.

The election of Lincoln was the lynchpin of secession.

News of Abraham Lincoln's election reached Savannah, Georgia and started a chain reaction that led to a vote for secession from the Union. A meeting at the town hall was hastily called. Without any prodding, in a matter of minutes, not hours, bonfires blazed, rockets resounded, and a flag of the first Revolution flew at a secession rally in Johnson Square.

This moment had been brewing for ten years. By 1850 the new nation had changed dramatically. New industry and invention were fuelling a booming economy. Political power grew exponentially as the population increased. The so-called Free States in the north had a population of 13.5 million. The South had 6 million whites and 3.2 million slaves. Lincoln's election promised a change in historical status that had existed before the founding of the Constitution. Slavery had been strongly debated before it was finally approved unanimously by the Constitutional Congress, and now the avoided question would be decided by war. The South was strictly in its constitutional right to secede from a nation that was divided on the very principle of a government that was too bureaucratic. Morality and politics was insoluble, destined to boil over into insurrection.

The following January 1861, Citadel cadets fired the shots "heard around the world" when they opened fire on the Union ship *Star of the West* as it entered Charleston's harbor. She was sent by the Federal government with relief supplies for the garrison of Fort Sumter. South Carolina had declared the first ever secession from the Union. The dye was cast on the waters of the harbor entering Charleston at Fort Sumter on April 12, 1861.

**Charleston
April, 1861**

Chapter 1

Robert Bruce Taylor, a young history major, had sold the family farm in Fredericksburg, Virginia nestled between Richmond and Washington. Bruce inherited it from his deceased grandfather and had moved to Charleston in the spring of 1861. The northern cities were getting too cramped and noisy. He'd heard so much about the South from his grandfather who owned a few acres in northern Alabama where he grew up. Bruce had harbored the idea of pleasant living, warm seasons, and fascinating places in his youth. And his studies of the South had finally lured him to that enchanting land below the Mason-Dixon Line.

    He took a position as night cook in a tavern near Charleston Harbor. Bruce didn't like war because his great grandfather was killed in the Revolutionary War. It was from those nights around a potbelly stove that his aging grandfather had told such marvelous stories of Washington, Madison, Franklin, Jefferson, and Lafayette, stories that his father had recounted to him over and over until he could repeat them by rote. These precious stories stuck with Bruce through his impressionable years.

ARABELLA

In his mid-twenties Bruce stood about six feet two inches on a lean, muscular frame. He was born in the backcountry hills in 1835, an orphan of three, was raised by his kinfolk. Farm life gave him very little learning as teachers were very sparse, although he had learned to read and write in the only schoolhouse in the county. More fortunate than most, he had received six-months of education; his handwriting was atrocious, and he blamed it on the writing surface of his slate.

Mr. Clyde Perkins, Bruce's supervisor was a fine Christian man who hired him when he came in to his tavern for a drink, and they discussed his situation, fresh from Virginia, no job. Bruce didn't really need the money that he'd received from the sale of the farm. He'd hidden the gold coins from the sale in a secret place that only he knew its location. He was frugal, intelligent, and honest, characteristics inbred by his father before he died at an early age from typhoid. His mother had died of a grieving heart shortly after her husband passed. Bruce decided he'd work for wages and saveed the farm money for a proverbial rainy day. Unknown to him, that day was on the horizon, according to the political pundits across the new nation. He walked to the tavern door as he said his goodbyes. His head was still turned in conversation as he strolled out the door. A sudden shadow danced by his face. He ventured a curious gaze at a beautiful woman riding past in a carriage. For some reason her image stuck in his mind.

Arabella Rhett was in town for purchasing supplies, and saw a handsome man as he left the tavern, and walked over to the merchandise shop. She knew everyone in Charleston, and had never seen him before. The image immediately harbored in her memory as she stared at his tall, lanky frame. "That's him, that's the one, the man from my dreams," she quietly whispered!

By the time she reached the shop, this interesting man had left by a side door. The proprietor of the shop said he'd just arrived from Fredericksburg, but knew nothing much about him. He was tall, dark, and handsome, and she deeply desired an introduction. She sprang into her carriage, and drove back to the estate, all the while devising a plan in her active mind to meet this striking man.

Arabella awoke early the next morning, and called Hattie into her bedroom. She desperately needed help to get her body into that darn hoop skirt. How anyone could breathe in the blasted thing was a mystery to her, a grueling thought that taxed her nerves. She was determined to get dressed in her most captivating outfit and go into Charleston to introduce herself to that good looking man she'd discovered yesterday.

Hattie positioned the whalebone staves of the corset around Arabella's chest poking the sharp ends in her armpits.

Arabella screamed, tightening her torso muscles. "Careful Hattie, I won't be able to put my arms around that man."

Hattie raised an eyebrow; it was only the second time that she'd squeezed Arabella into this monstrosity. The first being the evening her father took her to a dance at a meeting of the Cotton Association celebration.

"Lord, Miss Bella, dis thing iz frum de devil hisselfl" she gasped.

Dauntingly Hattie began the torturous process of lacing the umpteen numbers of eyelets one-by-one, crisscrossing each string. She tightened the string with every fourth eyelet as Arabella clung to her bedpost. Hattie's strength waned, her tongue pushed between her teeth adding no strength, which unnerved her resolve. Quickly she stepped in a chair reasoning the extra height would provide her leverage. She placed her knee in Arabella's back, huffing and puffing like a blowfish wrestling with the strings.

"Miss Bella, I ain't gots dah strength no mo. Dis darn corset don gots dah best uh me."

Arabella disregarded her comment, and sucked in all the air her lungs would hold. "Now, Hattie tie it off—quickly!" she panted.

Hattie's eyes brightened. "Yesum, Iz done it—hallelujah!"

After an hour of grueling agony, Hattie finally wiped the perspiration from her face with her apron. Arabella's hoop skirt was finally ready for an adventurous outing, yet Hattie was glad the exhausting task was over once more. Her mind flashed back to a dance when the child was sixteen.

Hattie wagged her head, thinking. *"That girl had buter git hur man fairly soon, cause Iz gittn' too old to dress dah pretty thing. Bless hur heart,"* she whispered to herself.

Arabella stood staring into a mirror all corseted up in a deep blue velvet dress, a webbed shawl over her shoulders, a French style hat on her head, and hair the length that she like it. She applied a little rouge on each cheek and a tad on her lips.

"Oh well," she whispered, "it will just have to do."

Danny Boy had her carriage ready and parked at the door. Arabella told him to watch for her return by noon, or come after her. He'd never seen Arabella so driven or so adamant. He wasn't sure about this guy, nor was he quite sure about her motives. He'd wait and watch as he'd promised the old Master.

Arabella drove her carriage into town and saw her "target" walking into Perkin's tavern. She parked the carriage across the street about ten yards up from the tavern door. Taking a deep breath she spit on her fingers and wiped her eyebrows, slid her tongue over her red-rouge lips, exhaled and straightened the hoop dress with all its crinolines. She strutted down the boardwalk toward the tavern twirling a parasol over her shoulder. She peeped into the window; she couldn't go in but decided to bump into when he walked out. She waited her turn, and timed her move just when the handsome man came out of the door.

They collided!

Arabella was knocked off the wooden sidewalk into a mud puddle.

She sat disconcerted, mud on her lace gloves and her face; her hoops sprung upward exposing her underclothes of muddy muslin. The mortified gentleman took her dainty hand, and pulled her out of the murky mess. She slipped, and he fell into the puddle with Arabella collapsed on top of him, her mud-smeared face six inches from his handsome, soiled countenance.

The stare of destiny had arrived.

"I'm so sorry," he pleaded.

Arabella had the best record of any girl in Charleston of crying at will; she couldn't have planned it any better, she thought. Forthright she began to cry; real tears formed in the corners of her pale blue eyes, and cascaded down her muddy cheeks.

The gentleman draped his coat over her shoulders. "Please allow me to take you home," he desperately requested.

She faced him, her face a mask of mud. "Well, if you insist," she feigned, "my carriage is right over yonder," she sniffed, mud dripping off her long fingernail.

"Why of course . . . I didn't get your name . . . ah"

"Arabella, Arabella Rhett," she sniffed, wiping her nose with a muddy knuckle.

"What a nice name," he stammered. "Excuse my manners, ah—Bruce, Robert Bruce Taylor."

As they rode along, his horse tied to the back of her carriage, Arabella asked Bruce a few probing, yet devious questions. "Do you have a place to stay?"

He gently snapped the whip over the horse's backside. "Why yes, I've rented a house near the harbor."

She paused momentarily. "Why don't you stay a while at my plantation, Hattie can make supper—it will give us time to clean up."

He focused on how cute she was all muddied up, her alluring attraction and witty charm. His inhibitions were strangled. "That's very kind. I haven't had a home cooked meal in weeks," blurted out of his mouth, his agreeing smile reacting to her fascinating appeal.

She returned his smile, her plan advancing. "Then it's all settled," she pleasantly replied.

Bruce finally pulled the carriage into the large open gate of the plantation, the name chiseled in a wooden sign over the entrance: **Rhett Plantation.** They drove up to the frame structure house, built in the early 1800's by Arabella's father and uncle. She knew nothing about the building of the house, but she was born there and knew all the rooms and hiding places. It was a variation of the plantation type with a rectangular plan and two stories. The gable roof had chimneys on each end. There was also a gable roof unit extended from rear, built especially for Danny Boy's quarters when Arabella was about ten. The exterior was covered in weatherboards cut from the trees on the plantation. The inside of the house was an asymmetrical two-over-two plantation style, with a winding staircase to an open balcony that led to the bedrooms with spacious twelve-foot ceilings. The inside finishing consisted of pine floors,

ARABELLA

wide-board wainscoting, plaster, and cedar beams taken from the swamps.

Danny Boy curiously rode his mare out and met Arabella and a young man. "Welcome home, Miss Arabella," he said as his eyes focused on her muddy outfit, and the strange man driving her carriage.

Arabella smiled with a wink as the dried mud on her face cracked like a map of Carolina dirt roads. "Thank you, Danny Boy, this is Bruce Taylor, he'll be staying for supper."

He saw Arabella's wink and knew the situation as he cast his surveying eyes on the young man, his clothes as muddy as hers. "Good to meet you Mr. Taylor," he nodded. "If you'll drive the rig around to the pump house, you can clean up a bit. I'll put your horse in the barn with a feedbag."

Hattie served roast beef, boiled new potatoes, and turnip greens cooked down in fatback, with a dessert of peach cobbler. Arabella came down the stairway dressed in a cotton print dress with flat shoes. Bruce stood by the stairs dressed in her father's clothes, which Danny Boy had provided. He escorted her toward the dining room, her arm hooked in his bent elbow. As they entered the large room, he saw a long table made of spruce, and a sideboard of mahogany. He pulled out a Chippendale chair and seated her, as he observed that she was a mature woman. He fondly remembered the mud pit and how delightful she was when they first met rather inelegantly just earlier that morning. Her beauty was beyond any northern woman he knew.

"You look stunning, my dear."

She smiled. The word "dear" tickled her ego, the plan was working, she thought.

"Thank you, Bruce," she grinned, falsely embarrassed.

They finished the meal without much conversation, Bruce wasn't the talkative type, she guessed. She coaxed him out on the front porch and they sat in the swing. The fragrance of blooming mimosa was intoxicating, but Bruce was as abstemious as one of her hogs. Finally Bruce stood, and apologized for the events of the day, his words clearly hesitating for clarity. He took her hand and kissed it, and thanked her for the wonderful meal and fine evening, expressing that he must get back to Charleston.

Arabella searched frantically for a reason to see him again. An answer suddenly surfaced from her busy brain.

"Perhaps Danny Boy could come over and help you unpack and get the house into shape—huh?"

"Why that's a good idea, say about eight in the morning," Bruce replied.

The sun was ablaze as arrows of sunlight bathed the meadow and kissed the wild flowers on the next day that Danny Boy rode his mare into town. The sky was baby-blue, no clouds, only the smell of the ocean blowing in from Fort Sumter, the waves crawling gently on the shore. The dreamy ocean was its own master, and Danny Boy casually wondered who the master of this young man was. He went directly to the house that Bruce had described last night, and saw him through the window unpacking boxes. A knock on the door alerted Bruce that Danny Boy was on time, and he opened the door.

"Good morning, Danny Boy—how about a cup of hot coffee?" Bruce said, ushering him inside.

Danny Boy smiled gazing around the room. It was a nice little bungalow with one bedroom, an entry foyer, front room, and the kitchen served double duty as a dining area.

"Thanks, black please," Danny Boy replied.

Bruce went to the fireplace and swung the coffee pot off the glowing embers. He gripped the handle with a hand stuffed in his shirttail, and placed it on the table. As he took two mugs from off a peg, he glanced at Danny Boy.

"Thank you for coming way out here from the plantation—how is Arabella this morning," he asked, handing him a steaming cup of black coffee."

Danny Boy's face glowed as he suddenly laughed. "She's washing her clothes—never seen her so joyful since her father died."

"She's a fine woman, all right," he said, sipping his coffee.

Danny Boy sipped a swallow of coffee and then sat his mug on the table as he cocked an eyebrow. "So Bruce, what are your plans?" he asked like a father, but he was Arabella's guardian, and he'd promised the Master that much.

Bruce surrounded the warm mug with his hands. "Well, I sold the family farm and moved to Charleston—just a change of climate. Lincoln's election has so many people talking, I guess I wanted to experience the calmness a little further south."

Danny Boy enjoyed his talk with Bruce, mostly because he wanted to check out his motives. Miss Arabella especially liked this man, and he had to be sure. He was her only protector, but more and more he believed she needed no one's help but her own.

They finally finished the unpacking and the house was ready for occupancy before noon. After Danny Boy left, Bruce went over to Perkin's tavern. He had taken off a day to get the house ready and he wanted to thank Mr. Perkins, perhaps have lunch.

He marveled at the blue sky and the warm breeze as he walked, the gurgling waves out in the harbor were metronomic. It seemed he'd made the right decision to move to Charleston. There was so much to do and so little time to do it. The thought opened his mind to Danny Boy and Arabella—nice southern people, he decided.

Perkin's tavern was a hangout for men to come and smoke around mugs of rum. They talked about most anything. Mr. Perkins told him that the place was once an armory for Fort Sumter, the munitions moved out to the fort. He managed to purchase the place and turned it into a tavern.

As he entered the door, Mr. Perkins greeted him, asking several questions about his move. It was nice of him to take such interest in a stranger that came into town, especially offering him a job. Most of the young men were signing up for army service, but he wasn't really interested for reasons harbored deep in his mind from childhood.

When Bruce came home that early afternoon, he surprisingly found Arabella dressed in a cotton dress, a red belt around her wasp waist seated on his front porch, her mind overflowing with thoughts of last night. Meeting Robert Bruce Taylor had transformed Arabella into a woman of desire.

He was extremely handsome, a kind face, a mellow voice, one who listened, not quick to judge. Oh, how she loved him at first sight, but kept her feelings intimate, her emotions controlled, if only she could. One day she might explode with all the information swirling in her mind, she thought. But she was about to learn that her emotions would wildly shatter in a nightmare.

Arabella spent two hours helping Bruce arrange the furniture. At a rest break she had suggested, Bruce opened up, and told her of his interest in history, a sort of expert in the military tactics of George Washington, and that he'd even studied under Robert E. Lee for a summer. And then he casually spoke the words she had longed to hear.

"I'd like for you to come by tomorrow afternoon."

Her heart swelled with joy, gripped by the inability to speak.

"I'd like you to meet my wife and son—they are coming in from Fredericksburg on the afternoon train," he smiled.

Arabella's olive skin suddenly shone ghostly white. She only heard the first few explosive words. The effect was devastating. Her life immediately collapsed into nothingness. She stood aimlessly, her speech erratic, her thoughts a blank, as she was desperate to leave this place of agony.

Bruce sat wondering as he stared into her ponderous face, assessing what he'd said that had caused such a reaction—a typical male reaction of logic.

She suddenly burst out the door, jumped into her carriage, and stormed back to her plantation with acrimonious thoughts exploding in her mind, a myriad of unanswered questions gnawing on her ego.

She whipped the horse into a full gallop, the wind blowing her hair like an avenging angel set loose to torment Charleston. Her injured heart beat rapidly, the agony of a deceived woman in distress— "No," she screamed aloud to the wind, she had deceived *him*—she hated what she'd done, but still she loved this man despite his marriage. How her heart ached, yearning with desire that had eluded her hopes and her innermost dreams.

She wanted to cry, but couldn't—she wouldn't!

Finally, she raced up to the house, and pulled back the reins in front of the steps. She leaped from her carriage, bounded up the steps, and ran through the door, slamming it shut behind her entrance. When she crossed the foyer, Arabella gripped the hem of her dress and ascended the stairs three steps at a time. Finally she burst open her bedroom door and crashed on her bed facedown, pounding the feather mattress with her fists, her legs wildly gyrating like a pair of snipping scissors.

Danny Boy stood rubbing her horse's mane, its leathery skin moist with perspiration. He'd never seen Arabella whip her horse before. He looked up at her bedroom window on the second floor and heard her sobbing. He dropped his gaze, and decided he'd best check on her—but what could he do, yet he must go to her.

Suddenly, Arabella raised her torso on one arm, her mind buzzing, devious thoughts tearing at the cortex of her hectic brain, accusing actions twisting in her tortured mind.

She wiped her eyes with her index finger, and stared into space for a moment of decision, her mind a maze of questions. She coursed to the window, her eyes staring vacantly over the distance the cotton fields, the curtains waving in a gentle breeze that had no affect on the heat.

Abruptly she bounced toward the armoire and flung open the door, jerked out her fancy hoop skirt, the crinoline petticoats, all the muslin, and French netting, and tossed them into the fireplace. She watched it burn, as her heart burned for the man she could not have, her hands stubbornly gripping both her hips.

She spun around, went directly to the hall closet, and threw out items of clothing left by her father. One handful after another, she tossed out shoes, shirts, and pants—finally a pair of overalls that belonged to her father. With both hands she held the overalls against her body, her unstable mind a jumble of disjointed thoughts. This would do, she thought— it must.

As if she had solved her dilemma, Arabella looped the overalls over her shoulder and pranced back into her room. In the top drawer of her vanity she found needles and thread. Arabella tightened her upper lip, sniffed, and spread the overalls on her bed.

A knock on her door interrupted her thoughts. "Danny Boy, is that you?" she correctly assumed. He always knew when she was upset.

The door cracked open. "Are you decent?"

"Come in Danny Boy, I suspect you know what's going on anyway."

He stepped in quietly, only the second time he'd been in her room, the first was when the Master was away and she fell, broke an arm, and her mother sent him for the doctor. He stood fiddling with the brim of his cap.

"You had some kind of disagreement with Bruce, I take it."

She released the overalls from her hand. "He's married, Danny Boy," her raspy voice squeaked, the words stuck in her throat, the meaning stabbed her heart.

He twitched his head. "I'm sorry Miss Arabella—really I am."

She sniffed. "Guess he's not for me." But in her heart it was a lie; somehow she'd find a way to get this man for her own, someway, someday sometime— before she went crazy.

He saw the overalls and the stitching items. "What are you planning Miss Arabella?" he asked, concerned about her welfare.

"I haven't made that decision yet Danny Boy, maybe tomorrow."

Tomorrow was a day of infamy, the day America went to war against itself. Brother against brother, north against the south, shame cloaked in the mist of war.

But Arabella was at war with herself.

Chapter 2

The next morning Arabella donned her stitched invention, a riding habit—of sorts; nevertheless, she pulled on the tightly fitting suit that she'd patterned after English riding pants. The only pattern she had was the memory of a distant cousin who had visited from England. She stuffed a cotton blouse into the pants, and maneuvered the CSA metal button into its reinforced hole. She sat down in a velvet covered chair and pulled on knee-high leather boots, stood and stomped her feet. The heels added two inches to her imposing height. She inhaled, swelling the blouse tightly across her breasts. Arabella liked how she felt, proud, independent, and ready for whatever was out there.

She pranced over to her full-length mirror, and stared critically at her new outfit. She had the waist of a wasp, but was still reminded of the farmhand girl when she had chopped her daddy's cotton, along with the slaves. She knew them all by their names, drank from the creek when it was hot, ate watermelon at the end of the cotton rows.

"Oh well," she sighed, "it will have to do." Somehow she must get the message through Bruce's thick skull, that he was meant for her and that's the way it was going to be if she had her way! Then her head turned at the thudding sound of a woodpecker in the tree next to the window, reminding her of his hardheadedness. And then the smell of mimosas silently drifting into her bedroom and brought back memories of the only night alone with Bruce when they had sat on the porch.

"Who are you kidding," she whispered to the image in the mirror.

The day that Bruce's wife and son rolled into Charleston on the train, Arabella rode Bruce in her carriage to the depot as she'd promised. She was dressed in a respectable yellow gown with several crinolines, the edges trimmed in lace, and a matching web-like shawl over her head. She had agreed to take him to the depot mostly because she wanted to feast her pale blue eyes on this creature who had stolen her chances to love Bruce. They said nothing during the trip, the squeak of the wheels resonating in the afternoon stillness, the clip-clop of the hooves adding cadence.

Bruce finally broke the silence as he briefly shared a whirlwind marriage to Marceline, which his mother had been persistently against. He bowed his head as he unveiled the unfathomable hurt in his heart, how Marceline, his Creole wife, had destroyed his mother's pride with the untimely announcement that she was pregnant, a primarily reason that Bruce had decided upon moving his family to Charleston. If the devastating news had gotten out to their friends, his mother would've died of embarrassment. He couldn't permit it.

He had met Marceline while on a business trip in New Orleans for his father. It was during Mardi Gras, when he'd carelessly entered a bar for a drink. Marceline stood behind a counter serving whisky at the bar, and somehow her voodoo upbringing beguiled him, and it seemed he was under her mysterious spell. He often had wondered how it had happened.

If the truth be known, he was intoxicated although he hadn't ruled out that she had drugged his drink.

Marceline hailed from a family descended from the French Colony at its founding when the city was named for the Reagent Duc d'Oleans. Her father was a Creole half-breed indigent of refugees when Andrew Jackson stormed into the French Quarter in 1815. The Spanish/European culture slowly Americanized during the cotton boom of the South, but ancient credos remained traditional, especially in the *Mardi gras* region of the city. Bruce ended his statement with the promise he'd given his father that he'd not divorce her because of the child, the ignominy of society.

Arabella turned her head and faced him admiringly. "Thank you for sharing your heart, Bruce—I understand."

Indeed she did.

A disappointing frown wrinkled Bruce's forehead. "You are a good woman, Arabella." His crushed ego kept him from saying what was buried in his heart. "I . . . I appreciate your kindness . . . . I really do."

It was all he was willing to say.

The carriage rolled up to the depot, and Bruce snapped a halter to the muzzle of the horse's mouth. Arabella felt it wiser that she stayed in the carriage, a parasol stretched over her head in the blazing sun.

She focused on the steam puffing from the train engine, and then a striking woman with a little boy stepped from the train onto the wooden deck of the depot. She was beautiful, Arabella admitted; slim, dark, yet somehow mysterious, the eyes, not her façade. Bruce approached the carriage with a five-year child gripping his hand.

Arabella's heart sank as she focused on reality, but she was not one who gave up easily. She still had her dreams—that was enough for the moment. Today she actually wanted to face it squarely.

Bruce smiled. "Arabella, this is Marceline, my wife, and Josh my son," he announced with a cautious grin, and turned and faced his wife. "Marceline I'd like you to meet Arabella, the nice lady who helped me get settled in our house."

Marceline cocked her imposing head and raised a contemptuous eyebrow unveiling her womanly disdain. "Please to meet you, Arabella," she suspiciously fibbed, accented with a Creole drawl.

Arabella ignored her obvious conceit. "Likewise I'm sure," she replied with reticence, and turned her attention to the cute little boy, bowing to his size. "Did you enjoy the trip, Josh?"

The little tyke smiled innocently. "Yes, thank you, Miss Bella."

Everyone laughed and released the tension, but a different kind of tension lay in Marceline's wicked heart; a wife's suspicion and scorn.

To keep her sanity Arabella attempted at becoming friends with Marceline, though it was hard convincing her that she and Bruce were only impartial acquaintances. She never breathed a word of her love for Bruce, as hot days stretched into long humid weeks. Arabella stayed at her plantation, considering her future. Her life was at an impasse, her dreams set adrift like an empty bottle aimlessly floating in the Charleston Harbor.

One Sunday afternoon after church services, Marceline left a gossipy group of women, and stormed out to Arabella's plantation. She had just confirmed her suspicion that Arabella was in love with her husband.

Arabella became inquisitive as she heard rapid footsteps on the stairway, and suddenly her bedroom door burst open. Marceline's dark shadow stood in the threshold, her Creole blood boiling. Her eyes were squinted almost completely shut like the moment a shark attacks. She rushed into the room vehemently staring into Arabella's eyes.

A nervous silence prevailed for a moment of excruciating intensity. Only the scratching of a twig on the bedroom window cut through the apprehension.

Suddenly Marceline forcibly slapped Arabella's face—viciously, with a few unintelligible French words.

Arabella seemed baffled as she rubbed her cheek, and then looked into the palm of her hand, blood; the voodoo ring on Marceline's finger had scratched her skin.

"I don't deserve that," she barked with squinting eyes.

Marceline's dark brown eyes smoldered ablaze. "You certainly do—you've been sneaking around with my husband," she snapped savagely.

"That's not true, and you know it—yes I love Bruce, but he doesn't know it. There has never been anything between us but innocent friendship," she admitted stubbornly.

Marceline's shadowy face steamed a lobster-red, her eyes bloodshot. Rage seized her arm and she swung an open hand. Arabella ducked, moving like a fox. She grabbed a handful of Marceline's long black hair, and crashed her body to the floor like a sack of flour. Arabella dropped to her knees and threw her arm around Marceline's neck, noticing a demonic tattoo. She locked her hands together in a bear-hold worthy of a professional wrestler. Marceline coughed and gasped suffocating from lack of air. Arabella relaxed her grip, and Marceline fell limply to the floor holding her throat, on bended elbow.

Arabella stood, her chest rising and falling, her mind grasping for words. Marceline rolled over, slowly erected from her knees, her legs rubbery. She faced her adversary, unaccustomed to defeat, her countenance the image of black magic.

"I will curse you from my grave!" she screamed in measure words.

Arabella grinned unafraid. "If you dare hit me again, you'll get there sooner than you think."

Marceline scoffed, and then turned and staggered aimlessly from the room navigating the stairway gripping the handrail for balance, her mind calculating her revenge from the mentally stored handbook of black magic.

On some days Bruce yearned for the beauty of the Blue Ridge Mountains and its breathtaking colors of the autumn season. Politics around the cracker barrel in the merchandise store was what he remembered most in his youth, and the first telegraph in the area, now somewhat common.

Virginia's undying pride lived on in Old Dominion, a name cherished by the state. The state had helped to forge the nation, and Bruce decided he'd move further south. He'd convinced himself that his decision centered on the growing abuse of the Constitution in Washington just eighty-five years from the date the nation was founded. From the memories of his childhood he recalled, the nights the family sat around the dinner table listening to his grandfather tell the stories of the Revolution.

The night air loomed cold and dank as Bruce ambled toward the small tavern under a waning moon. He was ready for the nightshift. A warm breeze from Charleston harbor wafted in his face and rustled the hanging moss laden on the magnificent sheltering oaks. He took a deep breath, and then shoved his thoughts into the back of his mind; perhaps he would join the army, too, he sighed, his inhibitions to war subsiding.

Chapter 3

The moon refused to release the dawn, still under the command of the planet's gravity. The flickering stars lingered in the dark sky, only an orange glow melted on the horizon in the colors of an artists' palette. Shreds of mist passed through the cotton fields and crawled through the rows, as threads of wavy vapor crept over the sandy ground, noiseless and bloodless. Suddenly the dew glistened on mint-green fields of tobacco, a gentle salve for the soul.

The ocean breeze drifted chillingly around the corners of Perkins tavern in the early hours of morning. Like the end of every workday, Bruce took off his apron and donned his cotton coat about 4:30 in the wee hours before the dawn of April 12. He knew the date because he'd checked his pocket watch given by his father that somehow displayed the date in a small window—the Swizz were master watchmakers, he'd been told by his grandfather.

He ran through the alley with the thoughts of the move to Charleston from Fredericksburg lingering in his mind. It was where he grew up in a reputable family, lineage back to George Washington. He was a gangly lad, eager to learn, and he loved history; especially the history of this young nation. Many folks saw a trend developing that was an affront to the Constitution; the unhealthy growth of bureaucracy that George Washington had succinctly warned in his farewell address. Hamilton and Madison had convinced Washington to run for a second term as President, declaring the thirteen states would collapse without his leadership. Reluctantly, Washington had agreed. On his retirement from political life, his personal funds were exhausted, and Washington had to enlarge his personal whisky production into a larger capacity distillery. Jefferson helped Washington polish his farewell address and it was printed in the newspapers. Ironically, following unanimous approval of the Declaration of Independence in Philadelphia, the Deep South held those founding days of the nation more patriotic than the North. Perhaps, he thought that was the major reason he'd moved his family to Charleston; although his wife figured prominently in the equation, now a hindrance caused by her jealous attitude toward Arabella.

  The nation was entering the age of invention in a technological expansion; the railroad moved steadily westward, a financial dream of a few wealthy northern barons. Life was good, but not as good as in his childhood; strange how life was always better in the past. And then he remembered his fascination with an older cousin from the Knox family as they grew up playing together. How they played among the clover, threw pears at each other, fallen from the fruit trees. Then they gathered the pears and fed them to the hogs. Having to wash jars for canning, cultivating the large gardens, the pantry bigger that the bedroom where he slept. As children they only wondered about the next day, never the next year—it was oblivion, a place of fantasy. As it happened, Bruce still found it difficult to comprehend that he had grown up and married Marceline, from a different culture with different values. And somehow he didn't resist his kindly thoughts of Arabella.

His thoughts suddenly vanished at the sound of cannon fire in the harbor—a single shell—that broke the stillness of the dawn. A cascade of red and white lights traced an arc across the starry sky. The noise of soldiers firing their rifles, several cannon roaring, and an outpouring of shells from the harbor fell upon Fort Sumter, echoing in the chill.

It was a signal for his friends to attack—he'd heard the rumors; the abhorrence of Federal troops housed at the Fort had finally erupted. After about fifty guns had fired on the parapets, a live canister ignited in a hot barrel, and touched off a cascade of explosions, killing one Federal soldier and mortally wounding five others—the first causalities of the undeclared American Civil War.

Maj. Robert Anderson, U.S.A. officer, who occupied the fort, gathered his ninety garrison troops into the streets after they'd suffered a 34-hour bombardment; his feeble response was hindered by exposed parapet cannon as Southern cadets quickly destroyed his gun emplacements. His barracks was ablaze and his ammunition nearly gone. Anderson wisely surrendered. He reluctantly agreed to terms on April 13. The Major marched his men out of the fort with full honors including a 100-gun salute to Sumter's tattered flag as they sang "Yankee Doodle", all granted out of respect by his former West Point pupil, Brig. Gen. Pierre G. T. Beauregard.

Anderson paraded his men over the rubble on the wharf, the swinging gate dismantled by a direct hit. They finally boarded a steamer that ferried them to the relief fleet, which had anchored powerlessly off the Charleston harbor during the skirmish. The terrible irony was how the federal soldiers stood on the decks of the steamer, and watched the enthusiastic celebration ashore. Revenge seized their dry throats as they watched the raising of the Stars and Bars over the fort; even worse, the Confederate gunners lined the beach and silently doffed their caps, as the Union steamer headed out of Charleston harbor.

Bruce's wife was certainly not in favor of his decision, but women had no voice in these matters. He gathered a few necessary items in a pillow case, and entered the bedroom, tucking the covers over his son, and then kissed his wife. He gripped the pillow case in one hand, a hunting rifle in the other, and exited the door. Bruce stuffed the pillow case in the saddle bags. He gripped the horn of his saddle, placed his left leg in the stirrup, and straddled his horse graciously given by Danny Boy. He looked back thinking of his son, grasped the reins, gently kicking the horse's stomach, and steered toward the harbor.

As Bruce approached downtown, he was surprised to find that Mister Clyde Perkins had opened his building to local women for sewing uniforms. Out on the lawn young boys were boiling water in a large iron kettle fired by chopped wood. The older lads were chopping golden shittum wood, a species of acacia, and throwing the pieces in the kettle for dying the cotton fabrics to a grayish hue.

Bruce tied the leather reins to a wooden rail in front of the courthouse. He took his flintlock and ambled toward the building, as he watched the excitement exploding around him; kids running down the dirt road, dogs yapping, horses galloping, and handguns firing in the air like the 4th of July.

The proprietor of the merchandise store stood on the wooden sidewalk with his hands propped on a broom handle. Bruce shook his head; he hadn't seen such excitement since he met Arabella. He found a soldier standing at attention in the entrance of the courthouse, and casually asked him where and how he might join the army. Another soldier, a CSA Captain, sat at a table reviewing maps and spoke up.

"I'm your man, sir."

Captain Adrian Austin, a self-made man formally from Atlanta stood tall and firm on a six-foot frame, the product of a military family whose father had served in the Mexican war. Unmarried and unattached, he planned a military career, the only solid occupation he desired. Working on a farm was not his idea of the future, and he realized that the southern lifestyle would be waxing to its end. Though he abhorred the prospect, his youthful pride yearned for the expectant future.

Bruce dropped the butt of the flintlock by his side and faced the Captain. "Thank you, sir."

The officer sized his gangly stature of six feet two inches, but gazed long on the flintlock. "Say, that's an oldie—where'd you get it," he asked inquisitively chuckling.

He shrugged. "Why, it belonged to my father, and his father before him," he barked annoyingly.

Austin smiled, realizing that he'd offended the young lad. They chatted for several minutes, and the Captain asked personal questions that Bruce had to think before he answered, much of it about his distant family and descendants, his training and education. The officer finally nodded.

"Follow me, Bruce."

Austin led Bruce up a stairway to an office on the mezzanine floor. The Captain knocked on the door at the end of the hall, and entered. Standing at a wall map, a finely dressed civilian turned his attention from the map, his keen eyes surveying the visitor's gangly stature.

"Sir," Captain Austin saluted as he stood at attention. "This is Bruce Taylor, Mr. President. He is a descendant of George Washington, and his cousins served with Lafayette in the Revolutionary War, and a former student of General Robert E. Lee."

The cultured gentleman had arrived overnight, having ordered the capture of Fort Sumter, and his elegant clothes were smudged and unkempt, his graying hair frazzled. He stretched out his wrinkled hand, not from age but from the rigors of war and years as a Senator, and shook the young man's hand. And then he raked his fingers through his graying hair. He gripped his chin with thumb and index finger, and words echoed in his Mississippi drawl.

"Taylor? Are you by any stretch of the imagination related to Zachary Taylor, my boy?"

Bruce sheepishly bowed his head. "A distant uncle, I'm told, sir."

He quietly nodded his head as a memory flashed into his mind of his deceased wife, but spoke commandingly as he shifted his stance and straightened his coat.

"Son, this war began in the early hours of this very morning. No one knows how long it will last or whether we all will be hanged—are you sure you want to serve?" His eyes were penetrating and convincing, yet the depth of his stare unveiled a long service life in the U.S.A. Army.

Jefferson Davis grew up on a farm in Mississippi; spent two happy years as the only Protestant in a Catholic boarding school, four peevish years at the West Point. He graduated in 1828, 23rd in a class of 132 with 327 demits on his undisciplined record. He was an antsy youth, humorous, and quick to defend his position. In 1835, discouraged by the rigors of Army life, he was allured by the beauty of Colonel Zachary Taylor's daughter Sarah Knox. He resigned the Army, and he and Sarah were wed in June; alas, malaria struck them both and killed her in September. For ten depressing years of lamentation he lived alone like a hermit with only a few slaves on a Mississippi plantation called Brierfield. Out of the horror of loneliness he married Virginia Howard, 18 years his younger; and, in 1845 his neighbors sent him to Congress. He rushed off to the Mexican War the following June as colonel of the 1st Mississippi Rifles, a volunteer group of the rich and highborn, and subsequently returned a hero.

Captain Austin tapped Bruce on the shoulder and his thoughts vanished. "Well, President Davis, what do you think of our Bruce Taylor?"

Bruce's eyes swelled wide open. It was true. He was talking with the President of the Confederate States of America, Jefferson Davis. He swallowed dryly.

The stately man scratched the back of his left ear. "He'll do as a lieutenant—see to it Captain," he said, turning his back with his hands clasped behind him, and stared at the map as he thought of Maj. Gen. Lee's assessment of his final decision to attack Fort Sumter and kick out the Yankees.

Bruce stood awestruck. Jefferson Davis, a man of the stature of Abraham Lincoln, he thought as Austin again tapped his shoulder.

Davis only had learned, much to his dismay, that he was appointed provisional President of the Confederate States of America in February 1861. Whether he accepted the appointment out of loyalty to the South, or out of his vaulting pride was a concern of Maj. Gen. Robert E. Lee, who acted as Davis' advisor.

The Captain again tapped Bruce's shoulder. "Come along Taylor, let's get you indoctrinated."

Lieutenant Robert Bruce Taylor received a freshly-sewn uniform on the second day of his meeting with Jefferson Davis, one of few Confederate uniforms that were issued in the war. Recruits wore their own clothing, rode their own plow horses, and carried their own hunting rifles. Ammunition was a desperate shortage, and they melted every lead instrument, utensil, or artifact they could find, and molded lead balls for their muskets. They melted church bells to mold cannon.

Bruce proudly stood in the tavern where he worked, talking with his Mr. Perkins. Even though they had often discussed the impending war, no one actually believed it had really happened. They talked mostly about his appointment to the CSA by Jefferson Davis, himself, and the complications of leaving his family in Charleston.

For some reason Bruce's mind shifted to all that had transpired. Was his chance meeting with President Jefferson Davis just that, or was something unknown afoot. Could Captain Austin be trusted, or was he a part of the mystery. And would he ever see his wife and son again. This was the albatross that hung around Bruce's neck, though his thoughts often drifted to the discontent between his wife and Arabella.

Newly recruited soldiers stood in line all day and received their gunnysacks containing Johnnie cakes and cush, a Rebel delicacy of hominy cakes; plus some salted pork, a privilege not long lived in the CSA regiments. The northern soldiers were better trained, equipped, and fed. The women were their support in many cases, and older men left at home made whiskey and rum. Some of the more mechanical-minded men pressed out metal canteens, and sharpened sabers.

The Captain sent a message for Bruce's presence at the courthouse. Bruce left the tavern after shaking the hands of the people he'd worked with and some he knew only casually. Mr. Perkins agreed to send his wife over to Bruce's house, and look in on Marceline and the child. It took a mountain of worry off his mind.

The Captain ushered him to a locked room on the first floor of the courthouse. As he unlocked the door, the wall was lined with rows upon rows of rifles that the South had smuggled into Fort Sumter after they were covertly purchased from a gunsmith in Richmond. Profit made strange bedfellows.

The Captain took a rifle from its wall position and faced Bruce. "This is the latest Springfield. That flintlock of yours will garnish a small fortune for your son when he grows up," he chuckled.

Bruce only shrugged, a returning thought nagged at his mind, reminding him that the wife of the Merchandise Shoppe owner had apprised him of the incident between Arabella and Marceline. The thought stuck in his craw and often gagged his comments, but the horrible image of Arabella's mistreatment faded at the sound of the Captain's voice.

"The trigger on these Springfield's requires a healthy squeeze. And notice that it's muzzle-loaded with percussion caps."

The Springfield was the most common weapon found on the battlefield. Most rifles at that time were muzzle-loaded with small lead musket balls or a molded ball rammed with wadding and black powder. The mini ball was developed in France and had considerably longer and more accurate range; these, too, were smuggled with the rifles, probably the last improved ammunition the CSA would receive. President Lincoln had already given orders to blockade the major ports. Charleston was high on the list.

Bruce threw a smile at the Captain, and unlocked the muzzle. "You seem to know a good deal about these newfangled rifles," he said matter-of-factly.

"Yes, West Point teaches you all you can learn. Take this Springfield for example. Even though it is still a muzzle-load weapon, it uses a percussion cap firing mechanism. It has a rifled barrel and fires a .58 caliber mini ball, much more accurate than the lead musket ball. The first rifled muskets used a larger .69 caliber since the oversized ball simply rifled the .69 smooth barrels when it fired. Now take this Springfield; she's the 1861 model, and has a 38-inch barrel with three pressure bands, making her the same length as the smooth barrels she replaced."

Bruce wagged his head. "Imagine that! War is truly the mother of invention."

Austin disregarded the trivial remark. "This baby also fixes a bayonet, since bayonet fighting is very important in hand-to-hand situations," the Captain added.

Bruce leaned against the wall. "Say, Captain, off the record. I didn't get your full name."

He shuffled his stance, realizing the importance of this young man to the cause; since he'd purposely withheld the reason for his selection. "Austin, Adrian Austin."

Bruce extended his hand. "I'm pleased to meet you, Austin."

He dropped a smile, and stood at attention, refused the handshake as sternness froze his cleanly shaven face. He coldly and aggressively replied.

"Austin is fine for now. In public and on the field it's Captain Austin—understand," he smirked.

Austin militarily reasoned that Bruce was an intelligent soldier. Intelligence was just what he needed in his command. A promotion was bound to come, and the man would need much training for his assignment. It was too early to tell him why he was chosen or the plans for his service by President Davis and General Lee.

Chapter 4

Late in the night Bruce was awakened by a Sergeant, and escorted to President Davis' quarters. The graying hair of the tired old former Mississippi Senator shone in the flickering candlelight as he entered the room. His wrinkled hand gestured toward an oak ladder-back chair by his desk. Bruce nodded, and ambled over and sat down as Davis rounded his desk. The old former Senator clasped his hands and placed his elbows on the desk.

"Bruce, it's time we cleared up this mystery buzzing in your mind—I have to leave in ten minutes, and I'll make it short."

He stared directly into Davis' deep dark eyes, expectancy written on his boyish face. At last, he thought, the secrecy was about to end.

Davis rustled in his creaky chair. "General Lee advised me that he needed viable intelligence on troop movements. It fell on me to find the man."

The President continued to describe the reasons for this intelligence effort, but Bruce heard little. He thought of his son if something happened to his wife; who would care for them, would he ever see them again.

The movement of Davis' seemingly muted lips suddenly resonated with sound, as Bruce's mind returned to the conversation.

"We often have seen erroneous observations misdirect troop forces. General Lee demands more timely and accurate intelligence, and needs a trustworthy officer to lead an intelligence group." President Davis stood. "Your interest in history and the tactics of the Revolutionary war places you in good stead for additional training by General Lee's staff."

Bruce sat now absorbing ever word, acutely aware of his destiny.

Davis spread a map on the desk. "Union troops are springing up all over Tennessee, Alabama, and Georgia. This General Grant is a nightmare about to happen." He sat and crossed his long legs. "You will report immediately to General Lee in Richmond. I think you will discover that the Virginian Theatre is a separate campaign than what we are experiencing in the Deep South. We must stop the Union surge here in the South before it strikes Virginia. That is why Lee needs good intelligence."

He stood and shook Bruce's hand. "May God protect you young man," Davis said as if he had given a death sentence.

Bruce's orders were explicit, his plans chaotic as he pondered the details of his assignment. And then it dawned on him just why he had been chosen: he was expendable. And yet it was an important assignment, too, and he wasn't about to be caught in the breach of a political decision. At this moment he was going home to his wife and son. This was on his mind.

Bruce held Marceline in his arms all night without speaking a word about the incident with Arabella. This woman had suffered greatly in his absence and deserved better, even though she had wrecked his love for her before they came to Charleston. But in fact, many wives and mothers stayed home and waited—waited for peace and the salvation of their sons. Bruce finally released her from his arms and kissed her on the forehead. The blank stare in her dark eyes revealed no remorse for her actions against Arabella; she'd never broached the incident with anyone, yet it seemed that she somehow discerned that Bruce also knew. It was a problem to which she had a solution, she thought as she touched the voodoo doll under her pillow, just to be sure it was still there.

Bruce covered her shivering body, and left her side. He went over to the handmade youth bed he'd made in Fredericksburg, and touched the cheek of his 5-year old son. He glanced into the Marceline's depressed face as he tucked a warm blanket around his little body. Reluctantly he gripped his jacket that he'd hung on the chair arm, and strolled to the door; looked back again, and closed the door behind his exit. His heart dropped into his stomach as he hesitated on the porch but thought it best not to go back. The sorrow was bad enough, the pain too piercing to bear, the emotions overwhelming.

Marceline rolled over, took the voodoo doll from under her pillow, removed a long pin from her hair, and stuck it in the doll's side several times. Her eyes were blood red, her heart cold as a witch, as she thought that at least Bruce wouldn't be in Charleston for Arabella to continue her affair.

Over in the Rhett Estates house, Arabella awoke with a pain in her side. What is it, she thought? And then she remembered Marceline's connection with black magic; had she actually cursed her, she wondered? She sighed deeply and arose, the night hot and muggy. Arabella stepped into the kitchen and made a pot of coffee. Finally she poured a cup, and went out on the back porch and sat in a rocking chair, thinking, reasoning, and finally made a decision. The noise in the harbor was unsettling, the curious pain in her side perplexing. She heard Hattie come into the kitchen, probably awakened by my stirring around, she thought.

Hattie found her on the porch. "What's a-troublin' ye, Miss Bella?"

Arabella turned as Hattie walked on the porch. "Hattie dahlin', I can't have the man I want, and it's gnawing at my stomach."

Hattie sat in a chair beside her and touched her hand. "Child, ain't no man worth your health."

She gnashed her teeth. "That's why I'm leaving this plantation. You and Danny Boy can have it—it means nothing to me now," she swore, moisture gathering in the corners of her pale blue eyes.

Hattie shook her head left and right. "Honey child, dis plantation stays right hur 'til ye comes back. I done seen it in doz blue eyes. Ye is leaving, dats da truth," she said, a tear trickling down her shiny cheek.

Arabella pressed Hattie's hand to her face. This sweet child she had played with in her youth and cried with, the wonderful times they had growing up together, the devious things they did in secret. And now, this war had changed everything.

"I will miss you Hattie, and Danny Boy, too," she paused. "Hattie, you take care of him, he's not a young man anymore for us to pull on as we did in our youth."

Hattie bobbed her head confirming a silent promise, and held the child's hand for a long while as they consoled each other.

"Goodbye Miss Bella, mah pastor will pray fur ye."

They held hands until Hattie broke the grip, and somberly walked back into the kitchen, and off to her rooms behind a door where she lived.

Arabella heard Hattie sobbing. She bent one knee into the chair and laid her chin on it, steam from her coffee rising into her nostrils. Somehow she couldn't believe that Marceline could haunt her, but she wouldn't worry about such nonsense as voodoo, too many other things were more important. She was firm in her mind that she was going to Washington, D.C. and visit with Uncle Rhett. She'd sent him a wire, perhaps he would know what she must do.

Arabella stepped off the train in Washington with one suitcase. She expected to visit just for a day or two. Her uncle's butler met her at the station and they rode into town in a carriage. She had only been to his house twice in the summer when she was fifteen, again at sixteen. And then she remembered it was three years ago she came here with her father while they talked about the plantation. Her father died the next month. The thought produced a deep sigh.

What she remembered most was seeing Constitution Hall, but the crowds were annoying.

When the carriage pulled up to the house, she'd forgotten the federal style frontage and wrought iron fence, but remembered a gazebo in the side flower garden. And she had to remember her manners; her aunt had died last year, and her cousin Isaac, older than she by five years, was a student of William and Mary.

The butler brought her suitcase into the front door and a maid ushered her to a room up the stairs. She was a new maid—a white lady—and Arabella didn't recognize her. She gathered that her uncle was still at his office near the capitol because the maid offered to fix her dinner in the kitchen. While she was upstairs unpacking her things, the maid called her down for dinner. Arabella donned a cotton dress, and pranced down the steps reminding her not to straddle the handrail as she had done when she was fourteen.

She entered the kitchen and stood by the fireplace as the maid set a plate on the small table.

"Thank you, will Uncle Rhett return soon?" Arabella asked.

She pulled up a chair, her face solemn. "Miss Arabella, your uncle was arrested shortly after he received your wire. The War Department is moving quickly to arrest southern sympathizers who own property in Washington."

A silent stare coursed between the two pair of eyes. Finally the maid broke the silence.

"It's not safe for you to be here, either. A businessman from Nashville came by to see your uncle last week. I think he is a client of your uncle—he's supposed to return today, perhaps he can take you with him."

"What's his name?" she ventured, her mind busily calculating.

"Nathan Bedford Forrest," I believe, "a businessman from Nashville."

"What do you know about him?"

"He's a wealthy planter—only seen him twice when he comes here to see you uncle on business."

The butler entered the kitchen and told the maid that a visitor was in the parlor. Arabella stood immediately, pushed her chair aside, and followed the butler. He led her to the front parlor, and opened the huge sliding oak doors.

Arabella entered ahead of the butler, but he scurried aside and introduced her.

"Colonel Forrest, this is Arabella Rhett, the master's niece from Charleston." He bowed and faced Arabella. "Madam I am pleased to introduce Colonel Nathan Forrest of Nashville." He turned and faced the visitor. "If there is nothing else, may I retire, Sir?"

Forrest stood dressed in business clothes, and nodded his head. "No, nothing, thank you. That will be all—unless the lady would like a drink," he ventured, gazing at a beautiful woman but suddenly dropped his gaze.

Arabella's left eyebrow arched. "Hot rum, please."

Forrest slightly cracked a rare smile. "Make it two."

The butler left the room, and Forrest asked Arabella if they might sit. She bowed from the waist and sat herself on the sofa. She cast her pale blue eyes directly at the man, measuring him top to bottom.

"What can you tell me about my uncle's misfortune?" she frankly asked.

He stared briefly at her directness, a quality he admired in men; a lady was new territory for him. "Your uncle confided in me that he had given military information to Jefferson Davis, and expected to be arrested."

"And what's your part in all this?" she asked demandingly.

Forrest was glad the butler entered the room with the drinks, because it gave him time to think on the question. Arabella sipped a bit of hot rum; her keen eyes observing Forrest's apprehensive stare.

"Well?" she smiled quizzically.

He covered his mouth shielding a relaxing cough. "Ah hum," he exhaled, his fist pressed over his mouth. "Your uncle handled some business deals here in Washington for me." He paused, leaned forward with an elbow resting on his knee. "Listen Arabella, the Yankees will be over this house like flies on molasses. They will confiscate this property and sell it for the war effort. My advice is for you to get back to Charleston as soon as possible."

She cocked an eyebrow. "What do you mean "take" his property—that's not legal," she screeched.

"Anything is legal in wartime."

"War?"

ARABELLA

He sat the empty mug of rum on the table directly in front of the sofa. "Winfield Scott issued the Anaconda Plan blocking Southern seaports. This in itself is an act of war, but Lincoln officially signed a document declaring war on the 19th of this month."

Arabella's mind heard but didn't comprehend. Her uncle had been arrested, his property taken from him—what could she do? She raised her head defiantly, and faced Forrest with strong resolve glaring from her eyes.

"Are you leaving for Nashville tonight?" she inquired.

"Yes."

"Do you mind taking a passenger?"

He stood. "My pleasure, young lady," he replied. "In fact, we will leave immediately, if you can be ready."

"I'll be right down in five minutes," she winked, setting her empty mug on the coffee table.

Forrest's tanned face featured another rare smile. Deep in his mind he wondered what this charming young woman was doing in Washington with secession riots around every corner of the city, and abolitionists ready to kill the first white person without escort. Yet somehow he was thankful he could take her out of danger. But deeper in the shadows of his business mind he pondered how she might help the war effort. Was it possible, a woman thrust into wartime danger? This woman in his judgment possessed a rare character of discernment somehow. Perhaps he would investigate this idea while they traveled on the train to Charleston, he decided.

Arabella went upstairs and changed her clothes. She quickly selected her riding habit for travel. Without Hattie to help her undress, she momentarily imagined a difficult task by herself. But she went directly to the suitcase as she pulled the gown over her head, tossed it on the bed, along with several crinolines. She stepped into the denim trousers, pulled the blouse over her head, and fastened the metal button. She released a tucking comb in her hair and her lengthy hair unrolled on her shoulders. She shook out the tangles, and fussed for a moment before a mirror. Finally she sat on the bed and pulled on her leather knee-high boots. This was the moment she expected Marceline to torment her, and she was not disappointed that she didn't.

Chapter 5

The Washington/Charleston train sat on the tracks of the Washington depot as a carriage arrived and two people stepped off, a man carrying a suitcase in one hand and a grip bag in the other. A woman dressed in a curious riding habit similar to the English foxhunters walked beside the man toward the depot station. A robust man stood in the shadows watching the couple. Arabella took notice of his eyes, circuitous and cunning. As they entered the door, she saw his shadow move toward them.

Nathan Forrest sat both bags by a seat, and went to the ticket agent window. While he purchased tickets, Arabella's keen eyes noticed the man walking directly toward her seat. As Nathan returned, the man detoured to the ticket agent window. Nathan sat beside Arabella with the tickets in his hand.

"I'll drop you off in Charleston, and take you home. I have some business there with Jefferson Davis," Forrest said.

She faced him with her best smile. "That's very kind of you, Nathan—her eyes rolled left, "don't look now, but that man at the ticket window is following us."

Nathan's left eyebrow elevated, as he took notice of her keen awareness. "Let's take a seat on the train," he advised.

He gripped the bags, and they strolled toward the depot door, and walked alongside the train to a passenger car, steam rising in the rear. The man followed in a run. Nathan dropped the bags, and turned to face the man, his right hand clenched in a fist.

He was greatly surprised when he saw the man on his knees with Arabella standing behind him, his arm twisted in her grip.

Nathan glanced at Arabella; his forehead furrowed with surprise, and raised the man to his feet. "Just why are you following us?"

Arabella held her grip and jerked on the arm. "He asked you a question."

The man's face scowled. "I'm a War Department agent—Agent Dillard. Let me go!" he demanded.

"Like hell I will," Arabella barked. "You're following us because of my uncle's arrest," she added, grinding on his arm.

"All right, I admit it. Turn me loose," he agonized.

Nathan nodded, his face stretched with a grin. He had never witnessed a charming woman with so much grit.

Arabella released her grip. The man wearily stood, massaging his arm. He reached behind his lapel, and quickly received a punch in the nose from Arabella's clenched fist.

"Ouch," the man screeched rubbing his nose.

"Careful!" she warned, her left eyebrow cocked.

He dropped his hand. "It's only my badge!" he exclaimed.

He was an agent.

Arabella gazed into his eyes, somewhat embarrassingly but held a poker face. "Now you tell me why you are following us."

He stirred his foot, shaking the fog from his head. "This man you are traveling with has been a frequent visitor at your uncle's home," he said nodding at Forrest. "We believe he is transporting military secrets."

A smile crossed her face. "Is that so? Well what secrets do we have that you should want?"

His eyes blinked. "We found smuggled goods in your uncle's basement," he smirked.

Nathan stood marveled at Arabella's interrogation technique, her quick hands, and her fearless ability. "Listen, agent . . ."

"Dillard," he injected.

"Yes, well Mr. Dillard, we have no knowledge of any smuggled goods. This young lady is headed back to Charleston. Unless you have a charge, we are leaving on this train—understand?"

Dillard deeply sighed, stepping back. "There is no official charge, I am only investigating."

Arabella smiled, gently fingering the agent's collar. "Mr. Dillard. We don't usually treat visitors in the South with such haughtiness. Why don't you come down and buy yourself a plate of chicken and dumplings, and a bowl of grits sometime—it'll change your outlook on life."

Dillard cracked a smile at her witty charm. "Well, ma'am, I might just do that?"

She winked. "See that you do."

They sat in a booth across from two properly dressed ladies as the train moved lazily along the tracks toward South Carolina. Arabella's outfit attracted a few curious looks, but neither of the ladies said anything. Nathan drew the most attention from the obviously unmarried girls.

He was handsome in a manly way, a well-manicured beard and the usual men's trousers and white blouse with a cotton jacket dyed blue, crowned by a Derby hat, and anchored with button shoes. He was age 39 approaching his 40th birthday on July 13, and was born in Chapel Hill, Tennessee.

Nathan removed the Derby and laid it on the seat beside him. "Well, Arabella, what brought you to Washington?"

She dropped her gaze at the two girls, and faced him. "Personal," she replied insouciantly.

He grinned. "I don't mean to pry, but it must be serious to bring you out of Charleston, the best protected harbor on the Atlantic coast."

She inhaled a deep breath. "A long story, but let's talk about you," she suggested, weaseling out of the limelight.

He massaged his beard. "Nothing much to tell, I'm a planter, deal in land sales, and have dealt in slave trade until the Northerners charged the South as being racists, when they have as many slaves as the South."

She snuggled closer, which provoked one of the jealous girls who rustled in her seat, her neck stiffened conceitedly.

"How does a girl like me, help in this impending war?" she speculated.

He crossed his legs, twisted his neck and faced her. "It's interesting that you ask that question. I have an idea that with your charm, aggressiveness, and fearlessness, you could gather a fair amount of information."

"What kind of information?" she ventured.

Nathan uncrossed his long legs. "Well, let's cross that bridge when we get there."

Chapter 6

The train finally arrived at the Charleston depot, and Arabella surprisingly found Danny Boy waiting in the estate carriage. Sometimes his sense of her need was uncanny; she remembered when he always arrived at just the right moment, the day she fell from a tree, and he caught her in his arms.

She and Nathan had a parting moment alone standing in the steam of the train engine. Nathan bowed his head, and then looked into her keen eyes. "If you are serious about joining the war effort, I'll get you set up with the Confederate Intelligent Service. When you decide what you want to do, give me a holler at the Nashville capital," he said, bowing like the southern gentleman that he was.

Danny Boy shook Nathan's hand and thanked him for taking care of Arabella. The exchange was warmly cordial. Arabella suddenly realized that she had left for Washington without telling Danny Boy, and he was worried sick. She later discovered that Hattie had to swill a quart of rum before he coaxed her to spill the trip to Washington.

Nathan faced the couple. "Danny Boy, you take good care of this woman—she's special," he said, looking into her attractive face, somehow wishing that she would call him, but deep in his business mind he doubted she would.

Arabella cocked her head. "Thank you, Nathan for the ride home."

Nathan gripped the brim of his Derby with a slight nod. "It was my explicit pleasure, Arabella."

They waited inside the depot until the train arrived for Nashville sharing the news from Washington, and Nathan's prospects of war. Arabella said her goodbyes to Nathan as the train pulled from the depot. Finally she and Danny Boy rode the carriage out to the estate.

Danny Boy snapped the whip and the horse pulled back from a gallop to a trot. He turned in the seat to her with a question on his mind.

"Why did you run off without a word, Miss Arabella? You know how I worry."

She faced straight ahead, her thoughts captivated about a decision she must make this very night. "I am sorry, Danny Boy. I went to see Uncle Rhett. I thought he'd give me advice on a decision."

He chuckled. "That's admirable, I mean you needing advice."

She shelved the comment. "They've arrested Uncle Rhett, threatening to confiscate all his property. These damn Yankees are beginning to annoy me."

"Now that's not too cleaver of those northern folks, I mean to get you all riled up," he smiled.

She faced him. "It's serious Danny Boy. Nathan Forrest says this country is actually at war, Lincoln has blockaded the harbors after the Fort Sumter squabble."

Danny Boy stopped the cat-and-mouse tactics, apparently she was serious. "So what are you going to do?"

She breathed heavily, confident in her decision as she looked into the face of the man that had taken care of her since she was able to walk. "My dear, dear Danny Boy, I'm going to join the war effort as an espionage agent for Nathan Forrest."

Danny Boy's eyes swelled wide open.

The large fortified Harbor of Charleston was the envy of the Union. Since the first day of the war when the federal occupants of Fort Sumter were kicked out by a belligerent handful of Confederates, Charleston kept slipping out of the hands of the Union navy and the army. Yet the pesky Rebels managed to hold the harbor and the important city for much of the war, a thorn in the flesh of President Lincoln. Ironically, it was a small but significant battle that stopped the first land attempt at taking the city of Charleston, and the last attempt until late in the war. But many admirals took the chance of firing their guns into Charleston as they sailed passed the harbor. Fortunately, the technology of long range cannons was not available, and the explosive canisters usually landed on the buildings near the harbor. Such an opportunist's admiral had just completed a twelve-gun salute; canisters loaded with heavy gunpowder grenades and added shrapnel.

A sudden silence awakened Marceline. She rose stiffly and swung her feet from the bed to the floor. The nettling quiet was unnerving, and then she understood the reason.

The cannons had stopped firing. Would they start again, was the question that nagged at her mind.

Quickly she grabbed her son from the crib, wrapped Josh warmly, and dashed to the door. As she stepped outside barefoot she noticed a Union naval ship out beyond Morris Island. She remembered her husband's advice: go to his former employer's tavern. She surrounded her arms around Josh, and stumbled over rocks and debris toward Fort Sumter in Charleston harbor, leaving her blood smeared on whatever rock she stepped upon. The ghastly silence was interrupted only by Marceline's heartbeat. Still she pressed onward until a partial clearing appeared like an island in a sea of debris. She thankfully spotted the tavern in the near distance but found there were only two walls still standing. But the cellar door was intact. She pounded on the door until her fist was bloody.

Suddenly it opened.

A voice from inside the cellar yelled. "Who is there?

"Marceline Taylor, please let me in," she pleaded. The door immediately swung open. Marceline held her son in one arm and placed the other hand on the rail. A woman, the wife of the proprietor took the child until Marceline was standing safely on the cellar floor.

The door swung shut.

The walls began to tumble in the old Rhett Estate home. Arabella heard Hattie screaming but couldn't get to her; a large timber lay across her legs. Suddenly she heard a loud crumbling noise. She twisted her torso around just before the chimney of her bedroom fireplace crashed through the roof, and bricks toppled over the beam trapping her legs beneath the rubble.

She bit her bottom lip rather than cry, the pain was excruciating. All she could think of was Hattie. Was she all right, and how about Danny Boy? Then another canister exploded beside the damaged house, several walls crumbled with the sound like thunder. When the dust settled, she heard a faint noise. And suddenly her bedroom door ripped from its hinges and collapsed on the floor. Danny Boy rushed through the splintered portal stomping over the debris.

"Are you all right, Miss Arabella?"

Her smile released a ton of worry. "Now that you are here, I am," she replied nervously laughing. "Can you get this beam off my legs?"

Danny Boy stretched his legs over her head, and settled in a cramped spot. He tossed several dozen bricks aside, and squatted aside the beam. He gripped the timber with his large hands, tightened his abdomen muscles, and then rose slowly on his powerful legs. "Quickly, now slide out, if you can," he grunted.

Arabella had very little feeling in her left leg, but she wiggled out clawing like a crab on her elbows. When she was clear, Danny Boy dropped the beam in a rumble of dust.

"How's your leg, it isn't broken, I hope."

She stood, jiggled the leg a few times. "Nah, it's all right—I'll manage. What about Hattie, have you seen her?"

"She's in the kitchen," he gasped.

"But I heard her scream."

He chuckled. "Twas only a gopher rat racing toward the door. I found her standing on the counter holding her dress over her knees wildly screaming."

Chapter 7

Bruce sat aboard a railcar bound for Richmond authorized by Gen. Lee, according to his verbal orders given by Jefferson Davis via Captain Austin. The train pulled away from the Charleston depot under a wave of cannon fire, about fifteen minutes after he'd returned his uniform to Capt. Austin, and explained that where he was going a CSA uniform would get him hanged. He only brought a change of civilian clothes.

As he sat dozing, he thought he detected sounds of more cannon blasts emanating near the harbor. He couldn't decipher the sound, and decided he only heard the rumble of the train's boiler blowing steam. It was a plausible quest the harbor was under attack again, but his mind automatically calculated a rebuttal: If he missed this train, he also missed his appointment with General Lee. It was too important to turn back. And it suddenly hit him: Turn back to what? His wife's personality had changed so abruptly since they had first arrived in Charleston, but it was his son that held them together. His mind cancelled the thoughts as he closed his eyes, exhausted from lack of sleep.

The railcar traveled all night as Bruce sat listening to the dreamy sound of the steel wheels bumping over spike-joined tracks. Clandestine pictures of his intelligence plan were forming in the back of his mind. The plan focused on gathering information quickly. Technology was limited. The telegraph was new and amusing to the public. Signal flags were a daytime possibility, and dirigibles were risky and cumbersome. Bruce confirmed that shoe leather was his tool. Go where the talk was loose. He planned on three, maybe four people in his group.

Bruce arrived in Richmond ahead of schedule, but Lee's men were waiting at the station for his arrival. He saw two men standing at the gate; he gripped his bundle of clothes, and moved to the exit.

Finally the train stopped, and Bruce was the third person to step down on the wooden deck of the depot. Two men in civilian clothes strolled up, steam cloaking their faces.

"Lieutenant Bruce Taylor?" one man asked.

"That's right," Bruce replied, scrutinizing the two men, one tall and thin, and the other robust his disfigured face hidden behind a well-trimmed beard.

"Come with us please," said the tall thin man.

Out in the yard a covered wagon awaited, hitched to a mule. Bruce slung his bundle into the wagon behind the driver. He placed a foot in a spoke of the wheel and lifted his body into the seat, and sat between the two men, as the robust fellow gripped the reins and drove the mule. The other man sat stoic as if his mind was a million miles away. The wagon moved out onto a dirt road for a lengthy time, and Bruce finally faced the stoic man, the driver snapping his whip on the mule's backside.

"Is this the road into Richmond?" he wondered.

The tall thin man stared straight ahead. "That's good perception; you must be familiar with this countryside," he said dryly.

Bruce's forehead wrinkled. "Not since I was a kid, but it hasn't changed much."

The man dropped his smile. "Oh yes, there are changes all right."

Bruce sensed something was amiss. He gripped the edge of the seat and spun to face the man. "Let me see your credentials, please."

He grinned. "Certainly," he barked as he pulled a badge from the inside coat pocket.

Bruce's startled eyes squinted. It was the badge of the Washington police. "Where are you taking me?" he growled.

"You'll find out," he announced authoritatively.

Bruce held his emotions in check, in no position to disagree.

The wagon finally stopped about twenty yards beside an old barn as the daylight waned, and the sky grew ominously gray. They walked to the barn just as a blanket of endless stars covered the countryside in a myriad of celestial lights.

The inside of the barn was dark, yet noticeably a single lantern lit a room at the end. Bruce was escorted inside the barn, both men holding his arms. An older, more distinguished man leaned against a straw crib as they approached, his arms crossed under his armpits. He scrolled his eyes from head to toe. "So you are Bruce Taylor, I presume."

Bruce, more antagonized than ever in his lifetime, looked into his bearded face. "What's that to you buster," he snorted. Suddenly he kicked the robust man in the crotch, and tossed the thin man against a roof-support post.

The older man dropped his arms to his side, an encouraging smile on his face. "Relax Bruce; we are on your side. This is General Lee's way of introducing you to your training. My name is Jason Doyle; I'll be working with you. These two men are attached to the regiment."

Bruce's eyes squinted almost shut, releasing the fingers of his fists. He shook his head as he dusted his trousers, and then stretched his hand to the robust man on the floor pulling him to his feet.

"Sorry, pal—I didn't know."

The robust man gripped his crotch and flashed a grin, unable to smile or speak. Bruce notice then his disfigured face had probably resulted from a gross burn as he grinned embarrassingly. He faced Doyle with a pointed finger.

"You certainly have a novel way of introduction."

They gathered in the room at the end of the barn and discussed Bruce's plans. Sitting on bales of hay, they made plans for establishing a spy ring and the covert mission of gathering intelligence. Since Bruce had not met with General Lee yet, they only made general plans, but Doyle was experienced, which Bruce sensed was helpful.

Bruce went across the street to a tavern, his mind buzzing with details of the meeting and his awestricken arrival, his throat dry from the railroad trip. The quiet walk sent his mind back to his wife and son. Somehow, it felt strange to be apart, but he had a job to accomplish for General Lee. His mind returned to reality, and reality was the sudden noise of people talking while drinking rum as he opened the tavern door. His eyes habitually drifted over the area, and focused on a man who somehow looked familiar, appearing that he'd traveled a long distance. The man sat at the table against the wall where other men were engaged in loud conversation.

Bruce sat at an empty table near the window and a waiter brought him a mug of rum. He took a swallow, and sat the mug down, positioning his ear to the conversation across the aisle. Suddenly he heard the familiar-looking man say, "Bull Run."

He quickly rose from his chair and walked to the table. As he stood beside the man, all eyes upon him, the man turned and faced him. Suddenly Bruce realized he was a former employee of Mr. Perkin's tavern, Thomas something or other.

"Why Mr. Taylor—say ye might be interested in what I hurd last week."

"Why yes Thomas, let me buy you a tanker of rum."

They left the conversation and went over to Bruce's table, as he waved to the counter. A rather pudgy man draped in a cotton apron waltzed over. "Another mug of rum, please," Bruce said.

Thomas sat fidgety, and Bruce placed his hand on his shoulder. "I want to thank you in advance for any information."

A mug of rum slid across the table and bumped into Thomas' hand. "List'en, Mr. Taylor. I wuz in Washington last week und Iz overheard sum fancy dressed men whis'pring in de cap'tol building. Lincoln iz redy fer war; he's don General McDowell thu man tu take Richmon'."

"You mentioned Bull Run," Bruce probed.

"Yes sur, Yankee troops er gath'ring dar now."

Bruce digested the information. If Thomas was correct, Gen. Lee must have this information as soon as possible. They discussed over mugs of rum entirely all he'd heard in Washington. Thomas gave one other bit of information: Union naval boats had moored off the harbor and launched explosive canisters into Charleston, yet he had no other information on the extent of damage. And then Bruce realized that he had indeed heard cannon fire in the harbor as he left Charleston, yet he kept focused on his mission.

Chapter 8

After Bruce left the tavern across the street from the Confederacy headquarters, he went directly to General Lee's office. The general's secretary informed him that Lee was in conference with one of his officers. Bruce sat in a seat impatiently realizing he'd have to wait. He used the time rehearsing his information.

Finally, the secretary called Bruce into the General's office. As he strolled into the expansive room he noticed a rangy soldier with long leather boots slouched in a seat. He nodded to the soldier—a General—and faced Lee's desk.

General Lee sat studying a large map. A magnificent beard adorned his face with the countenance of a refined man. Robert E. Lee, the *Marble Man*, was the son of Revolutionary War officer Henry *Light Horse* Harry Lee III, and a top graduate of the United States West Point. In the early days of abolition John Brown was rabidly against slavery. Brown and four of his sons and seven men dragged a pro-slaver and his two sons from their home, shot the old man and hacked the sons to death. In 1859, Brown led a few of his men to the covered bridge over the Potomac, cut the telegraph wires, and overpowered the watchman. Then they entered Harpers Ferry, and successfully took over the armory, kidnapped a number of people, and brought them into the fire engine house. Ninety Marines arrived, sent by President James Buchanan. Lt. Col. Robert E. Lee, U.S.A., took command of all forces, including the militia. Next morning Lee sent his aide, 1st Lt. J. E. B. (Jeb) Stuart to the engine house under a white flag of truce and called for surrender. Convicted of murder, criminal conspiracy, and treason against the Commonwealth of Virginia, John Brown was hanged at Charles Town on December 2, 1859. Among the 1,500 militiamen on guard to fight off abolitionists was a young actor named John Wilkes Booth.

Lee distinguished himself as an exceptional officer and combat engineer in the U. S. Army for 32 years. He went to West Point because it guaranteed him a free education and a salaried job. He spent most of his career in far-flung Army jobs, individualizing himself under Winfield Scott in the Mexican War. He was such a fine soldier that, when Southern states began seceding, Scott offered him command of the Union forces with the approval of President Lincoln. Lee agonized for a few days, but finally decided he could not raise arms against his beloved Virginia. He did not approve of the war, but he never regretted his decision. When Virginia declared its secession from the Union in April, 1861, Lee chose to follow his home state, despite his personal desire for the country to remain intact. He had originally served as a senior military adviser to President Jefferson Davis, but soon emerged as a shrewd tactician and battlefield commander. After both sides got off to a faltering start, Lee emerged as the first, and perhaps the most brilliant, military leader from the day he took over the command of the Army of Tennessee. He organized the North Virginia Army and received brigades from all over the Deep South who served him valiantly in protecting

Richmond. The legend was born, and with it the South's first hero.

Lee dropped his gaze on the map, stood, and extended a hand. "Good to have you aboard, Bruce. I hope your trip went well."

Nothing was well, he thought as he shook the General's hand. "Sir, Lincoln has given Gen. McDowell the green light to attack at Manassas—he wants to take Richmond at the onset of the war."

Lee slumped into his seat. This was the news he had been waiting for; all he had had were vague stories. But he needed numbers: how many troops, their locations. This young man was good at his work, he sensed as he gazed into his tan face, his tall frame, and bright intelligent eyes; then he recalled that he had taught this young man while he served as superintendent of West Point 1852-1855, the reason he had agreed with Davis. Yes, seemed Bruce had dropped out of school before graduation, something about his mother's death, he thought.

Lee rotated his head toward the General seated in the Queen Ann chair. "Well Jeb. We at least know where the battle is staged—it's no longer an assumption."

Brig. Gen. Jeb Stuart crossed his long legs as he fingered his bushy red beard; he'd stopped shaving, when he first realized he had a short chin. This flamboyant, Virginia-born eccentric had seen action at Harper's Ferry, engaged in capturing John Brown; played a role in several campaigns, serving first with Stonewall Jackson in the Shenandoah Valley, and most recently with Maj. Gen. Lee in the Northern Virginia Army.

He gripped his red-lined gray cape with a yellow sash, a red flower neatly stuck in a button hole as he coursed his penetrating eyes over the young Lieutenant.

"Bruce, thanks for the tip," he rasped like a file on steel, remembering his own youthful educated at home by his mother and tutors until the age of twelve; he'd entered Emory and Henry College when he was fifteen, appointed to United States West Point at age 17, after failing enlistment into the U. S. Army as underage.

Stuart uncrossed his legs, his back erect "General Lee if you will dispatch me and my men I'll identify the numbers and location of those Yankees in ten days."

Lee called his orderly into the office as he looked at the map on the wall. "Jeb this is about the location Bruce advises, right in the heart of the Shenandoah Valley. Take your men there and God's speed to you." If Bruce was his eyes, Jeb was his feet; he thought.

General Lee faced his orderly as he stood at his desk. "Cut orders for General Joseph E. Johnston to take command of the Tennessee Army."

Chapter 9

While Washington bureaucrats fumed over the Confederate takeover of Fort Sumter, the war shifted to blockading all the Confederate ports on the Atlantic and the Gulf coasts: Fort Monroe, Albemarle Sound, Fort Clark, Fort Hatteras, Fort Macon, Fort Fisher, Fort Sumter, Fort Pulaski, Port Royal Sound, and McAllister. Only a few federal vessels were available for patrolling the nearly 4000 mile coastline. The ironclad ships were employed in limited naval action, but Lincoln concentrated on major ports. He chose the ports where cotton exports and imports of war materiel fueled the Southern war effort; such as New Orleans, Savannah, Wilmington, and Charleston. Blockade runners still played the game with great profits.

The northern press and the public were eager for an advance on Richmond ahead of the planned meeting of the Confederate Congress in that city on July 20. Encouraged by the early victories of Union troops in western Virginia, and by the war fever spreading through the northern states, President Abraham Lincoln ordered Union Brig. Gen. Irvin McDowell to mount an offensive. Lincoln reasoned that a quick surge would open military action into Richmond and bring the war to a quick close.

The first major land battle of the War was staged in the fertile Shenandoah Valley at Manassas Junction along a river dubbed Bull Run by Union planners. McDowell was too cautious. Instead of taking the available experienced troops and storming into Manassas, he gathered 35,000 volunteer troops at the capital. During the lull, defense units of the militia and the 1st Connecticut heavy artillery moved out of the area into Washington, just 30 miles from the city's defenses. McDowell knew his young recruits were not prepared and pressed for a postponement, reasoning that the rebel army was no more fit than his troops. This was true, but General Lee was resourceful; he promoted Col. Beauregard to full General, and placed him against McDowell because of his credible leadership at Fort Sumter.

Although the Confederate forces seemed amateurish, Lee's intelligence network under a young intelligence officer named Lt. Bruce Taylor, the only officer not dressed in a uniform, gave them advance warning of McDowell's movements. Gen. Stewart placed the location of troops. Coupled with the slow movement of Union troops, Gen. Beauregard gained the advantage of dispensing his Confederate rebels just 35 miles away hidden in the forest. Gen. Joseph E. Johnston brought in 8,340 men and 20 cannon from Winchester in the lower valley and reinforced the Confederate deployment.

This land battle involved 35,000 Union troops faced against about 20,000 Confederate forces, and was destined to be the bloodiest single day of battle in history. The battle lines were drawn along the small river of Bull Run.

McDowell's forces struck first.

Their cannon bombarded the Rebels across the Bull Run River, while his field commanders crossed the river at Dudley Ford with more troops in a glorious charge of destiny. There were no memories of home, or the girls waiting for their return, just the magnificence of war.

After a harrowing two hours of battle, the dead, and dying were scattered over the fertile soil where plant life beneath the carnage struggled to the surface. A larger, more defiant force of Union troops mounted a surge. The Rebels retreated across the Warrington turnpike and up Henry House Hill under the protection of Johnston's artillery. For some reason McDowell failed in chasing the retreating Rebels while he had them on the run; instead, he dispatched a runner with orders for artillery to shell the enemy from Dogan Ridge.

In this lapse of time, Gen. Thomas J. Jackson's Virginia Brigade reached the hill. Jackson was a former professor of the Virginia Military Institute, and calmly organized his band of several cadets from VMI. The cunning General positioned his men along a marshy depression unseen by the Union commanders, which gave them cover against the artillery.

While witnessing the panic swirling around him, Jackson suggested to Brig. Gen. Barnard Bee that his men form with his brigade. The excited cadets charged into the retreating swarm of men, as Jackson led them to his preplanned location. From their position on Henry House Hill, Jackson's men and cadets turned back several attacks in daring military moves, genius moves of Jackson's brilliance. His bold antics earned General Jackson his famous namesake *Stonewall Jackson.* Legend said someone shouted, *"There stands Jackson like a stone wall—rally behind him."*

McDowell held to his plan of weakening the Confederate line with artillery, but his artillery men were taking too many losses for response. His mistake was a crucial element of defeat and humiliation.

Reinforcements of Jackson's growing brigade surged in on two sides, and shattered the flank attacks. They finally drove the Union forces into the open field with sword and bayonet, routing the Yankees from their hiding places. Beauregard saw Jackson's men destroying the flanks and ordered a general advance. As they charged forward, screaming the famous *Rebel yell*, the sound chilled the air like a coon dog treeing a fox.

Confederates broke through the line.

McDowell's troops retreated across the river, and licked their wounds. Caught in the breech like a black bear with its foot clinched in a trap, his men were too exhausted and disorganized; they had no fight left in them, only chagrin and shame. McDowell gathered his wits, and finally rallied for an escape as he moved his men back toward the city of Washington before another attack destroyed his entire command.

Beauregard thought his men might reach Centreville and cut off McDowell's retreat. But fresh Union troops held the road into the town. Yet Jackson's Rebels doggedly pursued the men and captured Union troops as well as Washington dignitaries who came to watch their Union troops drive the Confederates back into northern Virginia.

As if modern television cameras were broadcasting the battle to the international world, reporters, congressmen, and stupid onlookers watched the battle from the nearby countryside, while they drank rum and celebrated the apparent Union victory. But to their consternation, Stonewall Jackson had rallied the Confederate troops to victory with his little Army of the Valley. Lee was blessed with competent generalship, but the confusion of war would change that condition.

Lincoln and the nation learned on that historic day that the war would not end soon. The Union defeat had stunned the North. They expected an easy victory, and it convinced many nervous people that the Confederates were about to attack the city of Washington, too. And yet many politicians still thought Virginia was the real enemy of the Union; like a wayward child she had left her nest, and she sat in their front yard.

On July 22, Lincoln signed a bill calling for 500,000 volunteers. The city began efforts to rebuild the Army. It would be a long, costly war; the numbers of dead soaring to unimaginable totals, the wounded and maimed suffering even higher totals before the war ended, if it ever did. This infamous war would occupy the halls of history, but few would understand why it had happened. It was not actually a civil war in the since of total rebellion, but a war granted by the Constitution when a portion of its citizenship saw the encroachment of a growing government on its State's Rights.

Lincoln, a shrewd politician, set the attention of the country on the war as a slavery issue. And history recorded slavery as the sole reason for the secession of southern states. From the first days as President, most of his decisions were related to bringing the southern states back into the Union by political persuasion. He seldom left the capital during the war, and never forgot that Washington and the White House were targets of the Confederate forces, just as Richmond and Alexandria were the targets of the Union. Until Union troops would capture Alexandria, Virginia, the enemy was just across the Potomac River from the capital. Wherever he went bodyguards protected him. Lincoln kept in touch with his generals on the battlefields by using the telegraph in the War Department building, which was next door to the White House. The President would go down a private stair, walk through the basement and along a colonnade, and stroll across the White House lawn. Lincoln knew the White House was a symbol of freedom. He wanted to make sure the country knew that he was determined to finish the war, and keep the southern states in the Union. Because of this Lincoln kept the White House open to those who wanted to discuss war, or to tour the house. This showed Americans and the international world that the government was confident that the United States would survive.

The glory of battle summoned men to Bull Run, and glory surely kept them coming. But now overshadowing that glory was the reality of the battlefield: torn limbs, dying screams, cowardice, the living picking the pockets of the dead.

The first Bull Run battle convinced Lincoln that his worst fear was correct; the Confederates could mount an attack on Washington. Yet these same bloody soils were destined for a second battle. Lincoln reacted to this first debacle by reaching for a victorious General of the Army as he appointed Gen. McClellan, who replaced the aging Gen. Scott. Lincoln ordered McClellan to reorganize the army.

Chapter 10

General Lee summoned Lt. Bruce Taylor to his office immediately after he left the field with Gen. Thomas Jackson in charge. The intelligence that this young recruit had provided had saved thousands of lives, despite the mishandling of his orders on the field. He deserved a few days off, he thought, remembering that he had a wife and child in Charleston; this lull in the war could be the only chance to spare the young officer.

The General's orderly knocked on Bruce's door as he was busy packing his clothes, excited that the General had given him a brief furlough. General Lee had requested his presence over wine in his study. He dared not refuse the request, and closed his bag. He ambled down the hall to Lee's study on the mezzanine floor, tucking his shirt into his pants. Down on the first floor he noticed the General's planners scurrying around a desk. The orderly opened the door even before he knocked.

General Lee sat at his large desk, a history book cracked open by his thumb. He removed his spectacles and motioned Bruce to sit in the Chippendale chair by his desk. Bruce slumped in the seat, for the first time realizing how the telegraph news from Charleston had affected his stamina.

The General stood and walked around the desk. He settled in his seat, crossed a leg, and with his arms folded in his lap. His eyes were steady, resolved, and keen, years of military experience shone on his wrinkled brow. He surprised Bruce with an announcement.

"Bruce, I am promoting you to Captain. I want you to take this insignia; it was given me at West Point."

Bruce sat speechlessly humbled. He had learned so much under this man, a genius of military tactics, and a man who demanded allegiance.

Lee poured vintage wine into two brandy glasses. "Let's toast this new beginning."

They talked for an hour or more about the war, the dead, and the maimed. Bruce had pondered the new information Doyle had given him while he was packing, and reasoned he should share it.

"Sir, we now know that General Henry Halleck has been called in from the West as general-in-chief. Grant has taken charge of the Army of Tennessee in the West. Lincoln has also summoned Gen. John Pope to take charge of a new army in Virginia."

Lee raised his head musing. He had known Pope in the older days. He was a windbag who made vainglorious speeches, not a good leader of men in battle.

An orderly quietly knocked as the door swung open. "Sir, the Richmond train has been delayed by a skirmish on the tracks on the outskirts of North Carolina."

Lee smiled at Bruce and poured a second round of wine as he nodded at the orderly. He warned that the rails were being watched by northern security. Bruce already knew that Grant's men were taking over railroads for troop movement, and travel into the southern states was under surveillance; Doyle had reported higher security on the tracks.

As they drank wine, Lee reminisced. "Lincoln offered me the command of the Union Army. But when Virginia seceded, I felt my duty lay with my home state."

Bruce nodded. "I guess Fort Sumter finally opened the government's eyes that the South is tired of a runaway bureaucracy paralleling that of Rome at its fall."

Lee smiled. "That's the lesson of history," he replied, and then gazed into space. "We have lost sight of the reason for the Revolution, and have begun to perilously resist the Constitution." He dropped his gaze. "These are growth pangs, Bruce. If your son forgets how we gained our freedom in this land, then this war is all for naught."

Bruce sat his empty glass on the desk. "The South is clearly more patriotic than the burgeoning growth of the Northeast and expansion spreading westward—two different lifestyles, Sir."

Lee assessed his reply momentarily, and tossed a report on his desk. "This is excellent information, Bruce. It will save a lot of lives."

Bruce glanced at the title; it was his report on the Vicksburg fortifications. Lee had discussed the report last night when he was brought over to Lee's office. It was his staff's decision that Grant was perhaps six months from the bluff overlooking Vicksburg, depending on the delaying overland battles in middle Tennessee. Lee had his eye of a self-made Colonel out of Nashville by the name Nathan Forrest. This man had the genius that may delay Grant.

Lee took the report, laid it in his lap, and faced Bruce. "I hope this brief furlough will be fruitful in rejoining your wife and son."

Bruce bobbed his head. "Thank you, Sir—thank you very much."

Lee extended his hand. "Remember, you cannot depend on the railroad when you return—get back here as soon as you can, son—if Vicksburg falls, Richmond is wide open."

"Yes sir. The South will need good rifles, not those muskets, without ammunition."

Lee nodded affirmatively. Bruce was the same intelligent man he had taught years ago. "Yes, we have some patriotic men here in Virginia, too. I think we'll have a few excellent rifles."

Down in the basement of a house on the Potomac, an old English gunsmith sat at his wooden table working under the light of a whale-oil lantern. Beside his work table were six wooden crates, which he had packed with 100 Springfield rifles, Model 1861. As a gunsmith at the Springfield Armory he was able in the course of nine months to smuggle out these rifles for which a Southern businessman had offered five gold bars, each worth ten years wage at the Armory. He had a sickly wife with mounting quack-doctor bills, yet she probably would outlive him, and he had to provide for her livelihood.

He was at his wits end when this Southern businessman had approached him at a local tavern in Boston. After they had talked, the man gave him the first payment of one gold bar, the other two bars on delivery. The message that stuck in the gunsmith's mind was the stern warning should he not deliver the guns. The gunsmith was a patriotic man but he had to provide for his wife. It seemed to justify deliver of the rifles. He also sold cotton to northern businessmen and gave the money to the General Lee and the Northern Virginia Confederates. Someday he knew he'd pay for his sympathizing activity, but the payment for these guns would pay off all his debts and provide completion of a grand house on the Potomac. He had filed his last will and testament at the courthouse in Gettysburg, giving the house to his wife, Julie.

He sighed, and sealed the crates.

Chapter 10

Bruce sat in a seat beside the window in a train arranged by General Lee. Streaks of lightning threatened a southern thunderstorm. He gazed out the window at the lush green drifting by his window. The smell of wet grass oozed through the cracks around the doors with intoxicating freshness. He listened to the steel wheels pounding out a moving rhythm against the rail joints, felt the movement of the locomotive and the six cars that followed. Then the engineer pulled the throttle up another notch.

He felt too tired to sleep and bored with the tedium of the trip, so he composed a letter in his mind. As the words flowed from the synapses behind his forehead, sentences began to form. He described the storm outside, the lightning that flashed across his lap, the long distance to Charleston if the tracks were intact. He briefly sighed, the rhythm of the wheels returned. He suddenly realized the salutation of his letter was addressed to . . . Arabella! It was a rude awakening. It worried him deeply. Marceline was so jealous, he bitterly thought, and Arabella was a charming companion. It was a marital dilemma that he had to resolve.

Finally he arrived in Charleston after boarding two trains, hiring a horse, and riding to the next train depot. The Yankees were scattered in regiments at the border of Virginia and Kentucky. Some of the more ambitious regiments had destroyed several train tracks, which made his trip more difficult.

Bruce finally arrived in his neighborhood near the harbor, and found it had been heavily bombarded. His surprise quickly faded into anger when he discovered that a hole existed where his house once stood. His heart thumped wildly, his mind screaming, where was his wife and son?

He rushed over to the tavern where he once worked, avoiding the debris looking for his former supervisor. He stumbled over several fallen palmetto trees, zigzagging in and out of jagged rocks. Finally he reached the area, astonished at the sight of destruction.

Only two walls of the tavern were standing, the roof blown off. And then he remembered the wine cellar. He ran to the back area of the tavern, and found the cellar door cluttered with debris. He frantically tossed off the debris, and lifted a splintered wooden door. Carefully he descended the undamaged stairs. It was quiet, too quiet, and suddenly Mr. Perkins stepped out of the darkness.

"Oh, it's you Bruce," he sighed, lowering the barrel of his Enfield rifle. His face was unshaven, his shirt bloody. He looked as if he'd lost everything, and it seemed that he had.

"What happened here?" Bruce demanded.

He staggered to a crate and sat down. "About a week ago," he began as tears formed in his eyes. He sniffed. "Naval batteries bombed the area around the harbor with horrible exploding canisters."

Bruce's face suddenly froze. "My wife, where is Marceline?"

His eyes refocused from a nightmare, his thoughts slowly clarified. He suddenly stretched his arm and massaged his neck, a pain brought on by the uncommon use of a shovel.

"My wife finally suggested that Marceline and the child live with us. I mean their food was running out, the nights were too cold for the little boy."

"And then what?" Bruce agonized. It seemed an eternity before Perkins regained his confidence.

His head slowly raised, his hair frazzled. "Bruce, I'm afraid my wife and Marceline were both killed in that raid last week," he said in measured phrases.

Bruce's heart collapsed.

Yet he held his stance as if his mind could take the strain. "My son, what of him?" he cried as he grabbed Perkins by the shoulders, unconsciously shaking him.

"A woman who lived down your street took him. She told my wife she knew you, I couldn't take care of your son," he sadly admitted with a bowed head.

Finally Bruce's endurance lost control.

His mind went mad. He grabbed Mr. Perkins and drew him into his chest. They cried on each other's shoulder, until Bruce couldn't allow himself the advantage of crying any longer—not now when his son needed him.

Bruce retraced his pathway back toward the location of his obliterated house in the morning mist of the destruction, craning his neck over piles of debris. In the foggy distance he saw a tall man standing beside a black woman. As he walked closer he intriguingly realized it was Danny Boy and Hattie! Suddenly Arabella walked out of the shadows holding the hand of his son Josh!!

"Bruce Taylor," she weakly called.

He stood stunned. "Arabella . . . you have my son," he fervently replied.

"Yes. He's safe, a fine little man. We live in a room a few blocks from here," she amiably assured as Josh took his father's hand.

Bruce's knees buckled and his shoulders slumped. A curious peace quelled the bitterness, and the rage in his heart subsided. He lifted Josh into his arms hugging him tightly. It was a joyous moment although the evidence of sorrow was strewn all around the area. Finally he opened his eyes and gazed over Josh's shoulder into the dirt-smudged face of Arabella. His forehead suddenly wrinkled with compassion. "Thank you, Arabella. I don't know how I will every repay you for saving Josh."

"I'm glad I was able to keep him safe—you should be pound of him. The little fella never cried."

Mixed emotions suddenly strummed the frazzled strings of his tormented heart. His wife was dead, and standing before him was a vibrant young woman who had befriended him when he first moved to Charleston. He owed her something, but what did he have to give, he thought.

The thinly cloaked woman studied Bruce's familiar face for a moment of quiet longing. She confirmed in her heart that he was the only man for her, but sadly she kept silent; now he was free, but it was too close to the death of Marceline to tell him how she felt. She quelled the urge in her heart, swallowed her pride.

Bruce fixed his red irritated eyes on Arabella Rhett. "Arabella, I can't begin to thank you enough, and allow me to apologize for Marceline's indiscretion—I really don't know what possessed her."

Her head lowered sheepishly. "Bruce, I'm so sorry about Marceline's death. You owe me nothing— what are good friends for," she replied, her heart screaming—*nothing! Nothing, indeed! How she'd loved this man since they first met, her heart silently screamed!* The pain in his face caught her eye, and her heart acquiesced. She bowed to her intuition; it was too early for Bruce to consider another woman in his life, she would not embarrass him—perhaps herself, but not him. The bitter thought was a balm of truth if she were to survive without him. But existing without him was not in her plans—she'd wait for another day.

The cobwebs in his mind cleared momentarily. "Really, Arabella, I don't know what to say?"

Her head tilted. "Perhaps we should leave it at that," she replied, astounded at her remark.

Bruce puzzled. "Yes, well what are your plans now?"

She dropped her gaze, cleared her mind. "The plantation is a wreck, the house destroyed. I plan to put Danny Boy and Hattie on a train for Richmond if the tracks are open. I'm taking the train for Nashville. The Governor of Tennessee has asked Nathan Forrest to form a cavalry unit. I've decided to become a spy for his cavalry," she replied to a spellbound face.

An eyebrow arched. "Sounds dangerous," he smartly assumed, dropping his gaze.

She quoted the same information Nathan had given her. "Many women are joining the war effort providing military-sensitive information—I must do something, I'm not the type to sit and wait."

He had known Arabella long enough to realize that when she had made a decision, every element was calculated to the last decimal point.

"I think your decision is honorable—you will be careful, I mean . . . don't take any unnecessary chances," he advised dotingly.

His obvious fondness warmed her lonely heart. She sulked, stirring her foot on the ground, moisture blurring her pale blue eyes. If only she could tell him what was in her heart, she thought.

In their brief discussion she advised Bruce that General Grant was gathering his army to take Fort Henry, and that she suspected Grant would stage his operations along the Tennessee banks.

The information was important news for Lee, and Bruce assured her he'd see that Lee received it. He was astounded at her bravery, and yet many southern women were not satisfied to sit and wait; he'd noticed that in the Fort Sumter battle, how the women rallied together supporting their efforts.

"So you plan to work through Col. Forrest?" he replied, considering they might meet in the field and share information.

She inhaled a deep breath. "Yes, I hope we will meet again in this crazy upside-down world."

Bruce stood stunned, totally speechless at this woman's ingenuity. And it suddenly occurred to him what he could give her for all she'd done for Josh.

"How are you fixed for money?"

She thrust her tiny hand into a leather pouch, or was it a handbag, and pulled out a wad of Confederate paper money.

"This is the bank."

Bruce pondered for a second. "Where you're going you'll need gold. Let's tidy up here, and we'll go prospecting."

Arabella's head tilted. Maybe the war had touched Bruce's mind, yet he was still the most handsome man she'd even met, reminded her heart. She told Danny Boy and Hattie to wait and they would later go to the train depot.

Bruce led Arabella out where his house once stood, what was once the backyard near the stump of an old live oak that had shaded his backyard. Fortunately, if not divinely, he found a spade in the rubble, the handle half gone. Arabella held Josh's hand as he dug into the dry earth. Finally they heard the 'clink' of a metal box, a coffee tin.

"Ah, here it is," Bruce exclaimed!

"You buried your money" Arabella chuckled.

"Better than the bank; I sold the family farm before I joined up."

"Yes, I see," she thought, amazed that he'd found a buyer.

He twisted open the rusty top, and poured out thirty Double Eagle gold coins minted in 1861 by the New Orleans Mint.

"Here, you take twenty coins, and I'll keep ten; it'll get me and the boy back to Richmond."

"Gosh, Bruce, I can't take your savings."

"Think of it as payment for babysitting my boy," he smiled.

She squatted and hugged Josh. "Take care of your father, Josh—he's a good man."

Tiny tears swelled in the corner of Josh's eye. "Gosh, Miss Bella—I'm gonna miss you."

Arabella hugged Josh for a long moment and looked into his face. "I'm going to miss you, too, Josh."

She stood as she bowed her head facing Bruce. "It's a helluva war, destroying families, tearing the nation apart."

Bruce was somewhat taken aback by Josh's fondness of Arabella as he gazed relentlessly into her eyes. She reluctantly stretched out her leather pouch, and Bruce dropped twenty gold coins into the sagging bottom.

Arabella looked into his face and filed his image indelibly in her mind. "I've dealt with these Yankees before, and I'll do it again. You take Josh and be careful," she said as she pressed his hand against her cheek for what may be the last time she'd see him, touch him, or look into little Josh's face. Tears glistened in her eyes.

ARABELLA

She turned and walked away toward Danny Boy and Hattie for a short distance. Suddenly she stopped, spun around, and raced back toward Bruce. She leaped into his arms and planted a kiss on his lips. Finally, she released him, slid to her tiptoes, and looked into his startled face.

"That's just to remind you that I'm coming back," she smiled.

Bruce watched Arabella stroll off toward the railroad with Danny Boy and Hattie until they were out of sight. In the quietness of the moment he remembered the day he'd first met Arabella, so vivacious, so alive—alive, he thought, and stooped and took Josh in his arms, and rushed back to the tavern. He must bury his dead wife.

He found Mr. Perkins outside in the dimming dusk. Bruce discovered a suitable rock in the debris, and took it down into the cellar. He rummaged around until he found an old iron rail pin. He found a mallet, and began chiseling an epitaph in the rock: *Here lies Marceline Thibodaux Taylor (1837-1862) the mother of Joshua Abraham Taylor, and her unworthy husband, Robert Bruce Taylor.* He stood and took the tombstone topside, and over to the place in the garden where Clyde had buried the wives. He wedged the stone into the ground at the head of Marceline's grave.

Bruce sat in the dirt for the better part of an hour rereading the epitaph over and over again. Somehow he felt the pain of the nation. How he loved this country, especially the South and marveled at how young revolutionary Americans had died to secure its freedom. And now even the citizens had to fight just to live—it was the real epitaph—life among the dead.

His mind digressed. Who would be left to tell this story of the Old South—the proud people who loved their God, who lived by the sweat of their brow, who treated everyone as individuals—even the slaves of the era—took them into their homes, regarded them not as second class people, but human beings who eked out their livelihood as it was dealt them by God. Good people, good memories—good epitaphs . . . yet he thought of Arabella, because without her, Josh may not be alive? That thought he planted in his mind; it would germinate and blossom as uncertain time marched onward. It was a good anchor in a sea of trouble.

Chapter 11

Arabella left a telegraph station located in a nearby train depot outside of Charleston. Nathan Forrest had just answered her wire. She was glad he'd left word in Nashville should she call because he wanted her to meet him in Columbus, Kentucky in six days. They would discuss her desire to become his agent. She dropped her bag containing her riding suit and a few odds and ends, and strolled over to the ticket agent. Arabella bought a ticket to Columbus, Kentucky, and two tickets to Richmond for Danny Boy and Hattie, who sat on a bench watching. The agent told her the Columbus train would arrive in two hours, the Richmond train was delayed. She sat down beside her childhood friends, told them about their train, and handed the tickets to Danny Boy. She gave him a fistful of Confederate money, but didn't know if it would be acceptable now. The time together seemed solemn, the two hours only a few moments.

In that painful time Arabella planned what she'd wear over her riding habit. It occurred to her that she had a deep blue cape in her bag. That would do nicely, she decided. Danny Boy decided to remove himself and go outside before he burst into tears.

He strolled outside along a green pathway. His thought drifted to the war. In a few months there wouldn't be much greenery left when canisters of explosives fell and soldiers were marching over every blade of grass. He thought of Arabella, that little child now full grown, and he remembered that he'd promised her father to take care of her. And now it seemed she was taking care of him, he thought, and slowly walked back inside to wait for the train.

It was a solemn moment for these three friends from childhood, now separated by a war they had not asked for, nor actually believed that it had happened. Somehow they understood it may be their last time together, the sad circumstance of countless families trapped in a war. Danny Boy remained strong, though his manly pride was a bit wounded. Hattie cried on Arabella's shoulder.

Nathan Forrest had gathered about 700 men comprising an eight-company regiment commissioned by the Governor of Tennessee as the Forrest Rangers. They arrived at Columbus, Kentucky in the cool months of late autumn to begin rigorous training. Nathan received word that Arabella Rhett was at the depot, and he sent his Captain to bring her to his tent. The men had been drilling for about a month, and Nathan planned on moving out to Hopkinsville on the next dawn.

Arabella walked into Nathan's tent dressed in a gown gripping a small bag. He offered her a mug of coffee to warm the chill, and she sat more beautiful than he'd remembered. Her story that she'd told him back in Washington seemed tolerable, that is, she had a serious desire to do something for the war effort. From what he'd gathered she certainly was a victim of the secession: a woman with her good looks and witty charm, losing her family and the plantation, even the clothes on her back. But she was about the spunkiest woman he'd ever met, he believed and that quality was a rare necessity. She was well-built with good height compared to most southern women. She had the looks of a woman who could get information from a turnip if required. She would be on the road most of her time, not stuck in a home or entertaining the officers in Washington seeking information. It was a hard task, but Nathan believed she had the stamina. But he couldn't help worrying about the danger he was commissioning her into, a job most men would resist.

"So, you want to be an agent, Arabella Rhett?" Nathan asked.

She breathed deeply. "Yes, I do, or I wouldn't be here," she snapped.

Nathan saw that spunk coming out again. "I think you'd better get into something more suitable before chow," he grinned. "The tent is all yours."

Before eating, Arabella asked Nathan to join her in his tent. She was dressed in her stylish riding habit. More importantly, she had been busy devising a code they might use with sensitive information when the telegraph was unavailable. The two conspired together that Arabella would ride the area and discover Yankee troops, determine the numbers of soldiers, location, and destination. That kind of information would give any General the necessary evidence to prepare for battle or evasive action.

They sealed the plan with mugs of rum.

Nathan selected a horse from the corral where he regularly placed horses that showed up looking for food; they were useful when many mounts were shot from under his men, and he'd lost a few good mounts himself.

The next morning Arabella rode off with food in a sack on her first mission for Nathan Forrest's cavalry. Nobody was more confident than she, except Nathan Forrest. He believed in her ability.

Chapter 12

Bruce readdressed his plans when he found the railroad depot crammed with Union soldiers and armaments leaving the area westward. His spying credentials immediately came into play; it must be Grant's reinforcements, he thought. He was glad he was not dressed in a CSA uniform.

Bruce quickly entered a vacated house on the fringe of the city where he gratefully found foodstuff, his son in one hand. He opened the cupboards and found dried bacon and grits. He even discovered water in a bucket by the woodstove. After he and his son had gorged themselves, he surprisingly found a sack of coffee. Quickly he found a pillow case in the bedroom, but no weapons. Finally he crammed foodstuffs in the pillar case, and they ran outside.

Fortunately he discovered a saddled horse eating grass by the house, whether it had strolled from the Yankee lines or had escaped from a stable, it was a ride. Josh had wandered into the barn, and he went inside, reached down to grip his hand, when he heard a moan in the loft. He climbed up the ladder into the loft, and found a Union soldier with an injury of some sort. Upon investigation he discovered that he had a broken leg. Quickly, he descended the ladder and grabbed the pillow case with the foodstuffs. When he ascended the ladder, the soldier had a Colt revolver pointed straight at Bruce's gut.

"Hold on, son. I only want to help you. You have a broken leg."

The soldier slumped, his arm stretched out in the hay, his trigger finger engaged.

Bruce sat the pillow case beside him and kneeled. He retrieved a pocketknife from his pocket and slit the pant leg up to the knee. It was a compound fracture. Fortunately he had a bottle of whisky in the pillow case and uncorked it. He carefully took the soldier's bandana from around his neck and soaked it in whiskey. The soldier seemed calm but in pain, his face revealed he was just a boy of eighteen or so but a rank of lieutenant.

"Son, this is going to hurt," he warned and wiped the irritated flesh around the protruding tibia bone. The boy flinched, his face tightly wrinkled.

After a search of the loft, Bruce found a few broken pieces of a wooden crate. He wrapped the bandana soaked with whiskey around the leg, and fashioned two wooden slats on each side of the wound. Finally he removed his bandana from his neck and ripped it into three pieces and secured the slats with square knots.

"That's about all I can do for now, son. Are you hungry," he said to a pale face.

The soldier released his trigger finger. "Ah, thank you," he stuttered, readjusting his thinking process.

Bruce gave him a piece of hardtack and hard bread. His shaky hands seized it and he gorged his empty stomach.

Finally, the young lieutenant eased back into the hay. "I owe you my life," he admitted. "My name is Jeremy Hostetler, from Pennsylvania."

Bruce smiled, and stretched out his handshake. "Bruce Taylor, from Richmond."

The boy's face wrinkled. "I'm sorry, sir, your town is often bombarded by every Union ship that passes by the harbor."

Bruce bowed his head. "So that's what destroyed my house and killed my wife," he said, staring into space in a moment of reflection.

The boy slowing bowed his head. "I'm sorry—really I am—I lost my brother at Fort Sumter."

"That was the day that started this war—what does it all mean," Bruce mused.

The boy nodded. "And where are you headed now," the lad asked, a kind thought for a compassionate man.

Bruce sighed. "Virginia. I have a cousin there who I hope can care for my son."

"Well Mr. Taylor, travel carefully. General Grant is staging his Tennessee army at Pittsburg Landing along the Tennessee River. I believe he will combine the Ohio and Mississippi armies for this push."

Bruce filed the information in his brain. He left food for the wounded soldier, mostly beans and water. Their parting words were similar; war was hell, indeed, when would it all end. The soldier seemed sure that his men would find him and told Bruce to take the horse; he couldn't mount him anyway with a broken leg.

Bruce shook the lad's hand. He mounted the horse, grabbed the pillow case of food stuffs, secured it on the saddle horn, trotted to the house, and called out his son. He took Josh's arm, and slung him behind his back. They rode out under the cover of creeping night following a trail northward toward North Carolina.

As they crossed a railroad track in the open country under the light of the moon, Bruce had an idea. He sat Josh on a rock beneath a telegraph pole. Bruce climbed the pole and used his pocketknife to cut the telegraph wires. Using the blade he stripped the ends of the wire, and tapped out a Morse code message directly to General Lee's office. Now Lee knew Grant's intentions at Pittsburg Landing, the gathering of troops, and he would convey the news to President Davis, he thought.

On the way they bypassed the valleys, where Union troops were staging for a battle, and found safety in a cave at the front of a cave. Bruce trapped a rabbit with a forked stick, and cooked it over a fire set deep inside the cave for security. The boy needed protein, and so did he. A fresh, cool mountain stream provided water.

They left the cave as the wings of dawn lay a foggy blanket on the battle fields. After hours on the trail, they fortunately stumbled upon a farmhouse nestled in the mountains. As they approached Bruce spotted a farmer leaning on a pitchfork. Moving closer, he noticed that the man sucked on a twig.

The farmer spoke first. "Ere ye lost," he asked rolling the twig to the opposite side of his mouth.

Bruce smiled, pulling Josh into his arms. "Yes, you might say that—we are heading to Richmond."

They chatted a few minutes until the farmer seemed satisfied he was talking to a Confederate, not a renegade Yankee.

"Ye got a long spell on the trail. Won'cha cum into da house. I'll water and feed your mount in the stable."

Bruce immediately felt his compassion. "That's awful decent of you."

He took the horse's reins. "These ere times we hav'ta help our neighbors. I hears somewhere these ere times that try a man's soul."

Bruce smiled. "I think that was written in the Revolutionary War by Thomas Paine in his little book of *Common Sense*. Perhaps we don't use common sense anymore," he smiled.

The farmer spat a wad of tobacco on the ground, and wiped his mouth. "Ye got a point dar, friend," he said, and pointed to the door. "Let's see whut da womun of da house ere cook'in."

The farmer led him toward the house as Bruce grabbed his almost empty pillow case in one hand and Josh in the other.

The wife was setting the table for dinner as they entered the house. Her husband was a kind soul who often invited neighbors, even strangers, in for dinner. She saw the child and immediately took his hand.

The table was set with chicken and dumplings, green beans, and a pan of cornbread baked in an iron skillet. Bruce had not seen food of this quality in Richmond or Washington.

"Tis been a long spell since I held a child in my lap," the wife reminded herself as she wiped the boy's dirty face with her apron.

"This is very hospitable ma'am, we are indeed grateful."

She cracked a forced grin. "Tis all we has—thankful dat we has a roof over our heads."

The farmer laid his wooden spoon in his plate. "Our two boys ere serving with Colonel Jackson. We ain't heard a word since da left."

Bruce sat his mug of coffee on the table. "Colonel Jackson's cavalry horsemen are providing valuable reconnaissance. I feel sure your boys are safe—Jackson is one of the best Generals in Lee's command."

A moment of silence prevailed with the quiet sounds of eating.

The farmer finally broke the silence. "This war ain't nowhar neah ovuh."

The wife stood and took the boy and sat him by the fireplace. Bruce sipped his cup of coffee as he answered the farmer's questions. When he understood Bruce's condition, his attachment to General Lee with valuable intelligence, he instructed his wife to prepare food for his journey on the dawning morning.

The sun hid behind the mountain peaks, the area cloaked in a chilling fog as Bruce awoke to the smell of a country breakfast. He slid from the feather covers still in his clothes, donned his shoes, and entered the kitchen off the hall.

The wife smiled. "Breakfust ere await'n," she said gripping the handle of the iron skillet with a fold of her apron.

Bruce slumped in a chair, took a fork, about to demolish two fried eggs and grits. Suddenly he laid the fork down and looked up at the wife. "Ma'am, when I get back to Richmond, I'll check on your boys," he said and tucked a gold coin in her apron pocket.

She brought her apron to her face purposely hiding the tears. "Thank you kind sur," she sniffed as she felt the impression of the coin in her pocket. "Yez a good man."

"Ma'am, the unknown truth is the South has its good people like you."

The farmer entered the kitchen snapping the straps of his suspenders. He sat down, and they eat breakfast fielding questions about the war. There were so many things that Bruce wanted to tell them, but they were of military importance.

Finally, the farmer wiped his mouth with a cloth napkin. "Bruce, ye horse is saddled and ready. I took da liberty uh placing a sack of foodstuff over da saddle horn."

Bruce pushed his chair aside rubbing his tight stomach. The wife had finished feeding Josh, and gave him a coat she had saved from when her boys were his size.

The farmer brought Bruce's horse around from the barn where it fed on straw during the night and drank water from a trough.

Bruce shook the farmer's hand and doffed his cap to the wife. "May the Lord bless and keep you, ma'am. And when this war is over, perhaps the South will rise again."

Tears cascaded down the wife's cheeks. The farmer rolled a twig with his tongue to the opposite side of his mouth, an admirable grin on his tanned face. Bruce threw his leg over the saddle; the farmer lifted the boy, and sat him behind his father.

He took Bruce's hand. "Ye tells General Lee we ere with him, son."

Bruce and his boy rode off on a trail down into a hollow suggested by the farmer. As the sun dropped behind the hills, the hollow lit in the glow of dusk, they finally discovered a cave, and bedded down for the night. They found plenty of water in a stream flowing below the cave. Bruce searched in the sack for a light meal. They had to arise early if they were to reach the coast by nightfall.

Cape Fear appeared on the horizon just before dusk, the sunset so marvelous and colorful that Bruce forgot the war for a moment of peace. Tonight they would eat in town. The horse navigated the trail down into the area of the seafaring village. Bruce tied his horse at a rail, and lifted his son from the saddle.

They saw the lights glowing through the windows in a fisherman's pub down by the water. As they entered the front door, he witnessed a host of seafaring characters gorging their faces with fish and cornbread, chattering as if a flock of magpies. They took a seat at an empty table and finally ordered.

As they waited for their food, Bruce noticed a fisherman at the table next to him eating with his mate. The food arrived and they ate a delicious meal of sea bass with fried potatoes. Bruce wiped his mouth in a cloth napkin and rotated in his chair. "Pardon me, sir."

The bearded man turned his head. "What can I do for you and that lad?"

Bruce cleared his throat choosing the proper words when he wasn't quite sure of the question. "We need to book passage on your boat. I have important news for General Lee in Richmond. The trains are loaded with Union troops, all heading the wrong direction."

The fisherman took out his pocketknife and began whittling a toothpick as if he had not heard the stranger. A moment of purposeful pause, and the fisherman fixed his eyes on Bruce, pointing the blade at his nose.

"You ain't a lying Yankee, are ye," he said waving the pocketknife in Bruce's face."

Bruce gulped. "I'm from Charleston, and I just buried my wife. Me and my son here are headed for Richmond," he explained.

The fisherman's face wrinkled with remorse. "Ye say ye are attached to General Lee."

"That's right. Can you take us? The General will repay you."

He closed his knife. "I can take you up the Albemarle Sound, you'll have to make you own way to Richmond, and there ain't no charge."

Bruce's face beamed. "When?"

"We'll depart on the evening tide. My boat is moored in the third slip down on the wharf."

"Say does your mate need a horse and saddle?" Bruce announced abruptly.

A young man about twenty-five leaned forward, his eyes greenish, a scar on his left cheek, a bristled beard masking the extended edge of the scar, a seafarer for life. "My brother can use a good horse—what'cha wants fer him?"

"Nothing, he's yours."

The surprised man took the reins and suddenly saw the emblem of the U.S.A. Army embossed in the saddle. "Hey, wait a minute—this is a Yankee's horse," he barked.

Bruce smiled. "You might say I took it from a Yankee—does it matter?"

The man scratched his head. "I reckon not."

The fisherman smiled. This fella and his son needed passage, and he was the man to get it done. He certainly weren't no Yankee, he could see dat plain as day.

The sturdy one-mast sloop slipped quietly along the shoreline of the Atlantic. The fisherman extended the tubes of a telescope, and peered through the monocular lens. His eyes bulged open, and he lowered the scope.

"The harbor is blockaded. I'll put in here."

As the wooden boat sailed nearer the shoreline, the fisherman spotted the entry of a sheltered deep black creek, and angled the tiller. The sloop slipped into a thirty-foot wide waterway. The fisherman lowered his sail, and weighed anchor, as the bow nudged the shoreline about fifty feet from the entry.

"This creek is fed by a stream up yonder, and it should lead you to civilization," he advised as he off-loaded the bags.

Bruce took Josh's hand and slung the bag over his shoulder. "You have been a great help; indeed, sir. I can't imagine what we would have done without you. God bless you, my friend."

The fisherman doffed his cap. "Ye tells General Lee we won't fergit him."

Two hours of following the stream, and they finally entered an open plain enclosed by a steep hill, where they saw a mile-long trail of covered wagons rolling north, Bruce guessed to Washington.

After about two hours, they hopped on a covered wagon of refugees in a line of several dozen covered wagons headed to Washington for resupply. It was a clever idea; the mule driver wasn't too bright, he was in a hurry to get back to his regiment after transporting ammunition to the rail depot. After all his espionage movements Bruce had gained the uncanny ability to move safely through Union forces.

The wagon train finally reached Washington as dusk settled over the city. Bruce and his son got off, and thanked the lad.

The mule driver nodded. "Best of luck to you and your son, sir," he said, and whipped the mule's backside with a laureate.

Bruce bobbed his head, waving. They waited until the wagon moved past, followed by the stream of other wagons, and they walked into the edge of town. They entered the area where the wagons were parked in rows that seemed to reach for miles—so many of them. Bruce had an idea, though he hesitated at involving his son. Yet he had an opportunity and he must take it. They went to the rear of a barn where the ammunitions depot was fenced outside.

Bruce found a crawl space under the fence where a hound dog had slept, probably after chasing a fox. They crawled under the fence, and sneaked into the adjacent building. Bruce placed his son in the hayloft, while he snooped around. Near the barn door he found several barrels of gunpowder. He used his pocketknife to open the bunghole and tilted the barrel on its side. Carefully he rolled the unit toward the door where several canisters of munitions were stacked against the wall outside. As the barrel rolled it left a trail of gunpowder pouring out of the bunghole. He sat the barrel on end. Now he needed something for ignition, he thought. He found a stack of Springfield rifles against the inside wall opposite the barrels of gunpowder. He used his knife to pry off a percussion cap, and laid the cap on a rock.

Bruce climbed to the loft and whispered for his son to follow him down. He placed the boy at the door where they had entered the barn, and then he sneaked over to the percussion cap. He took his knife by its blade and hammered its base against the percussion cap supported on the rock.

The gunpowder ignited; a cone of fire crackled along the gunpowder trail toward the ominous barrel.

Quickly he pushed his son through the hole under the fence and snaked behind him, thankful he'd set a long burning fuse. Bruce grabbed his food sack, and they ran toward the railroad. They never stopped or looked back, and followed the track out of town heading for the hill country and Richmond. The moon was aglow, the city covered in a blanket of stars. Finally they climbed up a hill, and looked for a place or somewhere they might hide. The boy found a cave and they went inside.

Suddenly the stillness shattered by a massive explosion. The sky was ablaze in a billow of flame and smoke that rose a mile into the sky like the 4th of July. Debris tumbled from the heights and crashed over a large area of the town.

Chapter 13

Bruce and Josh finally reached Richmond. He needed lodging and a place for Josh to stay. In the back of his mind he had considered this situation and had managed to save a letter that his father had received a few years back. He pulled the tattered letter from his inside pocket and located the address written on the back of the envelope. The house was located on the southern side of the Potomac, perhaps two miles. He decided the boy was tired and he'd see General Lee after he settled Josh in a safe home.

He finally found the house and tied his horse on an iron ring at the edge of the road. Bruce ascended the long steps up to the house, Josh dangling at the end of his hand. As they stood on the porch, he wiped the top of each shoe on the calf of his trousers, and then patted away the dust with his hand.

A maid answered the door. She was of moderate height, and might have been very provocative except for her square-cut jay. A few words allowed his enter into the foyer, where he waited as instructed while the maid inquired of her employer; he wasn't sure of the situation in the house, nor his uncle. Paintings hung in the foyer but he recognized none of the people. Bruce rehearsed his thoughts; how he might explain his visit, yet he dared not expect too much. They were distant cousins, and had not made contact since they he was in knickers and suspenders in Fredericksburg.

Finally the maid returned and ushered him into an elegant room where he must wait again. Over the fireplace he saw a painting that he recognized. His uncle and the father of his cousin—oh what is her name, he thought: Julie, Julie Knox—yes, that teenager I used to play with, he remembered.

The wide door opened and a handsome elderly lady came into the room assisted by a cane. Bruce stood as she rounded the sofa. Their eyes met as they stood facing each other. Memorizes flashed through both their minds, as pigtails became curling hair, and freckles became a handsome man.

Finally she sat down beside Bruce. Her voice was soft and restful to the listener, a pleasant alternative to the sound of gunfire and canon, or the long nights of hooting owls and the ominous hiss of crawling things when he and Josh had slept in caves.

"Why Bruce, it's been so long," she remarked, her blue eyes scaled with cataracts.

Bruce sat mesmerized for the moment. It had been long, long enough for a teenager he once knew to grow old and apparently alone. "Do you live alone here, Mrs. Julie." It just fell from his mouth, no words to express his visit or the characterization of her title.

Her lungs filled with a deep sigh. "William died three years ago. And your wife—I assume you have married," she nodded.

Bruce finally regained his confidence. "That's the real reason I came. You see my wife was killed during a bombing at Charleston—.

"Oh I am so sorry," she interrupted.

"Thank you. Ah . . . I have a son of five years."

Her eyes bloomed. "Oh how wonderful. William and I never had children."

Bruce had no desire to ask the question he'd rehearsed. But Julie read his mind.

"Why don't you bring the child here? There is more room than I can possibly use."

Bruce sat speechless. "That's so kind of you Julie. But really I can't—.

"Nonsense. You arrange to bring him here, and I'll take care of it."

He smiled embarrassingly. "I'm afraid that I'm under false pretense, Julie. You see the boy is out in the hall."

Her face was aglow. "Why that's even more wonderful." She rang a tiny bell and the maid came in. "Marjorie will you take the boy into the kitchen and feed him, please?"

She bowed, "Yes ma'am."

Bruce's eyes followed the maid through the door.

"Why don't we have tea and talk about this," she suggested.

Bruce slumped on the sofa overcome with admiration and lack of sleep. Julie reached out and took his hand and led him to the sofa.

They sat around the fireplace, the logs flaming silently. Smoke curled up the chimney and the warmth of the fire brought back more memories. Julie said she would arrange for the boys clothing. Bruce felt intruding, an imposition his manhood denied. He stood.

"Would you excuse me for a moment? I have something in my saddle bags." The maid brought in tea as he passed her in the hallway.

Bruce returned promptly with a small burlap bag. He took a seat beside Julie, and she handed him a cup of tea as he sat.

The silence was too secretive for Julie. "What's in the bag—your dirty laundry?"

Bruce rolled back his head with laughter, the first time he'd felt so happy since his wife was killed. "No," he replied. "It's some savings I kept for a rainy day." He looked into her face. "I must say this is a bright sunny day, and I want you have this."

He placed six gold coins in her lap. She brought her hands too her mouth. She was running out of funds with the cost of operating the house left by her husband, and the wages for her maid. "Oh Bruce, you shouldn't."

He took her hand. "And you shouldn't have taken us in, either," he smiled.

They talked of those happier days in Fredericksburg for long hours into the night. She told him of William's death, their long years together, how the Union had stolen their property, and the house was all they had. Bruce was glad he had save the gold coins, and thankful for Julie's compassion.

Chapter 14

The summer temperature soared relentlessly in the south, as Maj. Gen. Leonidas Polk took over temporary command of the Confederacy's Heartland, that is, Tennessee, north-central Alabama, northern Georgia, and northeastern Mississippi, but not Kentucky, which still lay in Union hands.

The Confederacy had spread westward into Missouri, and they stood stern and ready for battle. They cleaned the barrels of their Enfield's, and honed the edges of their bayonets; the Union came at the risk of a fight to the death. In August, the Rebels marched on Springfield with 11,000 seasoned soldiers. Ten miles southwest of the town, 5,400 Union troopers intercepted the invaders at Wilson's Creek.

The hot summer sun singed the hands that held the metal implements of war, cooled only by the blood trickling down the saber handles. Death walked among the dying as arms and hands were slashed from its torso. Five grueling hours of fighting yielded the despicable carnage of 1,200 causalities.

The dusty dry earth was expensive, paid with the precious life of the dead, and the dying. The Federals pulled back, leaving a large chunk of southwestern Missouri land in the hands of the Confederates.

Union forces were staged in the west under the dictatorial leadership of Union Maj. Gen. John C. Fremont, that flamboyant Pathfinder of the west. He saw himself as ruler of the military domain beyond the homeland of Washington. While the Confederates actively recruited agents, Fremont announced his personal edict as he threatened immediate execution of any Rebel bearing arms. Further, in the nebulous pages of his unwritten edict, he confiscated the property of pro-Confederate Missourians and released their slaves. The purpose of Fremont's edit was to prolong a crisis. When word reached the White House, Lincoln annulled Fremont's edict, and removed him from command, a wise decision of a President yearning for unity.

As the weeks past, guerilla fighting tormented the Missourians. Despite the inconvenience, the lack of sleep, the nights of terror, and death always at the doorstep, Missouri remained a state of the Union, as did Kentucky when its governor ordered Confederates off its soil, another violation of property rights granted by the Constitution. The order was not challenged. Brig. Gen. Ulysses Grant had no direct orders when Maj. Gen. Fremont was relieved by Lincoln.

Grant began his military career at West Point at the early age of 17 in 1839. He served in the Mexican-American war under Generals Zachery Taylor and Winfield Scott, and retired from military service in 1854. With the onset of the Civil War in 1861, Grant was working as a clerk in his father's tannery shop in Galena, Illinois. He was called back into service, and trained Union military recruits at Galena. On June, 1861, he was promoted to Colonel. Maj. Gen. John Fremont observed Grant's "iron will" to win, and appointed him to commander of the District of Cairo. The Confederate army, stationed in

Columbus under Gen. Leonidas Polk, had violated Kentucky's military neutrality. Immediately, Grant landed troops from gunboats and transports, and took the Kentucky River city of Paducah without a fight.

The next day Grant set his sights on Columbus with 3,000 men transported on two gunboats sailing down the Mississippi from Cairo, Illinois. The gunboats sailed toward Belmont, Missouri, while a steamboat landed on the shore opposite Columbus. Grant captured Belmont. Polk responded with 5,000 men across the river and overwhelmed the Federals.

Grant's men retreated under protective gunfire from the gunboats, and they scrambled to safety aboard the ship. The raid accomplished nothing. But, indeed, it foreshadowed the tactical traits of Grant's keen eye for establishing a target and charging full steam ahead. His career skyrocketed from those meager exploits at Cairo.

Lincoln had not received an analysis of the Western Theatre battles as yet, nor had he heard of Grant's exploits. Instead, Lincoln concentrated his political charm in Washington, gathering political strength for passage of his Emancipation Proclamation. But the legislators longed for an end to the war.

Lee called Lt. Bruce Taylor into his office late in the afternoon as he sat at his map table planning a mission for Stonewall Jackson. Gen. Stewart sat in a chair across the room reading a book. Bruce stood nervous with thoughts churning in his active mind. Perhaps he should mention the observation of Davis' lackluster leadership, how Capt. Austin had heard rumors of disagreeable generals in the Western Theatre. He had discussed his reasoning with Austin, who thought Bruce's appointment was the proper time for voicing the leadership problem—but he wasn't sure of the timing, nor was he too keen on divulging a third-hand rumor.

After a period of introductions, Bruce decided he'd wait. Lee had something on his mind.

General Lee deeply sighed as he turned. "I haven't had the time to thank you for that intelligence on Bull Run. Thank you Bruce, you are doing fine work—by the way, a Union ammo dump on the outskirts of Washington exploded two nights ago—did you have anything to do with that?" he smiled.

"General, I'm afraid I am guilty."

Lee shook his head. "Nice work son, ammunition will be scarce for a while," he replied with a rare smile.

"Add to that about fifty crates of Springfield rifles," Bruce expanded, although his mind was on the safety of Arabella. For some reason his technical mind had not understood until now.

Gen. Stuart grinned, the smell of his cologne obvious. "Looks like you have another Thomas Jackson on your hands, sir."

Right now Bruce was more concerned about finding lodging in Richmond. He deeply sighed and stepped into the entrance foyer behind Gen. Stuart who placed his cavalier hat on his head, an ostrich plume waving in the air. Bruce gave his departing remarks to General Lee, and shook Brig. Gen Stewart's hand. "I assume we will meet again, General."

"Anyone who serves with General Lee won't have the time to meet on many occasions, my young friend."

Bruce only grinned as he bowed his head embarrassingly. Stewart gave several pointers to him, and Gen. Lee advised him on a few ideas, mostly he needed viable information on troop movement with numbers of cavalry. Before Bruce left, Lee recommended Doyle to show him the ropes, and thought it advisable to revitalize contact with the Maryland underground patriots.

More confident at this stage of discussion, Bruce returned to Austin's request. "General Lee, sir. I think you should talk with Capt. Austin. He has confided in me a plot to remove Davis."

Lee nodded his magnificent head. "This is not good for the war effort. I advise you to tell Austin to report to Davis himself and submit his claims directly," he replied as he motioned Bruce to step back into his office. He paced the floor with his hands clasped behind his back. Finally he sat in his chair facing his desk.

"Sit down Bruce."

Bruce closed his mind on the Austin request. From all he'd read and studied it was time he'd listen to the greatest general since George Washington. As his ears heard the quiet commanding voice of General Lee, he witnessed competent leadership unfolding in his presence. Lee pinched his bottom lip.

"What I am about to say is strictly between you and me," he said and rocked back in his seat. "Yes, Davis is the weak link in the South's war effort; I don't think he even wanted the inauguration. In his past he had a fistfight when he was a senator from Mississippi. The delegation from Mississippi spouted venomous words in the Senate chamber. Henry Foote scuffled with a Pennsylvania senator, threatening to hang a senator from New Hampshire, and, during a speech on the floor, he pulled a gun on Senator Thomas Benton, also of Missouri. Senator Davis got into a fistfight with Foot and challenged an Illinois congressman to a duel with muskets.

Lee paused, placed a knuckle under his nose anchored with a thumb under his chin.

"Such unscrupulous action is popular with the public but is not the proper action of a leader of the Confederacy."

Bruce sat amazed at the frankness and bluntness of General Lee. But he wasn't finished with his statement.

"For the record I am no longer an advisor to Davis. He is Commander in Chief of the Confederacy. My job is the defense of Virginia in the face of a hostile Washington government."

The room became deathly quiet as if the air had been sucked out. Lee poured a glass of wine and handed it to Bruce.

"Take this, you will need it," he said, and rocked back in his seat. "Bruce, since we are going to work together on a trustworthy basis, you must keep this thought in your mind." He paused, and inhaled a deep breath. "There is a terrible war coming, and young men who have never seen war cannot wait for it to happen, but I tell you I wish that I owned every slave in the South, for I would free them all to avoid this war."

Chapter 15

Bruce sat comfortably at a corner table in a Washington tavern in free sight of the door, except for the pungent smoke of tobacco and the candid words of Gen. Lee still buzzing in his head. Bruce was dressed in civilian clothes; a cap snuggled on his head shielding his eyes from the flaming candles of a cartwheel chandelier hung from the ceiling with a chain.

Jason Doyle sat beside him; a mug of rum cuddled in his hands. The crowd of soldiers, and rift-raft from the Potomac were emerged in conversations—mostly about the bombing of Fort Sumter, the Bull Run event, or the stormy election of Lincoln as President in 1860.

The cleanest dressed spokesman sat at a near table, one arm slung over the chair rail, the other arm balancing his third mug of rum. His speech was smooth, no slur, complete command of King George's English. His comments revealed that he was a southern sympathizer by the way he characterized Lincoln.

Doyle suddenly stood and ambled to the near table. "Sir, I perceive you have current knowledge of the war."

He raised his head from the mug of ale and swallowed. "And why, may I ask do you need this information," he replied with a cocked eyebrow.

Doyle smiled with a poker face. "My brother is attached to Major Anderson," he lied.

He smirked. "Kind sir, I hear many things in my profession—mostly criticism of that dastardly bloat these idiot citizens elected as President—a government stealing land from property owners, confiscating personal goods of men who have relatives living in the South."

His eyes suddenly gazed into empty distance, a decision churning in his obscurely demented mind. Suddenly he stood, gripped his lapels on each side of his cotton coat. He calmly looked left then right.

"Man is but a walking shadow, a poor player who struts and frets his hour upon the stage, and then is heard no more." He bowed and raised his hand, an index finger pointing upward. "And he won't be President long."

The proprietor refreshed Bruce's rum as he raised his head with a question on his lips that blurted out irrepressibly. "Who is that man over there," he asked, a finger pointing to the near table.

The proprietor wiped his hands in his dirty apron. "Why that's the actor who plays at Ford's Theatre—don't pay him any attention, he's always quoting Shakespeare."

Bruce rocked back in his seat as Doyle approached the table, their eyes melting together in a continuous stare. Great Scott, Bruce thought! That man was planning to assassinate Lincoln!

Bruce tapped the proprietor's hand. "I'll drop by here again soon; if he comes in again maybe he'll disclose where he lives. I'd like to talk with him," he uttered, and handed him two Union dollars.

The proprietor nodded. "If he shows up—one never knows when he comes here."

Bruce and Doyle left the tavern and walked outside. Bruce's mind stirred, and finally he told Doyle to check on this actor and he'd inform Gen. Lee's office. As Doyle threw a right leg over his saddle and galloped off, it occurred to Bruce that the Washington authorities should know about this actor. Bruce puzzled over an idea as he rode his horse down to the War Office. Bruce dismounted, found a rock, wrote a note, tied it to the rock, and hurled it through the front window of the War Office window, then casually galloped away, turning into the shadows between two buildings.

Even though Bruce realized the President was his enemy in war, he was the elected Commander in Chief of the Union, yet he sincerely expected that General Lee should be consulted on this issue.

General Lee sat at his desk pouring over maps, his back as straight as an arrow from a Cheyenne quill. Bruce was escorted to the office door by Lee's secretary, and warned not to interrupt Lee's concentration until he recognized him.

Bruce quietly walked inside, and stood in silence. Finally Lee lifted his head from the maps and nodded him toward a chair.

He filled his lungs. "Well Bruce, how's the team coming along?"

Bruce bobbed his head. "Just fine sir—sorry to interrupt you, General, but it seems we have a sticky issue here."

A graying eyebrow arched. "How so?"

"There's this actor in Washington who seems to admit he plans to assassinate Lincoln."

Lee's back stiffened. "You're sure of this!"

"No, I can't be certain, but we are following up on his whereabouts. I'll have a name soon."

Lee massaged his gray beard as he rocked back in his chair. "If this guy assassinates Lincoln, this war won't be over for generations to come—get back to me as soon as you can confirm this claim, Bruce."

Bruce stood at attention, and saluted. "Yes sir."

Bruce left Lee's office through the side door and crossed the street into the alley, looking both ways before he walked to a door in an adjacent building. He looked once more and knocked three times, followed by two knocks. The door slowly creaked ajar, two eyes staring in the crack. Then the door opened and closed behind Bruce's entry.

Doyle met Bruce at the door and they walked into his covert office with guarded excitement. Little Josh sat in a chair as his father instructed..

"His name is John Wilkes Booth. From what we can gather he is a sympathizer with his own game plan."

"That's good detective work, Jason. He may not be working alone—see if you can find any leads as to a meeting place; it's not the tavern, that's where this Booth guy gets his courage drinking rum—the tavern proprietor said he worked out of the Ford's Theatre."

Doyle was careful with his questions as he chased lead after lead, and finally discovered that Booth also received his mail at Ford's Theatre, and perhaps that's was the best place he'd start. But first he wanted to check with the Confederate underground operators in Maryland as Bruce had recommended.

Doyle found a ferry boat and crossed the Potomac to a shore about two miles from Ford's Theatre in the early afternoon. He hired a horse and galloped northward through a sparse neighborhood, until he suddenly spotted a man in the shadows that he'd met at the last intelligence meeting. He quickly pulled back the reins and dismounted.

"Hey, Walter—got a minute?"

A muscular man with broad shoulders who stood about six-two leaned from the shadows, and gestured his head for Doyle to follow him. Doyle dismounted and tied his horse to a rail.

The muscular man opened a door in the alley and motioned Jason to enter. The door closed behind their entry. Jason followed him through another door down a hallway, and hurried behind fast pace.

Inside a room lit with a candle, two men sat smoking cigars. Their features were so alike, he guessed they were twins, but actually they were first cousins. These guys were members of the Confederate Secret Service who smuggled recruits across the Potomac into Virginia, and relayed messages for Confederate agents as far north as Canada.

Walter introduced Doyle as an intelligence agent attached to General Lee. The atmosphere suddenly cycled from icy to convivial.

"Sit down," said one cousin, a glassy smile on his chapped lips.

"Doyle is checking out John Wilkes Booth," Walter responded, having chatted briefly with Jason in the hallway.

His left eyebrow lifted. "That actor? Why he's a grenade about to explode."

"What can you tell me about his friends, where he lives, that kind of stuff?" Doyle ventured.

He sucked in a deep breath. "Well, at times he works for us; he's attended a few meetings, even recruits members. Why only last week he recruited two friends as accomplishes, Samuel Arnold and Michael O'Laughlen. They meet often at the house of Maggie Branson. She's a sympathizer; works out of her house on North Eutaw Street in Baltimore," he particularized.

Doyle saw the enormity of Booth's involvement and played his trump card. "Listen, we have reason to believe he is planning a scheme to harm Lincoln. General Lee is concerned that the President's death will shift morale to the Union."

One cousin pinched his bottom lip. "You might have luck by talking with Booth's brother, Edwin. He has kicked Wilkes out of their house in New York because of his vehement speeches about Lincoln. But let me caution you—Edwin is pro-Union."

"So do you think the President is in danger at this time," Doyle queried.

He rocked back in his seat, crossed his hands behind his neck. "Can't swear to it—but I hear something about a kidnapping. Regardless, this Booth is capable of just about anything dramatic."

Chapter 16

Bruce walked into the War Department in Washington and asked to speak with the Secretary, his voice venturous, ready to take the risk of possibly disclosing his undercover motive. The office was stereotype, a couple of chairs, the picture of Lincoln hung on the wall over a small table, and a vase of cut flowers sat on the secretary's desk. The lady at the counter demandingly informed him that he had no appointment. Bruce looked into her battleaxe face.

"You tell your boss that the man who threw that rock through his window wants to see him."

Her face exploded with astonished expressions: surprise, trepidation, disbelief. "Just . . . just a moment please."

A man dressed in exquisite clothes stormed through the War office door. He had a jutting jaw, a Roman nose, cleanly trimmed beard, and a waistcoat with a missing button. A flowery collar sported a black tie that jammed his Adam's apple. His tanned hand held a lit cigar squeezed between his nicotine stained left index finger and thumb.

"Come in, please," a gruff voice bade.

He led Bruce into the office where two men sat behind a table, books, and pamphlets strewn about on the floor. The taller man stood and rounded the table with extended hand as Bruce walked inside.

"You are the gentleman who threw the rock threw that window," pointing to a repaired windowpane?" he asked as he shook his hand, gazing into Bruce's brown eyes.

Bruce shrugged. "Afraid so," he replied nonchalantly as he sat.

The agent reached over and took a handwritten note from the table. It was weathered, wrinkled, but legible, and Bruce immediately recognized his hand scribble.

"So do we have a name?" the agent asked pointedly.

"Bruce Taylor."

He forced a smile from a fading grin. "What do you know of John Wilkes Booth, Mr. Taylor?"

Bruce straightened his back, his head tilted like a cat ready to strike. "What makes you think I know Booth?" he barked annoyingly.

An eyebrow arched above a wrinkled forehead. "You aren't denying it, are you—we have ways of knowing," he replied as he squirmed in his chair.

"Well since you ask so nicely, I confess that I did my civic duty—yes, I wrote the note, and I tossed it threw the window," he grinned deviously as he crossed his arms across his chest.

The officer uncurled from his chair massaging his jutting jaw. "Now that's the question we have been asking ourselves—why, Mr. Taylor, why did you do that?"

Bruce wrenched in his seat. "I didn't want to get involved at the moment—that's all, and you are the people who need this information—not me."

The taller man who had sat quietly fingering a mug of coffee, suddenly dropped his gaze, and stood, placed his hands on his hips, and stretch backward relieving a pain in his back.

"My dear boy, if you can point out this man it's quite possible you'll receive a reward!"

Bruce smiled within his tattered spirit. He'd gotten away with his bluff, he reasoned. "If you take me to that tavern I'll point out Booth, if he's there, that is."

The taller man drained his coffee mug. "That's the stuff. You wait here and I'll call a carriage."

As he left the room, the two men poured glasses of water. Bruce noticed the outer door of the office was cracked open as he swallowed a gulp of water. He casually glanced at the movement of a dress that flashed passed an open space, the voices muddled. He'd seen it recently, but for some reason he couldn't recognize where, the colors seemed familiar. He filed the color in his mind for later recall.

Suddenly the man in the other room called the two men seated with Bruce, it seemed he had not found what he was looking for. However, as they left, Bruce leaned over the desk, and saw a file in an open drawer. Quickly he opened the file. It was a report on Gen. Grant and the plans for an invasion of Shiloh near Pittsburg Landing. He quickly closed the file and retook his seat.

The Tavern appeared in the dusk of the ending day, the shadows dancing on the leaves and branches. The carriage finally stopped in front of the tavern, and the taller War office agent stepped down on the wooden sidewalk. Bruce followed his steps into the tavern. The proprietor recognized Bruce from the bar, and met him at the door.

"That actor fella is here," he whispered.

Bruce nodded, but didn't look, not wanting to alert the actor who was drinking a mug of rum at a table in the back of the tavern near a rear door. Instead Bruce whispered to the War officer rolling his eyes toward the suspect. The agent grinned, and motioned for the carriage driver to guard the front door.

Suddenly the actor recognized the agent, jumped from his seat, and dashed toward the back door through the kitchen. The officer pushed Bruce aside, and pulled out his Colt revolver as he leaped over a chair, running into the back area.

With the officer in chase, Bruce winked at the proprietor and vacated the premises. Once outside he quickly hopped into the carriage. He snapped the whip, and the horse leaped to a gallop.

When he reached the area of the Potomac, he stopped the carriage and tied the horse in front of a livery stable a couple of blocks away from Julie's house. Funny how he thought of Josh, and how gracious of Julie to keep him at her home.

Bruce made his way through the alley to Julie's house, huffing and puffing. He banged on the door and the maid let him inside. He rushed toward the main sitting room and Julie met him in the hallway, wrinkles of worry on her forehead.

"What is it, Bruce?"

"War Department agents questioned me, I need to gather my things and vacate your house soon as possible," he gasped, without further explanation.

Her face registered disagreement. "Must you go?"

He took her by the arms. "You must not be mixed up in this, Julie."

"Mixed up in what?" she pleaded.

Her face frowned with questions, as he took her arm and led her into the sitting room. Her mind continued to whirl without answers as they rounded the sofa. She sat silently for a brief moment as Bruce poked the logs in the fireplace, his elbow propped on the mantle. The silence was too imperious for Julie.

"Bruce, I don't care what you've done in the past, but you must tell me why you are running away."

Bruce replaced the tongs in its caddie, and sat beside her, his thoughts sorting what he could tell her from what might endanger the mission.

Finally he faced Julie. "I am a Captain in the CSA attached to Maj. Gen. Robert E. Lee in Richmond."

The meaning of his statement twisted in her mind and finally uncoiled. "Then you are in undercover work."

He only nodded in silence, but his keen ears heard a sound at the door. He whirled. It was the maid entering with cups of steaming tea. She sat the tea on the table in front of the sofa, and a plate of teacakes.

"Thank you Marjorie," Julie said.

As the maid departed, the hem of her dress flapping, Bruce's mind downloaded the vision he had seen in the War Department office. It was the same dress, the same shoes. He stood.

"Marjorie, may I have a word, please," Bruce said demandingly.

She stopped in her tracks, and stood with her back facing Bruce. Suddenly, she bolted out the front door.

Julie stood. "Why Marjorie—you come back here," she yelled.

Marjorie came back, but with her arms handcuffed, Jason Doyle pushing her forward.

"Thought you might need assistance, this woman has been under surveillance for almost a year," he grinned. Then the grin dimmed as he looked into Julie's face. "Ma'am, your husband was killed for his sympathetic activities, and we suspected this woman was the informer."

Julie faced her maid with defiance, a helpmate she had hired after her husband had died—was killed, she suddenly thought.

"Why you strumpet," she barked vehemently," as she slapped her face. Immediately her eyes flooded with tears, and she fell into Bruce's arms, weak from too much excitement.

The maid's head bowed in muted silence.

Bruce rubbed his hands over Julie's back. "I saw her this morning at the War Department office—she must be a Union spy."

Julie's white face blushed blood-red, her eyes puffed by tears. Her mind was a quandary of nerves; she knew that her husband was a southern sympathizer; she now had closure, his murderer had been caught.

Julie pushed back from Bruce's arms, and broke the silence. "My husband was a gunsmith, and financed foodstuffs sent to Charleston in 1858, and he purchased Southern cotton and sold it to the mills in Pennsylvania—the money he gave to the Confederates."

Doyle shifted his stance. "Ma'am, your husband did more than that; he supplied Springfield rifles to the Northern Virginia Army. Gen. Lee knew your husband quite well, ma'am," Doyle added.

Bruce informed Jason that he was staying overnight and would report to him in the morning. Doyle nodded and left with the maid, and listed her as a Union spy subject to interrogation and incarceration at Libby Prison in Richmond.

Chapter 17

Bruce tied his horse on the concrete post outside of Lee's office. In his mind he sorted all the information that he'd discovered at the War Department. Somehow he felt he should get out into the field, this city stuff was giving him the creeps. He opened the outside door and walked into the lobby. Lee's orderly met him quickly to warn that Gen. Lee was in conference with Stonewall Jackson. Bruce nodded and took a seat in the lobby. As he sat idly for the first time in weeks, he allowed his mind's eye to focus on the image of Arabella's face indelibly imprinted in his memory. More and more he thought of her, and the reality of Marceline's death; the only bright event of their time together was the birth of Josh, and now he had no mother. He'd certainly made a mess of his life, charging off to Charleston because Marceline had destroyed his mother's self-respect when she told her she was pregnant.

The sound of the orderly's voice broke the vision of his thoughts. "You may go in now, Captain Taylor."

As Bruce walked into Lee's office, his eyes immediately focused on a striking man seated by Lee's desk holding an old foraged cap in his lap. He wore a field uniform, quit dingy, a saber strapped to his side, the image of a cavalry horseman was burned into his countenance. He had a hero's look about his high forehead, a long slender nose, a beard that set off his natural leadership persona. His appearance was exactly described by Lee's picture of "his right arm."

Gen. Thomas A. "Stonewall" Jackson had used ridges, gaps, and roads of the Shenandoah Valley to baffle Federal forces and to stall their advance on Richmond. With about 17,000 men, he defeated units of three Union armies, more than twice his strength, in five battles known as Jackson's Valley Campaign waged in the spring of 1862. His men earned their name "foot cavalry," marching 648 miles in 43 days engaging the enemy in unpredictable cleaver movements. He always inflicted more wounds than he suffered. His admirers crossed the battle lines, Grant and Sherman heaped praise on his tactics, yet men like Nathan Forrest, and Robert E. Lee admired him the most.

Lee stood. "Bruce, I'd like you to meet Gen. Thomas Jackson."

Gen. Jackson never took a furlough during the war and never slept outside of his camp in all that time, and as the greater part of his strenuous army life was spent in the saddle, he rarely saw his wife and little girl. He was afraid for them traveling in the winter, especially with contagious diseases in his camp.

Bruce nodded his head. "General Jackson, I feel as though I know you like the back of my hand. Gen. Lee has had fine words about you."

Jackson shuffled in his seat. "Well, you know Bruce; the general is a little biased."

Bruce spread a broad smile. "Yes, I see your point. But let me add that more scholarly people than I have studied your tactics."

"You are too complimentary, my boy—Lee had some kind words of you, too."

Lee interrupted. "You had something to discuss, Bruce?"

Bruce gathered his thoughts. "Yes, general, I've arrested the maid of my cousin. She is a Union spy planted right under my nose."

Jackson smiled. "You are learning fast, Bruce. That's where the enemy is, right where you least expect him. The trick is to find him and eliminate him fast."

Bruce chortled. "General Lee, you recall the rock I threw through the War Department window concerning John Wilkes Booth?"

Jackson exploded with laughter. "Well, Bruce you should come with me, your antics will keep my men in good spirits on the battlefield."

Lee exhibited a rare smile. "You can't have him just yet, Thomas. Now what is this about, Bruce?"

"I decided to go over to their office, thought I might pick up something useful."

"And, what did you discover," Jackson asked with added interest.

"That's when I heard Julie's maid in the other room, heard her voice, and saw her shoes and the hem of her familiar dress."

"Quite observant, my boy," Lee replied.

Jackson saw the glitter in Bruce's eyes. "There is more General—the boy is not finished."

Bruce nodded. "When the officers questioned me about the note, they finally stopped the third degree and said I might receive a reward if the information panned out."

"A reward," Jackson barked amusingly.

Bruce swallowed dryly. "When the men left the room, I spotted a file in an open drawer of the officer's desk. It was a file on General Grant, his mounting of an attack at Pittsburgh Landing near Shiloh. The reason I feel the information is real, a young Yankee lieutenant told me the same story when I returned from Charleston—completely forgot it until now."

Lee pressed his bottom between thumb and index finger. "It could be a trap, Bruce."

Bruce sat back in his chair, rehearsing his answer before he spoke. "Forgive me, sir. But I disagree. The lad told me the information after I set his broken leg."

Jackson stormed from his seat, the scabbard of his saber rattled against the chair. "The Captain is correct, General Lee. Grant is a smart tactician. If Lincoln engages him to lead the Union army, we'll have a real battle on our hands right here in the Valley."

Lee sat stoic, massaging his gray beard. "Better inform Jefferson Davis," he thought aloud, and called in his orderly.

Lee wrote out a message for wiring, Davis was out of state in Nashville. He instructed Davis to appoint Gen. Albert Sidney Johnston and Brig. P.G.T. Beauregard; these were the best available commanders to go up against Grant, and probably Sherman, too, he reasoned.

While Lee was writing the message, Bruce turned to Jackson. "There was another notation in the report, but I had no time to read—something about Fort Henry."

"That's Tennessee territory," Jackson snapped.

Lee turned his head concentrating on the message to Davis. "What's this about Tennessee?"

Bruce faced Lee. "I saw another name in the file but had no time to read further."

"Explain," Lee replied.

Jackson spoke up. "It's Fort Henry along the Tennessee River, General. If I were to guess, I'd say this is all about Grant, too. Gen Halleck has turned him loose to take Tennessee—Forts Henry and

Donelson are the last fortifications before Grant storms into Virginia."

Lee stood. "Bruce, I want you to go to Nashville and meet with Davis. Apprise him of what you've uncovered."

Bruce stood. "Yes sir." He turned and greeted Jackson. "It was invigorating, sir."

Jackson rotated his impressive head as Bruce left the room. "He reminds me of you in your earlier days, General Lee."

Lee cocked an eyebrow. "He was a good student, all right."

Bruce left General Lee's office and went by the Potomac home. He met briefly with Julie, and had a quick meal. Doyle had already left for the train depot checking on the schedules to Nashville, and was expected back in less than an hour. As he ate, Julie brought Josh down from upstairs. After Bruce finished his meal, she called him to come into the front room by the fireplace.

As they sat chatting, she reported that she'd placed Josh in a class taught by her church. There were children his age and he'd develop social skills plus English and reading.

Bruce had much on his mind but he heard what she had said. "I owe you so much Julie. Thank you just for being available."

She smiled. "Josh needs a mother around him, Bruce, and I'm trying to fill that void."

He took her hand. "You'll make a fine mother, Julie. This war brought us together again; I just hope it doesn't destroy you."

"Bruce dahlin, what a Christmas present for Josh if he had a real mother—I think that's your job—find him a mother, Bruce."

They heard the door open and Doyle walked into the room. He'd checked with the

Nashville/Chattanooga Railroad, and reported a train departing for Nashville in three hours, but there were reports of Union soldiers scattered over the vicinity. Bruce assumed these were troops gathering for travel to Fort Henry, and then he realized the battle could be sooner than he thought. Immediately he left with Doyle, who took him to the train depot.

Chapter 18

The night was extremely cold, even in the cabin of the train. Bruce sat listening to the rhythm of the rail junctions bumping under the train wheels. He had told the conductor to awaken him if Yankees were in the area. He dozed off to sleep as he thought about John Wilkes Booth. Somehow he was glad he'd given that case to Doyle with top priority. It was his last thought as he drifted off to sleep. Rarely had he dreamed in his many restless nights. Deep from the caches of his mind the image of Arabella flashed on his retina. His eyes fluttered beneath the eyelids. The image focused. She stood dressed in a hoop skirt, a soft breeze rustling her hair. She was more beautiful than he'd imagined. Bruce's eyelids relaxed. And then the image blurred as a tall imposing figure drifted from the shadows of his dream. It was Marceline with a knife raised about to plunge it into Arabella back! His eyelids fluttered wildly.

Bruce was awakened by the conductor. He shook his head, blinked his eyes. When his mind cleared, he realized it was all a dream. But still there cobwebs of despair lingering in his consciousness.

The conductor realized he must have had a nightmare; these were the times of great desolation, nightmares were the norm.   "Sir, there are Union soldiers up ahead at Fort Henry." And then he explained there was an immediate question as to whether the depot in Nashville had been assaulted by Union troops. Bruce rubbed the sleepiness from his eyes.

"Do you have telegraph facilities on this line Mr. Conductor?"

"Matter of fact, we do, a check-in key at the next juncture."

Bruce stood from his seat. "It's urgent for me to wire a message. Fort Henry will be attacked within a few days, and then Donelson will follow, leaving middle Tennessee wide open for Grant."

"And you are?"

"Captain Bruce Taylor attached to General Lee."

"Do you know Morse code?"

Bruce nodded. "I've got to get a message to Jefferson Davis in Nashville."

"Come with me, Captain."

The conductor led him to the baggage car. "You wait here. I'll check with the engineer—should be within eyesight of the juncture now. When we stop you can leap out of the door." He placed his hand on Bruce's shoulder as if the next words were the most important.

"The telegraph key is in a box bolted to a pole," he said, as he fingered his vest pocket. "This key opens the pad-lock on the box. The train will wait until you've sent your message."

Bruce focused directly into his eyes. "Sir, you are a credit to Virginia—bless you, sir."

The train pulled into Nashville depot. Bruce leaped off and unlocked the box. He gripped the key and tapped out a message to Jefferson Davis' office. As he replaced the key and locked the box, he suddenly noticed a host of soldiers, all Confederates gathered with horses saddled. He handed the key to the conductor standing by the car, shook his hand, and then walked down the wooden floor toward the horsemen. Two his great surprise, he saw a familiar face standing by the depot talking to a Confederate Colonel. Immediately his mind replayed the dream he had on the train. He walked over and stood about twenty paces from the couple. The woman suddenly broke conversation when she saw a familiar shadow on the ground and immediately spun around. She squinted, her eyes facing the high sun. It was him! She ran and leaped into his arms. Forrest stood astonished that she had left him in the middle of a conversation. And then he realized this must be Bruce, the man she had told him about on many occasions.

Arabella looked into Bruce's eyes, her arms tightly wrapped around his waist. "Where did you come from, how I've missed you, longed for you," she confessed, her face spread into a broad smile.

Bruce placed her face between both his hands, drew her to his lips, and kissed her. The temptation was too strong, the desire overpowering, and his loneliness too desperate. They clung together for what seemed an eternity, lost in the tantalizing mist of rhapsody in the turmoil of war.

They heard the Colonel's cough, but ignored a response. Suddenly Bruce felt a heavy hand tapping his shoulder.

"Captain, we must be off to Fort Henry, either let her go, or one of men will saddle a horse and you come with us".

Arabella placed her head against Bruce's chest. "Bruce Taylor, may I introduce Colonel Nathan Forrest."

He was a tall impressive man perhaps six feet two, and about 200 pounds, not a day over 40. Though he had lots of hair it was distributed on each side of his crown anchored with a healthy beard. His dark eyes were piercing and Bruce felt he looked right into his mind.

Bruce extended his hand. "Pleased to meet you, sir."

Forrest acknowledged his reply with a nod, measuring the man he'd heard so much about. "So you are the gentleman who sent Arabella to me. I thank you, sir," Forrest acknowledged.

Bruce extended his hand. "I've heard about your cavalry, Colonel Forrest. Yes, I think I would like to go with you. What better place to get information for General Lee."

"Lee's a good man. Welcome to the cavalry, Bruce Taylor—let's see if you are as good a man as Arabella thinks."

Bruce cocked an eyebrow, squared his stance. "Say Colonel Forrest, what's the situation at Fort Henry?"

"For one thing, the fort is poorly sighted and is often undulated with rising river water."

"Why does the river flood this far inland? I thought the Tennessee was a calm river."

"She is, but she's interconnected with the Mississippi, the Ohio, and the Cumberland. Torrential rains and snow-melt add to the problem."

"I see," Bruce replied, but he didn't quite understand, nor was he trained in water hydraulics.

Nathan enjoyed the exchange, wasn't often he had the opportunity of expressing his views of old Tennessee. "Thought we'd ride over and check out the situation at Fort Henry."

Bruce touched Nathan's shoulder. "If you don't mind, I must talk with Jefferson Davis first— where do you suggest I find him?"

Forrest nodded his head toward the statehouse. "At the courthouse in that building," he replied.

"Good. You might delay that trip to Fort Henry for an hour; I'd like to tag along."

"Be right here—but no longer than an hour, mind you Taylor."

Arabella smiled. She'd have more time with the man she loved, she cheerfully thought. It wasn't often she had the chance to be with Bruce. She would relish every moment while she had him with her. Things were so uncertain with the war raging in Tennessee.

Forrest's men handed a horses reins to Bruce, and he rode to the courthouse and tied the mount outside. He turned up his collar, the air was getting colder. The large doors were approached by six or so steps. He entered the building, immediately sensing the warmer environment. An officer pointed to the second floor where he'd find Davis, and he climbed the several steps.

Three Confederate guards stood at a door near the end of the hall. Bruce introduced himself and a guard escorted him into the front office. A lady at the desk asked for his identification, and he gave her his message.

"Well, Capt. Taylor, it's good to see you again. I've been with President Davis since his inauguration—I remember you in Charleston," she explained.

"I'm blessed, ma'am—is it possible to see President Davis? General Lee sent me here."

"Let me check," she said, and walked to a door behind her desk, gently knocked with her knuckles. Presently, the door opened and she entered. Only a few seconds passed. She exited the office, and waved at Bruce.

Bruce quickly met her and she pointed to the door. "He'll see you right away, Capt. Taylor."

As he opened the door, a familiar face stood behind his desk and strolled up to him.

"Well, my boy, it's good to see you once more. General Lee tells me you are doing splendid work."

"Thank you sir, you are too kind."

"Won't you have a seat over here, Bruce?"

He followed Davis to a chair staged in front of his desk. Bruce sat and gathered his thoughts, eager to discuss a situation.

"Sir, Lee is concerned about Gen. Grant out of Cairo now assigned to the Western Theater. He believes that Grant is the man that Lincoln has been looking for to command an attack on Virginia. And that attack will come through middle Tennessee."

Davis rocked back in his seat, hands placed in his lap. "Well I quite agree on that point. Thank you for the wire, the Board estimates that Grant will be pressing down on Nashville inside six weeks."

"Sir, I have intelligence that Grant is massing forces at Pittsburg Landing at this moment. I believe he may attack Fort Henry first, and then push to Donelson. Grant has involved the Union navy and its gunboats, plus a hundred Napoleon cannon."

Davis pinched his bottom lip. "Well, Captain this is an important observation. A scout party has reported a group of Yankees at Shiloh."

"Shiloh—that's the sight of the battle, according to a report I read."

He nodded. "Could be you are right, Captain. I'll call the Board together immediately," he said, as he scratched a note on pad and called his secretary.

"Sir, I've met Colonel Nathan Forrest here in Nashville, and plan to travel with him to Fort Henry. Nathan has tactical concerns about both Forts Henry and Donelson."

He bobbed his head, unkempt gray hair waving in a breeze from an open window. "Colonel Forrest is the best cavalry man in the theater. He is highly underrated, and I plan to see if we can get him promoted. I welcome any information you have after your trip to Fort Henry."

Forrest's crew finally arrived at Fort Henry in the late afternoon. The river had subsided, leaving dried mud on the trails around the structure. She was a five-sided, open bastioned earthen structure, about ten acres on the east bank of the Tennessee near Kirkman's Old landing. The fort was sited about six miles below the mouth of Sandy River and Standing Rock Creek.

Forrest took Bruce with him as they walked around to the Fort entrance, and talked with Brig. Gen. Tilghman. Colonel Forrest wasn't satisfied with the fort's continual flooding, nor with the armaments. He felt that if Grant attacked, and it was a strong possibility, the fort probably couldn't stand a gunboat bombardment. After a long discussion about the Western Theater leaders, including this brash General Grant, the neurotic Sherman, and the old goat General Halleck, Forrest left the meeting. Nathan and Bruce walked beside each other, both silent as they chewed on the information.

Bruce ambled up to his horse, Forrest following as he gnawed on the conversation with Tilghman.

Bruce thought Forrest might have read between the lines of their conversation with the General, anxious for his interpretation on the fort's condition.

"What's your take on the situation, Colonel?"

"Tilghman doesn't like the defensibility of the fort. But I don't think he's aggressive as he should be in this situation. My guess is he will surrender in a single day if attacked—we'd best head back to Nashville before it gets dark," he advised.

Gen. Foote's naval flotilla, consisting of ironclads and wooden ships, bombarded Fort Henry as Grant's troops began the landing. Tilghman surrendered before Grants major force attacked on the 5th day of the bombardment, although approximately 3,000 Confederates escaped before the surrender. The fall of Fort Henry opened up the Union war effort in Tennessee and Alabama. Finally, Foote's naval fleet steamed to Fort Donelson while Grant moved overland twelve miles east to attack Fort Donelson. The 3,000 Confederate escapees joined the command of Gen. Albert Sidney Johnston's corps in the defense of the Cumberland Fort.

Chapter 19

Albert Sidney Johnston faced some tough choices. The logistics were cumbersome: Grant was located between Johnston's two main forces; Beauregard at Columbus, Kentucky with 12,000 men, and William J. Hardee at Bowling Green with 22,000 men. Fort Henry had been a prominent safeguard in the line defending Tennessee, because the Yankees had removed the railroad ties just south of it. This situation restricted reinforcements defending against the larger opposing Union army. Now that Grant controlled Fort Henry, nearby Fort Donelson was ready for capture, with only about a 5,000 man garrison.

The predicament: Grant might attack Fort Donelson, and Nashville was wide open, or Grant might link with Maj. Gen. Don Carlos Buell in Louisville with 45,000 men. Grant played the wild card, and followed Buell into Fort Donelson.

Johnston decided upon a non-aggressive course that forfeited the initiative across most of his defensive line, tacitly admitting the Confederate defensive strategy for Tennessee was a complete disaster. He met a council of war held in the Covington Hotel in Bowling Green, and decided upon abandoning western Kentucky by withdrawing Beauregard from Columbus, evacuating Bowling

Green, and moving his forces south of the Cumberland River at Nashville. Despite his misgivings about its defensibility, Johnston agreed to the advice from Beauregard suggesting he should reinforce Fort Donelson with another 12,000 men, knowing that a defeat there meant the inevitable loss of Middle Tennessee, and the vital manufacturing and arsenal city of Nashville.

Johnston chose Beauregard for command of Fort Donelson because of his admirable performance at Bull Run, but he came down with a sore throat, unable to serve.

Before he left Nashville, Bruce Taylor telegraphed Lee's Richmond office with information that Johnston had given command of the Fort Donelson battle to Brig. Gen. John B. Floyd, one of Lee's western Virginia generals after Beauregard fell into sickness. After he sent his telegram, Bruce chatted with Arabella for a long while, until she rode off on her horse eager to get back to surveillance.

Lee's orderly brought Bruce's telegram into his office, and Lee immediately sent a wire to Johnston regarding Floyd's background; he was a wanted-man in the North for alleged graft and secessionist activities when he was Secretary of War in the administration of President James Buchanan. His background was political, not military but he was nevertheless the senior brigadier general on the Cumberland.

Bruce confronted Johnston on his choice of Floyd. War had its strange bedfellows, just as politics, he thought. Johnston had little substantive comment, and Bruce didn't push it. His job was intelligence.

Maj. Gen. Henry W. Halleck, Grant's superior as the commander of the Department of the Missouri, was also apprehensive. He had authorized Grant's capture of Fort Henry, but now he felt that continuing to Donelson was risky. Despite Grant's success to date, Halleck had little confidence in Grant, considering his recklessness. Halleck connived against Grant in an attempt of convincing his own rival, Don Carlos Buell that he should take command of the campaign and get his additional forces engaged. However, Buell was as passive as Grant, but was highly regarded by Johnston as a tactical opponent. Grant never suspected his superiors were considering his relief, but he was well aware that any delay or reversal might push Halleck over the edge and he'd cancel the operation to take Fort Donelson. Grant was not about to let that happen.

Rains had resulted in miserable conditions on the roads around Fort Donelson and the flood waters had submerged Fort Henry anew. Early in the morning on February 11, Grant held a council of war in a nearby house.

Up in the attic of the abandoned house, a woman curled in fetal position straining her ears at a knotty crack in the ceiling above Grant's meeting. Their speech was garbled, but Arabella pieced together the message and stored it in her analytical mind: Grant's generals supported his plan for taking Fort Donelson in a single day, all except Brig. Gen. John A. McClernand, who disagreed.

Arabella lay in the attic until the dusk of dawn. The meeting was over, the house quiet as an ossuary. She opened the attic access door and lowered her body to the floor, holding the supported edges of the frame, stretching down until her feet dangled near the floor. She sneaked to the rear door, and quietly ran into the bush and out into the woods where she had tied her horse.

She mounted her steed and galloped into Murfreesboro. As she rode into the town she noticed a group of Yankees camped by the courthouse. She dismounted and walked between two buildings into a back alley, where she tied her horse. Instantly she noticed the back door to a merchandise store was cracked ajar. She sneaked inside and spotted a telegraph key behind the counter. The key man was cooking his breakfast in the back room, and she didn't know if he was friend or foe. Arabella had no time to waste and stepped behind the counter. She activated the key, and wired two coded messages to Nathan Forrest in Nashville, one on the Donelson raid, the other on occupation of Murfreesboro by the Yankees. The smell of the man's sausage and eggs aggravated her taste buds; besides that, her horse needed feeding.

She had passed a livery stable at the edge of town, but before she left the store, she commandeered a sack of flour a dozen eggs, and a side of bacon, a useful ploy that Nathan had taught her. Arabella sneaked out of the back door. She carefully stuffed the merchandise in her saddlebags and led the horse through the alley until she was out of earshot of the Yankees. She exited the alley near the livery stable and fed her horse on hay and unshelled corn. Her mare sniffed out a water barrel and sipped her fill.

Arabella rode off into the twilight looking for a hidden location to cook the eggs and bacon, and make some biscuits.

Col. Nathan Forrest moved his cavalry to the outskirts of Murfreesboro just after midnight. Arabella's message was correct. The Yankees had a regiment of about 1500 men; some camped west of town, the command headquartered in an inn, the balance holding up in the courthouse. A resident of the town told Forrest that the jail was full of citizens and some Confederate soldiers scheduled for hanging the very next day.

Col. Forrest sent his Texan brigade stampeding into the enemy camps at the east end of town, and the Georgia brigade to engage the enemy at the west of town. Forrest led the rest of his regulars on an attack down the center of Main Street. He divided the remaining men in three small groups: one to capture the Yankee General at the Inn headquarters, another to free the prisoners from the jail, and the other group to engage the enemy in the courthouse.

At sunrise the next morning a three-prong attack commenced. Screaming horsemen sent a shock-and-awe fear into the hearts of the sleeping Yankees, startled by the now familiar Rebel yell charging toward them on three fronts simultaneously.

Col. Forrest led the charge through the center of town with the escorts of two companies from Tennessee and Kentucky. The Yankee general and his staff were quickly taken into custody, but the fighting on the outskirts of both ends of town was fought to a bloody stalemate. Finally the Federalist soldiers were too wasted to fight.

Forrest sent a man under a white flag and offered them to lay down weapons and become prisoners or they would die within the hour. The Federalist surrendered with 400 troops and carnage of over 1000 men.

Chapter 20

Fort Donelson was a flat area, clear of trees and brush with tall earth walls enclosing the fifteen or so acre compound. It sat high above the Cumberland River, and its heavy guns protected the fort from enemy invasion. Col. Nathan Forrest received Arabella's coded message and wired Gen. Gideon Pillow at Fort Donelson. When he arrived at the fort, Gen. Pillow immediately put him in charge of about 300 mounted men. As ordered, Forrest took a squad on reconnaissance to the west and located the enemy moving in from Ft. Henry. About 5 miles out they spotted a detachment of Union cavalry. Without hesitation Gen. Forrest sent his unit into battle hollering, "Charge men—Charge!" They attacked headlong in the face of the bluecoats. The area was wooded heavily and very brushy, and Forrest men were scattered. Several bluecoats lay dead, and when they heard the bugler sound for halt they fell back. Suddenly, Forrest saw a large body of Union infantry ahead which set up impossible odds.

Despite the odds, Gen. Nathan Bedford Forrest attacked with uncontrolled dynamism, a man possessed by the demon of war, but in fact he was aware of everything on the battle field. Without military training, he insisted that 15 minutes against the enemy was better than three days of tactics.

Forrest inflicted damage, physical and emotional, and ordered his squad back to the fort. His men formed a horseshoe off the steep bluffs of the Cumberland. They had delayed the Union advance by a solid two hours, giving time for Gen. Pillow to assess the number and placement of men and artillery.

Grant arrived in the afternoon and established his headquarters near the left side of the front line, at the Widow Crisp's House. All logistics were in place, and Grant met with his generals that night. In the deep shadows of the candlelit house, Arabella Rhett crouched in a dark corner beneath the staircase, looking for information useful for Nathan Forrest. She heard the generals pouring wine amidst idle chat, and then Grant directed the strategy, gave his personal schedule, but left no one in charge as he exited by a rear stairway. Arabella took note of Grant's absence.

Although the weather had cooperated up till then, a snow storm arrived the night of February 13, with strong winds plunging the temperature down to ten degrees Fahrenheit, and deposited three inches of snow by morning. Wagons were frozen to the earth. Because of the proximity of the enemy lines and active sharpshooters, the soldiers were forbidden campfires for warmth or cooking. Many had arrived without blankets or overcoats.

At 1:00 a.m. on February 14, Brig. Gen. Floyd held a council in his headquarters at the Dover Hotel. The only protection the fort possessed was the river battery overlooking the Cumberland River, not adequate against an Army of infantry. Gen. Pillow was chosen for a breakout attempt, but lost his aide from a Union sharpshooter, and postponed the breakout because they were detected by the enemy.

Although Floyd was furious, it was too late for the completion of the mission.

Grant finally arrived down river and tied his horse to a log on the Cumberland shoreline. He boarded his flagship, and sought out Flag Officer Foote. They discussed Grant's strategy, consuming whisky poured in Foote's private English china. Grant was satisfied with the plan, but he'd made an uncommon mistake by not leaving someone in charge while he was away.

Col. Nathan Forrest approached Gen. Pillow with Arabella's information on Grants absence. Armed with this report, Gen. Pillow prepared for a dawn attack against McClernand's division. The Confederate plan went into action at daybreak. Pillow's men sounded the Rebel yell, and pushed McClernand's men out of the way for an escape route. Col. Forrest mounted a flanking attack that sealed the route. McClernand sent messengers for assistance by Gen. Lew Wallace, but Wallace refused action without orders from Grant. McClernand had no choice. He had to withdraw.

Yet, not everything was going so well for the Confederate's advance. By midmorning, Col. Nathan Forrest urged Bushrod Johnson for an all-out attack on the disorganized Union troops. Johnson was too cautious, the bane of indecision, but kept the infantry moving forward. The Confederate offensive stopped around noon, when Col. Thayer's Union troops formed a defensive line on a ridge astride Wynn's Ferry Road. Although the Confederate's assaulted three times, they failed, and withdrew to a ridge one half mile back.

Grant galloped seven miles over icy roads and finally reached Wallace's headquarters. He was utterly amazed at the confusion and lack of leadership. By his nature, Grant did not panic at the

Confederate assault; instead, he sent word to Foote for a demonstration of naval gunfire, assuming that his troops were demoralized. The blast of naval guns was a sweet sound of confidence.

No such leadership existed in the Confederate ranks at that perilous moment, save one: Nathan Bedford Forrest. Had they heeded his advice, they would be twenty miles south by now. From that moment Forrest made a default decision in his mind; fight his battles where he did the most good, in the byways of the southern states, no longer would he trust the upper commanders with the lives of his men.

Grant moved quickly. Despite repelling repeated attacks, the Confederates lost the earthworks. By nightfall all the Confederates were driven back behind their original trenches. Grant was already planning his attack for the next morning. However, Floyd and Pillow telegraphed Gen. Albert Johnston in Nashville that they had won a great victory, unveiling there confused command of events.

Grant's plan strangled the last hope of Confederate victory and escape. Gen. Buckner met with his team and pleaded for surrender. Pillow escaped by small boat across the Cumberland that night. Floyd left the next morning on the only steamer available. Disgusted with their cowardice, Col. Forrest announced, "I didn't come here to surrender my command." He stormed out of the meeting.

On the next morning Gen. Buckner surrendered Fort Donelson. Buckner sent a note to Grant requesting an armistice and asking negotiation of terms of surrender. Buckner had hoped Grant might remember how he had given him permission to return to his home in Illinois sometime after Grant resigned his commission because of alcoholism before the secession. However, Grant showed no mercy towards men he considered rebellious against the Federal government. Instead, Grant offered "Unconditional Surrender."

The Battle of Fort Donelson was the turning point for the North, the stake in the heart of middle Tennessee. Grant's victory gave him the notoriety he needed to gain the attention of President Lincoln. It was the first army he had captured, but several more battles waited in the wings of the war. Cannon fired and church bells rung throughout the North. The capture of Forts Henry and Donelson were the first significant Union victories of the war, and opened two great rivers as avenues of invasion into the heartland of the South. Grant was promoted to major general, second in seniority to Henry W. Halleck in the West. Nearly all of Albert Sidney Johnston's forces were taken prisoner; Grant had captured more soldiers than all previous Union generals combined. But Grant was no fool, he had his eye upon Nathan Forrest, a man who thought and acted like himself. Alas, Kentucky-born Johnston bore the stigma for Donelson. Beauregard's sickness would not stop him from meeting Grant another day.

Col. Forrest escaped from the Fort Donelson capitulation with about 700 of his cavalrymen and a few other horsemen who had joined from Fort Henry. They rode toward Nashville through the shallow, icy waters of Lick Creek. Colonel Forrest had sought out a local boy from Dover as guide, and sent him and two of his men to scout out the flooded condition of Clarksville road, which led to Lick Creek. They came back in an hour filthy and half frozen, reporting to Forrest that the road was dangerously passable but unguarded. The local boy warned that the ford was icy and probably three-feet deep.

Forrest informed his officers he wanted them ready with rations of salt bacon and corn bread rolled into blankets. The horses were saddled awaiting the Colonel's orders. By this time eleven hundred horsemen had assembled behind Forrest, each recognizing his leadership capabilities. They walked through the freezing wind without seeing the enemy, and finally passed Dover. They came to the banks of Lick Creek, the black icy waters flowing about a hundred yards wide. Col. Forrest rode out front as usual, hesitated but a moment, and slowly wade his horse through the current, the thin icy cracking as he went. He reached the other side, and sat on his horse and watched every horseman safely over the creek.

Because of the uncontrollable conditions it took the better part of an hour for all the men to cross the creek, the freezing water extended up to the saddles in places. Forrest provided no rest, and spurred his men on toward Nashville. By this time these men would follow Forrest through hell and back. They rode all day into the night, and finally Forrest ordered halt, and they rested, lest he'd end up in Nashville with a group of soldiers down with pneumonia. Forrest allowed the men to build fires if they found dry wood. Fortunately they found plenty of wood and dried their clothes while they sat wrapped in blankets. Some dried their clothes, others made the food. It was a cold night, but they stoked the fires all night. It was good to be off the mounts, good to follow a man who was a leader, not like those misfits back at Fort Donelson.

Early the next morning they rode into Nashville. Many were sickly, but alive, thanks to Colonel Forrest. They had lost 400 of their men at Fort Donelson, the army lost 12,000, and Gen. Buckner was captured. And now the Yankees patrolled gunboats and transports at will up and down the Tennessee and Cumberland Rivers.

Chapter 21

The cavalry of Nathan Forrest stayed in Nashville a week resting, some with gun wounds and saber stabs, many more with frostbite. The surgeon who rode with the men fixed the boys up and bandaged their wounds. The next day Forrest sent his major to Murfreesboro along with the men who were not wounded. The morning they left the other men prepared the quartermaster stores and loaded them on wagons. Most folks believed the Yankees would attack Nashville soon.

Arabella Rhett rode up on her horse and went into the hospital tent where Forrest was resting out of sight of his men. His left eyebrow elevated, when he saw her.

"Sit down Arabella, thank you for the info on Grant's absence at Donelson—you're the best," he said as he poured her a jigger of whisky. She had saved over 2,000 of his men with her coded information, handled an Enfield better than most of his men.

"Nathan, I'm sorry about Fort Donelson. Some of these generals are wimps."

"Yes, I gave them a piece of my mind—Listen Arabella, you've been busy sending wires, but now me and my men will be most time on the road, so I appreciate it when you can meet me on the road."

She nodded. "Can do—the reason I dropped in. Grant has pushed 35,000 men into Corinth. Gen. Albert Johnston could use your cavalry if you can get there in time."

Nathan bobbed his head. "If it's possible we'll get there—we're moving out tonight."

She leaned back on Nathan's saddle, cross her boot-laden legs. "Johnston believes the surrender of Fort Donelson has given Grant's men a boost in morale."

Nathan grunted. "Grant needs to be taken down a notch—heard he's addicted to cigars."

Arabella's eyes glowed. "Yeah, maybe I'll just slip him a cigar loaded with cyanide," she chuckled.

A rare smile crossed Nathan's face. "Why don't you rest here? I'll leave a guard outside."

"Thanks, Nathan—listen, if something happens to me, you know. Would you contact Bruce?"

Concern blazed across his bearded face. "He's a good man, held his position well while he was with us for a few days. Where will I find him?"

Her eyes sparkled. "He's attached to General Lee in Richmond as his intelligence officer."

He nodded affirmatively. "It's the least I can do, Arabella—but you take care of yourself,—you hear."

She touched his arm. "Right."

Union Maj. Gen. Ulysses S. Grant moved his army deep into Tennessee along the Tennessee River. He made his encampment at Pittsburg Landing on the west bank. The thick woods in these parts required clearing for his artillery, the swamp areas were a potential problem for his foot soldiers. Believe it or not, the mosquitoes were bigger than humming birds, according to a Captain with huge whelps on his face.

Grant sat at his map table smoking one of his 18 a day cigars. He poured a jigger of whiskey, downed it wholly, and wiped the back of hand across his fuzzy beard. He had summoned his young Brig. Gen. to his tent for a conference. The flap of the tent suddenly opened and a Captain ushered Sherman inside. He promptly saluted.

"You called, General?"

He shuffled. "Give me your Shiloh plan."

His head cocked, unkempt hair quivered. "Nothing extravagant, Sir, find the enemy and charge."

Grant poured another jigger of whiskey. "Listen Sherman, Johnston is not going to fight as you were taught in War College. He's a guerrilla tactics man, strike you where you least expect," he snarled and downed the whiskey, his Adams apple wiggling.

Sherman's beady eyes stared indifferently. "Should that really concern me, Sir?" he rasped.

Grant's unblinking eyes enlarged. "Well, it damned well concerns me! Your arrogance is worse than mine, Sherman. Be realistic—Johnston is a good general," he barked, like a dog chewing on a bone ready to bite his intruder.

Sherman bobbed his head of bushy frowzy hair. "If you insist, Sir—would that be all, Sir."

Grant lit another cigar. "Just this, you are on detail at the camp tonight."

Sherman saluted, about faced, and walked out of the tent, scoffing under his breath.

Clouds moved in from the northeast. Winds stirred into gusts, and dark clouds formed with distant booms of thunder. Grant had called a war council in a house behind his lines. They were meeting upstairs with a maid who served drinks.

Outside in the swilling debris the rain had drenched the ground; puddles of standing water dimpled the yard. A horse trotted up in the distance and the rider tied the reins to a post in the backyard. The rider moved stealthily toward the house, staying hidden in the bushes planted by the path. A candle in the window dimly lit the rider's face.

Arabella opened the backdoor and sneaked inside. She sat under the stairs hidden in the dark listening to Grant talking to his generals. Suddenly a door upstairs opened, a shaft of candlelight poured down the steps. A woman's voice echoed a few words, and the door closed, the downstairs again sealed in darkness. Arabella released her breath.

She sneaked around checking each drawer and shelf, and finally arrived at the fireplace. Her hand fingered a box of sorts, and lifted it from its hiding place behind a small clock. It was a box of Grant's Havana cigars. She fiddled with the cigars for a moment, and placed them back in the exact spot.

Arabella crouched and moved to the backdoor, and gingerly swung it open. She stepped off the porch and entered the safety of the bushes. Suddenly a mist grew into a white cloud with a large image suspended in the air. She looked and the image turned to face her.

It was Marceline, the deceased Creole wife of Bruce!

Arabella smiled, remembering that Marceline had declared she would haunt her. Suddenly two Union soldiers rushed around the corner of the house, Springfield rifles elevated. They ran directly into the huge facsimile of a Creole woman. Her dark red eyes shone like a demon, and long black hair streaming wildly, with a hatchet in her raised hand.

Suddenly the image lowered into their pathway, thunder clashing, lightning flashing.

The two horrified men fell to their knees, dropped their rifles, jaws drooped wide open, eyes ogling, trembling as if on a frosty wintry morning. Her booming voice cackled like the sound a thousand booming cannon reverberating up and down the valley, as the hatchet swung in a deathly scythe. The two men lay prone shivering from fear, unable to move.

Arabella mounted her horse, pulled the reins around, and looked up at the image, shaking her head.

"My, don't you look ugly," she whispered as she galloped into the stormy night.

Startled faces were staring out the upstairs window. Yet Grant coolly slouched in a chair and nodded at his orderly. The injured Sargent obeyed his nod and approached with a limp. He straddled Grant's extended leg with his backside facing the General. Grant firmly positioned his other foot in the orderly's buttocks and thrust his leg forward with a gasping grunt. The dirty boot squeaked from a soiled soak, toes wiggling. The orderly pivoted and removed the other boot in similar fashion with another grunt from Grant. He lifted the boots from the plank floor and limped to a side room. Presently he returned with a pair of deerskin moccasins given to Grant by an admiring Major serving in the Western Theater.

Suddenly the door to the room opened, and a woman came in with a platter of mugs balancing on her open hand. The Generals at the window heard her enter and strolled over to the table whispering thoughts of what they had seen down in the front yard.

Grant dismissed their babbling as he swilled a mug of rum. He sat the mug on the table, and removed a cigar from his shirt pocket. The Sargent struck a match across the table and lit the cigar. Each General took a mug in turn and settled back in their chairs. Grant removed his cigar and surveyed the men he'd called to this meeting. In his mind he had planned a strategy to take Tennessee.

Smoke swirled in a cloud over the table as several other Generals lit cigars. On into the night they chewed on the details of Grants strategy. Each man added his thoughts, but they all knew Grant had already decided on the final plan. It was his way of bouncing his ideas off his staff.

Arabella camped just outside Kingston, the one-time capital of the state. The weather changed sunny and warm most of the trip, and she was tired. She found a mountain stream nearby and took the chance of taking a bath in the heat of the afternoon. Nathan had given her several bars of home-made soap, and now she had the chance of using a bar.

She disrobed behind a large pine tree, and dipped a foot in the cool water. It was tantalizing just to think she could finally bathe. She slid into the water up to her armpits, and began rubbing the soap over her body, even her hair. The feeling was invigorating. As she rinsed her hair, her mind focused on Bruce. Where was he now? In her mind she could almost reach out and touch his hand and draw him into her arms. The vision vanished as she flung her head back and squeezed out the water in her hair. She dipped her hair in the water once more and squeezed it again. She trudged to the shore.

She lay naked on her saddle blanket for a restful hour as she dried. Somehow she wanted to sleep, but knew she had to move on. Finally she rose and redressed, tied her hair back with a ribbon she found in her saddle bags. She went over where she'd tied her horse, and replaced the folded blanket in the saddle bags. Her horse raised its head, his nostrils vibrating. He smelt something, and Arabella had learned to trust her mount's sense of smell.

A twig snapped.

Arabella whirled toward the sound in the bush. As she slowly walked into the bush another twig snapped, she spun in that direction. And then a man stood ten feet in front, his face passionately grinning.

"What's on your mind?" she said.

His studied calm cracked slightly at the edges of his beard; a taunt flush touched the wide cheekbones as he smiled lustfully. "You are a pretty picture on that blanket," he grinned. "Come closer, and I won't hurt you, but I don't mind if you fight," he said as he raised a Colt revolver.

Her eyes squinted. "You'd better not," she barked. Suddenly Arabella kicked dirt into his face. The gun fired, as she twisted the Colt from his hand, fell on her backside and jerked the trigger twice.

The man fell dead, two bullets in his midsection; his deathly dark eyes staring blankly.

"That ought to teach you some manners," she muttered boldly as she pushed his limp body to the side, suddenly grabbing her arm, a twitch in her eye. A bullet had lodged in her lower arm. She struggled to her saddle, fumbled in her saddlebag and tore a piece off her blanket, and then wrapped it tightly around her arm. Then she tore another longer piece and fashioned a sling.

She had to get to a doctor, enemy, or friend. She'd seen the result of wounds like this before—gangrene, and she'd die without medical attention.

Nathan Forrest's cavalry remained in Nashville for a week, longer than he'd stayed in any one place. The hours of marching were horrible, but he always knew what he was doing, and wasted no time or men in doing it. He was wounded in the arm with one of those miserable French lead balls that accounted for the long stay in Nashville. The mini ball had cut a hole in his arm the size of a walnut, and he bled like a stuck hog.

Most of Forrest's men were as tough as he, or at least they pretended so just to show respect. Even after Forrest was wounded, his men kept on fighting right beside Bedford with his slashing saber. But his men were mighty glad the surgeon said he wouldn't lose the arm. They'd seen those surgeon's tools, nothing more than the common tools you'd find in a country barn.

Even while wounded, Forrest came by the hospital a several times, as he did for many of his wounded soldiers. A couple of days ago Capt. Kelly was sent to Murfreesboro where their army was joining together. The wounded men surely didn't want to miss the action, but the surgeon kept some of them back. Forrest sent most of the stores of food and ammunition south by rail and wagon. He felt the Yankees would invade Nashville and he didn't want to leave anything behind they might use.

Forrest was right when they moved into Nashville; the local people thought war was knocking at their door right behind them. The army had sent no batteries for protection. If the Yankees came storming up the Cumberland River to take the city, all hell would break loose. Many of the fearful citizens—hundreds of them—crammed onto the trains to Chattanooga.

The city leaders hopped on the trains, too. The state government closed, even the young ladies attending the Nashville Academy were sent home indefinitely. The newspaper closed shop after printing their last front page. Every bank packed their cash and certificates, into cases including gold and silver, and locked the doors. The merchants packed up what they could carry and opened their doors for anyone to take what they wanted, especially the poor. Forrest planned to burn all supplies and foodstuffs before he left.

When the time came to leave, Forrest gathered them all in a warehouse where they loaded the wagons, but a hungry mob banged on the door, and finally broke the door barricade. The crowd stormed inside. A big stout fairly drunk Irishman grabbed Forrest by the collar and yelled into his face that they had as much right to the foodstuffs as the army. Forrest quickly drew his pistol from its holster and whacked the man hard upside the head. This calmed the wiser minds in the crowd.

They continued loading the wagons, and finally another fired-up crowd came into the warehouse. Forrest quietly had us drive the wagon outside. He commandeered four soldiers and they pumped a blast of ice-cold, dirty river water into the crowd using the steam-powered city fire engine.

The mob saw their leaders blown down the street like bales of hay under the watery power of the fire engine, wallowing in the mud. Many laughed until their eyes were red with moisture. Finally, the crowd calmed down and left the warehouse.

The surgeon ordered Forrest back into the hospital in fear that he'd never ride again. He was defiant as usual but decided that he'd obey the surgeon at the overwhelming approval of his horseman.

Late that night, a soldier walked into Forrest's room. He lay in pain but was glad to talk with someone in his group.

"What's on your mind, Mark?"

"Sir, a squad of our men just brought in your favorite spy."

Nathan rose up straight in the bed. "Arabella! Is she all right?"

"Doc Cowan is attending her now, Sir."

"You mean she's in this hospital?"

He stirred his foot on the floor knowing how the Colonel cared for this woman. In the last three weeks she was wounded twice, healed like a pro.

Nathan slid his feet off the bed and stood wobbly. "Speak up soldier."

"Yes sir. She's down the hall."

Nathan slid his arms into a housecoat, and marched down the hall with added strength. Two of his men were standing at a door about twenty feet up ahead. One of the men ran to him and assisted him by the arm.

"Miss Arabella has been shot in the arm, Sir."

Nathan stared him in the eyes. "That's the third wound. Will she live?"

"Doc has removed a Colt 45 bullet—she's as spry as a pullet in the barnyard, Sir."

Nathan walked in her room without any assistance. He saw Arabella lying on the bed with her wounded arm outside the bedcovers. Her eyes were closed. He sat in a chair, and fanned the hair out of her eyes. He touched her forehead and she awakened.

She turned her head on the pillow and smiled. Just seeing the strength in his face was so comforting to her.

"Well, what are you in here for, Nathan—too much Grant?" she winked.

He touched her hand. "Dang it Arabella, you'll be the death of me yet."

She weakly blinked. "If Grant doesn't get you first, you devil."

He swallowed. "What happened—how did you get shot?"

She closed her eyes. "A woman keeps some things to herself."

Nathan asked no more questions. He knew she'd tell him if need be. Since the first day he saw her in Washington, he sensed Arabella had the makings of a soldier. But he also knew she had a dangerous task, a task few men could accomplish. He admired her spirit more than he dared admit. He decided he'd take her with him when they moved out. The both needed rest.

Chapter 22

Major General Halleck, commander of the Department of Missouri, had ordered Grant's advance. This was in response to the withdrawal of Johnston's Rebel forces into western Tennessee, northern Mississippi, and Alabama.

Halleck apparently harbored animosity toward Grant and had previously ordered his stay at Fort Henry. Halleck somehow envisioned he'd take personal leadership of the army, push toward Memphis, and siege the railroad link to Charleston, a vital supply line for the Confederates. However, reality restored the better part of valor in his aging mind, and he recanted, finally giving full command to Grant.

Confederate scouts located the encampment after mountain hunters warned them. The hunters admitted that a woman by the name of Arabella had given them the information since she was in a desperate hurry going somewhere. They reported to Gen. Pierre G. T. Beauregard, assigned under Gen. Albert Sidney Johnston. After critical losses in February, Jefferson Davis ordered Albert Sidney Johnston's relocation in an effort to shore up the Confederate Line that ran from Mississippi to the

Alleghenies. His troops needed a rest and he turned command over to Beauregard.

Johnston served as commander in three armies; the Texan Republic of Texas Army, the United States Army, and the Confederate States Army. He was one of the most experienced Generals in either war, and was considered by Jefferson Davis as the highest-ranking General in the Confederacy before the emergence of Robert E. Lee. When his adopted state of Texas seceded, he retired from the U. S. Army. Johnston moved to Los Angeles with his family where they stayed at the home of his wife's brother. Early in the Civil War, Confederate President Jefferson Davis decided the Confederacy should protect its Confederate line. Johnston, a former classmate of Davis at Transylvania University in Lexington was selected to command the Western Theater with less than 40,000 men spread throughout Kentucky, Tennessee, Arkansas, and Missouri.

On the first day of the battle of Shiloh, Johnston launched a massive surprise attack against Grant with his concentrated forces. The Rebels overran the Union camps, Johnston seemingly was everywhere as he personally led and rallied his troops like a madman in the devil's saddle.

Confederate forces clashed with Brig. Gen. William T. Sherman near Mill Springs. Without sufficient troops, Johnston used guerrilla actions attacking the Union lines, inflicting casualties, and then retreating into the woods, over and over. Small units sneaked into campfire areas, slashing soldiers with sabers as they slept in their bedrolls. Night after night guerrilla squads entered the camps, exploding artillery emplacements, and bayoneted soldiers.

Brig. Gen. Sherman became so exasperated and unnerved that Grant removed him from his command, but he'd warned Sherman. It was a bitter moment for Grant, but a shameful mark on Sherman's record; perhaps the spark that lit his scorched earth strategy.

At mid-afternoon while leading one of many charges against a Union camp near the "Peach Orchard," Johnston was wounded; he took a bullet behind his right knee. Disregarding the wound he sent his personal physician to attend some wounded captured Union soldiers instead. Finally Johnston felt dizzy, and gave temporary command to Beauregard.

Beauregard intended driving the Union forces into the swamps of the Snake and Owl Creeks beyond the river to the west. Intelligence reported that Maj. Gen. Don Carlos Buell's U.S.A. army was approaching from Ohio, and the Confederates pushed for defeat of Grant before his arrival. The battle lines became muddled in the confusion of the ferocious fighting, and Grant's forces fell back to the northeast, instead of westerly into the swamp.

The Union men regrouped in a sunken road known as the "Hornet's Nest," defended valiantly by W. H. L. Wallace's divisions. In this critical time, the rest of the federalists stabilized under the protection of numerous artillery batteries. In the first day of fighting General Johnston's wound kept him incapacitated, and Beauregard decided against assaulting the artillery position in the darkness of that night.

Over the night Beauregard's men slept and rested. He provided proper food for nourishment from a nearby farm. Beauregard feared that Johnston's condition would completely incapacitate him, and his charisma was greatly needed at the coming dawn. They slept apprehensively, even heard the rattle of Yankee canteens in the distance. The battle line was just 2 miles away from the Union camps.

Early in the dawning hours, Johnston's army was strategically deployed for battle, straddling the Corinth Road. Johnston seized command as he sat on *Fire Eater*, his favorite horse with his saber drawn, eagerly ready for battle despite Beauregard's warning of his weakened condition, but somehow grateful for Johnston's leadership.

No one was more astonished than Johnston that they had surprised Grants forces; there were no warning patrols, and Sherman who guarded the southern flank had no idea that the Confederacy would attack at all. Sherman was wrong in his assessment, but in reality Johnston had no unified plan. He simply pushed the attack on the right flank, preventing the Union army from capturing the Tennessee River, its vital line of supply and retreat.

As commanded, Beauregard stayed in the rear and directed men and supplies as needed. In effect, that order gave the direction of the attack to Beauregard who had a different battle plan: push Grant's army into the swamps.

The attack progressed forward in a three-wave approach, but in reality had no central push without the weight of artillery. Still numerous federalists of Grant's rather new army fled for safety to the Tennessee River. Some regiments fragmented entirely, and those on the field were stranded and attached themselves to other companies. Sherman had unwittingly placed his men along the river and picked up the stragglers and bravely pushed them on with staggering casualties. Apparently he had regained his senses after his removal from command.

Overall Johnston's forces made steady progress until noon, rolling up union positions one by one. As the Confederates advanced, many threw away their flintlock muskets and grabbed Springfield rifles dropped by the fleeing Union troops.

Sherman was wounded; had three horses shot out from under him; this action greatly enhanced his record, but it was unclear if Grant had even filed a report. Grant was injured when his horse fell and pinned him underneath; he convalesced, unable to move without crutches. But Johnston did not survive the Shiloh battle. The bullet in his knee had clipped an artery, and his boot was partially filled with blood. He was seen fainting off his horse, his face turning deathly pale. His officers lifted him out of his saddle, and he bled to death minutes later. They wrapped Johnston in a blanket, hoping not to demoralize the soldiers if they saw their dead General, but there was no shame in his death, he fought bravely to the end. They took Johnston and his wounded horse to the field headquarters on Corinth road, where his body remained in his tent until the Confederate Army withdrew to Corinth the next day.

Grant sat in his tent, madder that he been since his wife stole all his cigars and demanded no smoking in the house. He felt horrible after they pulled him from under his fallen horse. That was the second horse he'd lost in battle since he arrived in Tennessee. He sighed deeply and asked his orderly to have Sherman come to his tent.

Grant had just lit a cigar when Sherman pulled back the flap of his tent and walked inside.

"Sit down Sherman," he said, and poured two jiggers of whiskey, blowing a puff of smoke. "How's the wound?"

Sherman swigged down the whiskey and gestured for another. "Just a scratch, bullet only grazed my arm."

"Well Johnston didn't fare as well," Grant replied as he poured two more jiggers.

Sherman's eyes squinted as he remembered his arrogance at Grant's warning concerning Johnston's tactics, and now he knew better.

"He was a damn good general—a maverick who never played by the rules," Sherman said agonizing over his poor showing against the deceased general.

Grant settled firmly in his chair, his face a sullen gray. "Yes, Johnston was a good man—I met him in the Mexican-American war, along with Jefferson Davis and General Robert Lee. Damn tragic that we are wasting our future military brains," he said, puffing the last cigar in his pocket.

Sherman released his empty whisky glass, musing. Grant seemed to be more presidential every day, he thought.

Chapter 23

Lieutenant Gen. Nathan Forrest, newly promoted ace cavalry commander had arrived from Tennessee as ordered. Forrest was the best reinforcement any commander could want, but he had just been released from a Memphis hospital with a lead ball in his spine. His men would be Beauregard's cover until he could devise a functional plan.

The doctors gave little hope that Forrest would ever ride in a saddle again, but they just didn't know the fortitude of this wizard in a saddle; he was the modern Daniel Boone. After a two weeks leave, he dressed himself and walked out of the hospital to the astonishment of the doctors and nurses. During his absence his cavalry regiment was assigned to Gen. Beauregard's army. Many of Forrest's men were barefoot, and Beauregard had managed to supply shoes from the ladies assembly in Charleston.

At the end of May, Forrest was back at his regiment in his saddle dressed in full uniform. His men suspected he was in pain, and that he wasn't fully recovered, but it made him more respected to his men. No general had a closer following by his men, though Forrest rarely said much to them. He was a man of action, and they loved him; he never required them to do something he wouldn't do himself.

Forrest went to the commissary and got his men new spurs, boots, gauntlets, riding gear, ammunition, and nourishing foodstuffs. As his regiment moved out, the men upfront noticed Forrest bend from his saddle to pick up something; he reached for his back and winched in pain, but stayed in the saddle.

They were on patrol for a week since Forrest returned to the regiment. In the heat of the day, they road their horses across a small creek, and then jumped on a log on the opposite bank. When Lt. Gen. Forrest jumped, the lead ball in his spine shifted and paralyzed him in pain. He barely moved a muscle screaming in torment. Two men walked beside his horse supporting him seated in his saddle until they reached camp.

They brought Dr. Cowan to his tent, and he said he'd operate right then or he'd die. The doctor cut off his jacket and shirt as Forrest lay face down on his bunk. Dr. Cowan opened his bag and pulled out a scalpel, and doused it with alcohol. He made a cut over the colonel's lower spine. Gen. Forrest took no anesthetic, no whiskey. Four men held him by the wrists and ankles as he gnashed his teeth. Dr. Cowan spread the skin apart, and then probed with two dental-like tools. He found the lead ball wedged against the spine between two discs. He gripped the ball with forceps and pulled it from its improper place. It was flattened by impact. He worked at least thirty minutes on the wound, and finally told them to let him rest.

The next day he was sent back home to Memphis for a resting spell. The men hung their heads thinking what manner of man he was. This was the man who had walked the aisle of the hospital talking to each wounded man, speaking words of encouragement. But in contrast they had also seen him flare up; knock a man down for cowardice; they'd seen him shoot a man in the back for running from battle. Then in the midst of a battle he was a devil with a saber and revolver. He'd killed more men hand-to-hand than his men had counted; they had lost track after 30 Yankees had died from Forrest's knife. And yet, he'd not allowed his horse to be mistreated. They'd seen him rise from his saddle and slash with such violent hatred that he'd dismembered four of his enemy with his saber and gunned down as many more before he even realized it; the man had gallons of energy. The anger and fury of the man was frightening, but much more to the enemy. Four horses were shot from under him, and many times he'd been thrown to the ground. Yet he'd bounce up like an avenging devil slashing with his saber.

The men had been in the saddle under Gen. Beauregard for the best part of three weeks, no time to write back home. They had arrived with Forrest as ordered, seated in saddle for 350 miles from Chattanooga; standing was a bit more comfortable than sitting at present.

Beauregard finally devised a plan for the defense of Corinth: he'd save his men by deception. Stage one; three men took the plan over to the Union officers to set the trap, claiming they were deserters. Stage two: Bombardment began. Gen. Halleck was a cautious man, and waited for Beauregard's move as his division commanders maneuvered for position.

Forrest marched his men back and forth past dummy Quaker Guns staged along the earthworks. Campfires were kept burning, and buglers and drummers loudly played. The rest of the men slipped away undetected, withdrawing to Tupelo, Mississippi. Forrest's cavalry covered the rear, marching behind the retreating men all the way to Tupelo.

When Union patrols entered Corinth on the morning of May 30, they found the charred campfires, but the Confederate soldiers were gone.

The Union began suffering from lack of an experienced leader of the troops. The South had proved at Shiloh it did not lack of riders, and had men ready for battle; yet the Confederates were short of horses and nails. Lincoln removed Gen. George B. McClellan as general-in-chief and retained him as commander of the Army of the Potomac. His assignment: March on Richmond.

Two events had changed the odds. (1) Joseph Eggleston Johnston, had commanded the Manassas Battles, but he was wounded in a battle at a railroad station called Fair Oaks near Seven Pines, fighting desperately to protect the Richmond capital, and was convalescing. (2) Robert E. Lee had taken Johnston's place, knowing the next series of battles could very well decide the war.

McClellan favored war in the East. He proposed crushing the rebellion in one campaign by taking Richmond, Charleston, and other cities. Grant was in his camp considering the idea of crushing the rebellion, but he saw Gen. Robert E. Lee's point, and he respected him as a good soldier. Perhaps McClellan's accolades were too embellished if he had known that he was to face Gen. Lee in his push to Richmond.

Grant, McClellan, and Lee were now set for the historic battle series at Richmond. Grant's orders were to take Richmond at all costs. Lee was determined to protect his beloved Richmond.

Chapter 24

A series of six major battles of intense fighting over a seven day period near Richmond, Virginia, culminated as the Peninsula Campaign. The opposing armies were comprised of almost 200,000 men, potentially the largest battle of the War, including six generals in each camp. McClellan landed his Army of the Potomac at Fort Monroe and moved up the Virginia Peninsula in early April. He prepared for a quick advance but was met with surprise by Brig. Gen. John Magruder's defense positions on the Warwick Line.

Thereby McClellan prepared for a siege of Yorktown. He planned his advance along the Williamsburg Road in the direction of Richmond. The first fighting began at Oak Grove, but he attempted micro-managing the battle by telegraph from three miles away from the action. Ironically, McClellan achieved a minor tactical offensive against Richmond, gaining 600 yards at the cost of 1,000 casualties on both sides.

The next stage of the battle was destined to be disastrous with the loss of a tremendous number of men. Lee's plan called for Maj. Gen. Stonewall Jackson's attack on Brig. Gen. John Porter's flank. Meanwhile, Maj. Gen. A. P. Hill was to advance when he heard Jackson's guns, quickly clear the pickets from Mechanicsville, and move up Beaver Dam Creek. Hill was to charge in and support Jackson, while Magruder demonstrated his deception before the four Union corps on the frontline.

Lee's intricate plan went awry. Jackson's men were fatigued from a lengthy battle and ran four hours late. Hill grew impatient and began his frontal attack without orders. Union Brig. Gen. Porter repulsed the advance of repeated Confederate attacks with defensive positions entrenched along Beaver Dam Creek and Ellerson's Mill, while he added six more artillery batteries. Substantial casualties mounted moment by moment, a killing field of bodies.

Jackson's troops arrived late in the afternoon, and ordered his men bivouac for the evening, while a major battle raged within earshot. Was it wise? Jackson was no fool. Exhausted men could not fight. In fact, his close proximity to Porter's flank prompted McClellan's order of withdrawal fearing an immediate attack. He moved his men into the eerie darkness behind Boatswain's Swamp, five miles east. McClellan thought the buildup on his right flank was a plan to cut his supply line on the Richmond and York River Railroad, and he shifted his supply to the James River. He falsely believed the Confederate numbers were quite larger than actual. Hill and Longstreet continued their attack, despite Lee's order to hold ground. Consequently, lack of discipline by his field commanders cost heavy casualties. The Seven Days War at its conclusion stood as the bloodiest battle of the war.

McClellan drew down his Army to the southeast and never regained the initiative. He swore under his breath as he stood alone watching his shabby men withdraw—ragtag not from the fight, but poor leadership.

"Colonel, get General Porter over here—now!" His mind seethed at the prospect that Lee may upstage him. General Porter rode up to his field tent.

"You called, General."

"I want you to hold Gaine's Mill at all cost."

The general removed his hat. "But sir, it will cost too many lives, why not open with artillery and soften Lee's advance."

McClellan's eyes were bloodshot with indecision. "I don't care what it costs, you hold that position—if you disobey, I'll put someone in your place that will obey," he screamed.

The next morning, the Union forces concentrated in a semicircle. Lee launched the largest Confederate attack of 51,000 men. The battle of Gaine's Mill was the only clear-cut tactical victory of the Confederates; McClellan's order was a drastic mistake. However, nothing was clear-cut for the parents, sisters, and brothers of the fallen dead. McClellan lost 7,000 men, and Lee lost 8,000.

McClellan withdrew his entire army back to Harrison's Landing on the James River. Lee watched the battle unfolding from a hill as Captain Bruce Taylor rode up beside him.

"Sir, Union troops have abandoned their defenses of the Richmond and York River Railroad, including the White House supply depot on the York Rivers."

Lee mused over the information, and stationed his army at Gaine's Mill until he knew McClellan's intentions. As he sat on his horse he reviewed the situation, and it stuck in his throat how his generals had disobeyed his orders.

Gen. Magruder had ordered Brig. Gen. Robert Toombs' brigade forward, hoping for a reaction. However, Toombs, a Georgian politician with a disdain for military officers, launched a sharp attack at dusk on Garnett's and Golding's Farm. The Union soldiers easily repulsed the arrogant attack.

The next day Toombs again was ordered on a reconnaissance mission but he turned it into an attack over the same ground at the Garnett farm. Blindingly, Toombs commandeered Col. George Anderson's forces with him. The assault was vigorously counterattacked by the infamous 49th Pennsylvania and 43rd New York brigades. Nothing was accomplished; only the death of 156 Confederate soldiers.

The following day, the bulk of McClellan's army was staged around Savage's Station on the Richmond and York River Railroad preparing for a difficult crossing through White Oak Swamp. This was the very spot that Lee thought McClellan would stage his men. Lee's forces finally clashed with McClellan at the Battle of Glendale.

Lee had his best and last chance of defeating McClellan at Malvern Hill. He ordered Hill's divisions in a loop back toward Richmond, then on to the crossroads of Glendale. His orders were explicit. Holmes's division would head farther south and approached the outliers of Malvern Hill. Magruder's division would move east to eliminate the Federal rear guard. Stonewall Jackson's three divisions were scheduled to rebuild the burned-out bridge over the Chickahominy, and then head south to Savage's Station. Magruder would link forces with Jackson, and then apply a strong blow to the retreating Union army.

Lee's plan was brilliant, but unseen incidents had occurred always at the wrong time. About midmorning four regiments clashed 2 miles west of Savage Station. Malvern Hill offered good observation and artillery positions. Both campaigns wanted it. Believing all his officers were in place, Lee attacked directly. However, all the chess pieces were not in place, bogged down by mud, and other delays. Jackson was delayed at the bridge, Magruder's guides sent him in the wrong direction.

Eventually the line was formed with Hill's division. Brigades of Brig. Gen. John Bell Hood, and Col. Evander Law were staged for battle on the Quaker Road.

It was a bloodbath.

The battle produced enormous causalities in the face of futile attacks against infantry and artillery. Lee lost about 20,000 killed, wounded, or missing. McClellan lost around 16,000 in his retreat, abandoning tons of supplies and leaving 2,500 wounded men in a field hospital. However, the steadfastness of the Rebels despite the poorly execution of Lee's plan had dashed the Union's hope of quickly capturing the Confederate capital.

Lee calculated that McClellan had suffered too many casualties, and would not resume his threat against Richmond. Therefore, he moved his battered Northern Virginia Army back to Virginia still anticipating a second attempt upon Richmond. Deep in his mind he replayed the plan of attack he had so meticulously explained to his Generals a week ago in his Richmond office. He pulled out his pocket watch, the time 6:00 o'clock in the evening. Soon he expected his Generals to meet him on the hill overlooking the Shenandoah Valley. Indians called this valley "daughter of the stars." But to most Virginians she was known simply as the Valley, and Gen. Lee called her his beloved Richmond, the Old Dominion.

Lee dropped his musing, and placed his busy mind on the battle line of the expected second attack on Old Dominion. Uppermost in his mind was Captain Bruce Taylor who arrived two days ago with valuable information on troop placements and numbers. Taylor had been wounded in his left arm, and Lee ordered him to the field hospital. He was extremely grateful that Bruce had clarified McClellan's withdrawal. According to Captain Taylor's information, Lincoln was dissatisfied with McClellan as leader for the second strike on Richmond, but he had not been removed yet.

The gallop of hooves shattered his thoughts. It was his Generals as expected. His favorite military men were Thomas Jackson and Jeb Stuart, men who carried out his orders to the letter if humanly possible. They didn't stand behind excuses, they admitted their mistakes—honest men them both. With Bruce's information and these fine men they were sure to defend Richmond, or die trying. If they allowed Pope to take Richmond, then Virginia was lost. Jeb Stuart's axiom was fight to the last man, or let no one come back alive. Stonewall Jackson's adage was to give him some men who were stout hearted men, and they would fight for the land they loved—old Dominion.

Lee decided then that he had to trim the incompetent fat from his command.

Chapter 25

Bruce sought out his distant cousin after leaving the Richmond office of General Lee. He needed rest for his wounded arm, and he took the time to find room and board for his son. First he had to find the address. All he had was a letter that his father had received a few years back. He pulled the tattered letter from his inside pocket and located the address written to a house on the southern side of the Potomac.

He finally found the house, and tied his horse haphazardly with one hand on an iron ring at the edge of the road. As he ascended the long path of crushed gravel up to the house he noticed it was a two-story Federal style built of bricks. As he stood on the porch, he wiped the top of each shoe on the calf of his trousers, and then patted away the dust on his clothes with his hand.

A maid answered the door, a new maid that Julie had hired. She was of moderate height, and might have been very provocative except for a square-cut jaw and her hair bundled on the top of her head. A few words allowed his entry into the foyer. She led him to an anteroom across the hallway. In about three minutes, the maid ushered him into an elegant room where she told him he must wait. Over the fireplace he saw a painting that he recognized. His uncle and his brother, the father of his cousin—oh what is her name, he thought: Julie, Julie Knox—yes.

The wide doors suddenly slid back into the walls, and a handsome elderly lady came into the room assisted by a cane. Bruce stood as she rounded the sofa. Her appearance reminded him of an older teenager when he was in knickers and suspenders in Fredericksburg. Their eyes met as they stood facing each other. Memorizes flashed through both their minds, as pigtails became curling hair, and freckles became a handsome man.

Finally she sat down beside Bruce. Her voice was soft and restful to the listener, a pleasant alternative to the sound of gunfire and cannon, or the long nights of hooting owls and the ominous hiss of crawling things when he and Josh slept in caves.

"Why Bruce, it's been so long," she remarked, her brown eyes scaled with cataracts, the wrinkles of age sagging beneath her powered chin. Her tired eyes casually focused on his arm in a sling. "Oh my dear boy, you've been wounded."

Bruce sat mesmerized for the moment. It had been a long time, long enough for a young woman that he once knew to grow old and apparently alone.

"Just a scratch," he said and dismissed the thought. "Do you live alone here, Mrs. Julie." It just fell from his mouth; no words could express the reason for his confusion.

Her lungs filled with a deep sigh. "William died three years ago." She dared not say he was killed, for she couldn't prove it, only vulnerable circumstances for a sympathizer. "And your wife—I assume you have married," she nodded.

Bruce finally regained his confidence. "That's the real reason I came. You see my wife was killed at Charleston—

"Oh I am so sorry," she interrupted, her forehead wrinkled with the same horrible expression when she learned of William's death.

"Thank you. Ah . . . I have a son, he's nearly five old years."

Her face beamed. "Oh how wonderful. William and I never had children," she reminisced momentarily.

Bruce had no desire to ask the question he'd rehearsed. But Julie read his mind.

"Why don't you bring the child here? There is more room than I can possibly use."

Bruce sat speechless. "That's so kind of you Julie. But really I can't—.

Her queenly head tilted. "Nonsense, you arrange to bring him here, and I'll take care of it."

He smiled embarrassingly. "I'm afraid that I'm under false pretense, Julie. You see the boy is out in the hall."

Her brown eyes glowed. "Why that's even more wonderful," she replied, ringing a tiny bell.

The maid entered the room. "Marjorie will you take the boy into the kitchen and feed him, please?"

She bowed, "Yes ma'am."

Bruce's eyes automatically followed the maid through the door.

"Why don't we have tea and talk about this," Julie suggested.

Julie reached out and took his hand and led him to the sofa, flanked by a fireplace. Bruce slumped on the cushions overcome with admiration and lack of sleep.

They sat gazing into the fireplace, the logs flaming silently. Smoke curled up the chimney and the warmth of the fire brought back more memories. Julie said she would arrange for the boys clothing. Bruce felt intruding, an imposition his manhood denied. He stood.

"Would you excuse me for a moment? I have something in my saddle bags."

The maid brought in tea as he passed her in the hallway, again securitizing her attire.

Bruce returned promptly with a small burlap bag. He took a seat beside Julie, and she handed him a cup of tea as he sat.

The silence was too secretive for Julie.

"What's in the bag, your dirty laundry?" she said as a wrinkle stretched on her forehead.

Bruce rolled back his head, suddenly laughing, the first time he'd felt so joyous since he'd buried his wife.

"No," he replied. "It's some savings I kept for a rainy day." He looked into her face. "I must say it's a bright sunny day, and I want you to have this."

He placed six gold coins in her lap. Startled, she brought her hands to her mouth. She was running out of funds with the cost of operating the house left by her husband, and the wages for her maid.

"Oh Bruce, you shouldn't."

He took her hand, enclosing the coins. "And you shouldn't have taken us in, either," he smiled.

They talked of those happier days in Fredericksburg for long hours into the night. She told him of William's death, their long years together, how the Union had stolen their property, and the house was all they had. Bruce was glad he had saved the gold coins, and thankful for Julie's compassion and hospitality. This pleasant time of rest was a balm of healing and hope.

Chapter 26

Bruce left the Potomac home and went on a mission trip near Danville, Virginia scouting and gathering information of troop movement in the Western Theater that might push down toward Virginia. His arm was well enough for travel, and he knew Gen. Buell had bivouacked in Alabama following the Corinth retreat, and may move to Chattanooga soon. He crossed a railroad when he noticed a tavern, and thought he might wet his whistle before he wrote his report. He'd just sat down at a table when a young woman walked into the bar.

He couldn't believe his eyes.

It was Arabella or her twin. He stood and waved. She caught his gesture and went to his table, and then he noticed the sling on her arm.

Bruce stood and took her hand. "Of all the people in this war, you are the one I thought I'd never see—sit down," he reveled, "what's with the arm," he ask curiously, realizing that he'd taken off the sling of his arm only three days ago.

She smiled, and placed her hand over his. "A ticket of freedom for this moment," she said, her eyes blurred with moisture.

Her smile was irresistible. Bruce unknowingly caressed her hand as his mind soared back to Charleston on the day of the bombing, the day she had saved Josh. To be honest with himself, he'd missed her presence, her contagious smile, her warmth.

"Well, what brings you into Danville?" he said, taking a sip of his cup of rum.

"Gen. Forrest should be in this area soon and I have information for him," she said, noticing that her arm had stopped hurting when she sat down close to him."

"So Forrest has been promoted. I'm pleased."

She nodded and breathed a sigh. "Bruce, dahlin, this may be our last chance to be together. I don't want to waste it on talk," she said, and placed her free arm around his neck.

Bruce couldn't resist her lips so close, the thumping of her heart against his chest. He placed his arm around her waist and drew her into his arms.

They kissed.

The weight of the war fell to the floor and vanished through the board cracks; the rhapsody around the table shielded them from the world.

They kissed again.

Finally he released her. "I never thought I'd miss you so much, Arabella," he confessed.

Her blue eyes blinked. "Separation is what brings people together, Bruce—how is Josh."

He settled back into his chair, still holding her hand. "I have a distant Aunt in Virginia—he's living with her."

"That's nice, I'm glad for you." Her voice cracked, she bowed her head.

He placed his fist under her chin, and elevated it to the level of his eyes. "What's troubling you, Arabella?"

She wiped the strands of hair from her face. "It's the war I guess . . . oh that's not it, Bruce, it's the loneliness, the nights alone, the risk of never seeing you again," she gasped.

Compassion seized his heart.

He pulled her into his arms and rubbed his hands up and down her back. How his heart ached, his mind stressed; a memory surfaced, he shoved it to the rear of his mind. It was chivalry, plain and simple, more than that: he loved Arabella, but felt he had no right to forget Marceline—was it she that he held in his arms? Reality gripped his loneliness. No, this was Arabella. Somehow it didn't seem to matter—Arabella was real, alive, and present.

They sat alone wrapped into each other's arms, shielded by the screen of eternity, the minutes expanded into hours. The evening sun finally sank beneath the horizon in blue and purplish colors accented by the fading cosmic light. Only the twinkling flame of the candle on the table revealed there intimacy. Love had triumphed over war in an insignificant tavern somewhere in the cherished phase between peace and war.

A latent chill liberated a blast of November wind as the fingers of night released the autumn season to an early winter dawn. Danny Boy and Hattie boarded a railroad car cloaked in the early mist. This was the third train they had selected since Miss Arabella had instructed them to leave Charleston, although they had hidden in deserted houses along the way due to the presence of Yankee soldiers. In fact, they had stayed in Wilmington for almost several months with a distant cousin of Danny Boy. This train was scheduled to depart for Raleigh, North Carolina, if the tracks were intact. Danny Boy had heard that Gen. Nathan Forrest was in the area, and knew he was a master of twisted railroad ties—the friend of Miss Arabella.

The couple huddled in a seat near the window as the train pulled away from the battered depot. If only they could reach Raleigh, Danny Boy's home town they were safe.

His mind digressed.

It was the old master Rhett who had hired him when the severe winters had limited the rains, and the family crops of tobacco suffered. Just as cotton was the money crop of the Deep South, tobacco was the money crop of Kentucky and North Carolina.

He remembered as a youth how he had to plant the tiny plants of tobacco in a bed covered with gauze to shield the tender plants from the cold. His family had the first tobacco barns in his area, where the harvested leaves were hung on sticks for curing; just before he had left the farm with Mr. Rhett, his father had installed cold-oil burners to speed the cure.

Chapter 27

Lieutenant Gen. Nathan Forrest's cavalry regiment had marched for umpteen days from the hills of North Carolina and had just settled down near Danville, Virginia, their horses and men in greatly need of rest. A horseman doused the campfire as Forrest laid his head on his saddle and pulled up a blanket over his legs. Suddenly he heard the musical cadence of a horse's hooves playing on the hard ground and rose on an elbow with his Colt revolver cocked. When he saw who it was, he released the hammer with a rare smile.

"One of these days you're gonna git shot, Arabella."

She dismounted. "Congratulations on your promotion, Nathan."

"Pull up a stump and sit a spell."

The horsemen were accustomed to Arabella's appearance from out of the blue, and felt she calmed Forrest. It suited them just fine; when the General was in good spirits, so were they.

A soldier brought Arabella a cup of coffee, and she enjoyed a few soothing sips, the steam rising into her nostrils.

"According to Capt. Bruce Taylor, Buell is heading to Murfreesboro," she advised, as she rubbed a throbbing in her arm.

Forrest nodded and filed the information in his mind, another issue occupied his thoughts. "Listen, Arabella. Jefferson Davis needs information on Lincoln's plans located in the White House. You are the best one to get it."

She thought but for a moment. "I'll need help."

"Name it."

"Bruce Taylor."

Forrest gripped his bottom lip between thumb and index fingers. "I see, so what's your plan?"

"Well, neither of us can get into the Capitol dressed as Confederates spies. I'll need a gown and female stuff, Bruce will need a Captain's Union outfit."

"I can't wait to see you in it," he chuckled, as he gripped his bottom lip with thumb and index finger. "I'll get your Captain's outfit; you'll have to scrounge up the gown and other stuff."

A spirited black mare appeared in the distance about ten miles from Richmond and rode into the woods. Over near a small stream the female rider dismounted and scooped a handful of water, brought it to her mouth and drank. A noise aroused Arabella and she looked up from her dripping hand in three directions. She started to turn, but too late. A gun was poked in her back.

"Turn around slowly," a gruff voice said like a rasp on a file.

Arabella turned, and faced a Union sergeant with a Springfield rifle stuck in her ribs. He looked as though he was hungry. His face was unshaven and he reeked of tobacco smoke, probably lost from his regiment, she thought.

"I need your horse, young lady," he growled.

"Take it, I can find another," she said smiling broadly.

He backed step by step, the rifle aimed at her gut. His back bumped into the tree where her black mare was tied. He untied the reins with one hand behind his back, stepped into the saddle, lowering the rifle.

He doffed his cap, the rifle supported in the bend of his elbow. "Thank you ma'am."

Arabella nodded as he rode off. She positioned her lips and whistled.

The mare reared pawing her front hoofs in the air. The sergeant fell from the saddle, but caught his balance as he brought up the rifle.

"Neat trick, but I still need the horse," he replied and threw his leg over the saddle once more, still aiming his rifle at Arabella's midsection.

Suddenly the dense forest formed a mist and then a large white cloud. Arabella shook her head; she'd seen this cloud before.

Marceline appeared with a voodoo doll in her hands. Her waving hair was black and stringy, wildly blowing in a unseen storm with roaring wind, beady eyes staring with devilish vengeance.

The sergeant's eyes enlarged, the rifle fell to the ground as the mare reared on its back legs. He leaped off the saddle and jumped, stumbling, his eyes glued on the horrifying image. His legs seemed not to touch the ground as he scampered into the dense bush like an Olympic star of field and track.

Arabella looked up at Marceline with her dark Creole face glowing. The image seemed to smile, but one hand was sticking pins in the doll. Arabella couldn't distinguish the image of the doll, but she'd wager a dime that she was the image, yet she surprisingly felt nothing. She gripped the reins of her horse and looked up at the image.

"Either you've lost your power, or I'm immune to your antics. Why don't you just disappear, Marceline?"

ARABELLA

Arabella gripped the reins of her horse nudging her arm, mounted, and pulled the reins in the direction of Forrest's camp in Tennessee.

Chapter 28

The first Battle of Murfreesboro occurred in mid-July and was fought in Rutherford County, Tennessee, by Confederate troops under Lt. Gen. Nathan Bedford Forrest. The Second Battle of Murfreesboro culminated with a three day battle at Stones River at the end of 1862.

On June 10, Union Maj. Gen. Don Carlos Buell commanding the Army of Ohio started a leisurely advance toward Chattanooga. Brig. Gen. James S. Negley and his force had previously threatened the city on June 7-8.

In response to the threat, the Confederate government sent Lt. Gen. Nathan Bedford Forrest to Chattanooga to reorganize a cavalry brigade. By July Confederate cavalry under the command of Forrest and Col. John Hunt Morgan were raiding into Middle Tennessee and Kentucky. Forrest left Chattanooga on July 9 with two cavalry regiments and joined other units on the way to Mooresboro bringing the total force to about 1,400 men. The major objective of the Union was to strike Murfreesboro, and recapture an important Union supply center on the Nashville & Chattanooga Railroad at dawn on July 13. Forrest led his cavalry toward Murfreesboro.

ARABELLA

The air stirred hot as blazes in the July heat. Forrest's ragged band stopped for a spell and rested in a bed of needles beneath pine trees. They'd led invading Union federals in a wild goose chase over rugged Tennessee territory. It was the first time they'd stopped after three days of running nonstop.

They'd done nothing but run and stop since they arrived close to Chattanooga. They were plain tuckered out, and the horses were plum worn to a frazzle. Yet they had destroyed several dozen bridges, cut miles of telegraph wires, twisted railroad tracks all over middle Tennessee, and had captured tons of army supplies.

Forrest was never one who trusted the upper command, and he sent out Arabella, his female spy to assess the situation. It began to rain before she left, and Forrest gave her his poncho. He watched her ride out, wondering how she had withstood the dangers of war. He bowed his head, and thought how much he trusted this woman. He wasn't a praying man, but he removed his hat and lifted his head skyward, "Lord, I ain't much on praying, but would you look after Arabella?"

Late on the second night, Arabella rode her horse back into Forrest's camp. He called her out of the rain into his tent, and gave her a cup of hot coffee. As Forrest sat beside her, she reported that the Murfreesboro Union garrison was camped in three locations around town and included detachments from four units comprising infantry, cavalry, and artillery, under the command of Brig. Gen. Thomas Turpin Crittenden, who had just arrived with reinforcements. She suggested that Forrest's cavalry attack the Union garrison located east of Chattanooga on Woodberry Pike.

News passed down the line that the attack was scheduled before dawn. Rain fell in a steady downpour; the buckets of heaven were open wide. The Confederates huddled under their knapsacks, fearful of the coming dawn. In the early hours of night a private woke the troops because he thought he heard the Yankees approaching. A hundred men quickly grabbed their carbines and aimed at the head of a Yankee horse dragging his broken tether without a rider. These were the times that their nerves were jittery; hands shook uncontrollably—the symptoms of war.

The rains finally stopped and left a sky imbued like a wet blanket shielding out the sun. As if an omen the overcast was penetrated by dim shafts of light from a sliver-orange sun on the east horizon.

Suddenly a barrage of artillery fire pierced the silence and they heard the Rebel yell echoing from their comrades as orders came down from General Forrest: hold the ends of the flank.

Forrest's cavalry surprised the union pickets on the Woodbury Pike, and quickly overran a Federal hospital and the camp of a detachment from the 9th Pennsylvania Cavalry Regiment. Confederate infantry troops attacked the camps of the other Union commands plus the jail and courthouse. Arabella's judgment was correct, Forrest thought, but never found her information any otherwise.

His embattled horsemen advanced on Sunday morning through the once peaceful churchyard. In the hearts of 17 and 18 year old boys reared as regular churchgoers they must've wondered what God thought of how they were treating the Sabbath. Bitter fighting raged across the once white cotton fields, now tarnished with blood, mud, and guts. But the Union ranks were falling back in great numbers, yet they had fought a bloody battle without much organization.

By midday, after hours of fighting the regiment was still far away from the front battle lines because they were protecting the flanks. They soon arrived at a ghastly scene of intense fighting; hand-to-hand with bayonets. Maj. Gen. Benjamin Cheatham and a brigade of Southern boys were engaged in close quarters with a major Union force. Body upon body fell into gruesome piles, dismembered limbs, lifeless faces, and open eyes blankly staring. Chilling screams from all around were heard above the noises of battle.

Lt. Gen. Forrest rallied his boys and pointed toward a battery of cannon firing on the hillside. He ordered them to take the hill. The bugle sounded, and Forrest raised his saber and bolted straight ahead in the face of artillery. The men raised their carbines and dutifully followed their defiant leader. Explosive shells killed a number of the charging men, and unhorsed a number others. But they pushed forward screaming the Rebel yell at the top of their smoke-filled lungs. The boys on foot charged the hill, and surprisingly the Yankees pulled back their cannons.

Forrest led his army to the crest of the hill and ordered dismount, every fourth man holding the reins of their horse. Forrest tightened his cap on his head as he rotated in his saddle, and peered down the line of his men—good men, all of them. He slowly raised his saber.

The battle ensued.

They charged down the hill and drove the entire Union force back to the cliffs of the Tennessee River. The shooting suddenly stopped following a general order of cease fire. Although the enemy had about fifty cannons circling the bluffs for retreating purposes, they did not fire. Forrest stood facing the cannons with his saber drawn, daring them to fire. But the Union soldiers had had enough. The fighting was over.

Chapter 29

Two days of terrifying fighting was the unenviable destiny of the once beautiful Shenandoah Valley in Virginia. Manassas, the target of the Union's second attempt to defeat Gen. Robert E. Lee's Northern Army pitted against Maj. Gen. John Pope's Union Army of Virginia, ironically fought upon the same ground as before. The troop numbers were larger than before waging 62,000 Union soldiers against a Confederate force of 50,000 Rebels.

Lincoln, the Commander in Chief, wanted a victorious general in command. The political choice was Gen. George B. McClellan. But the collapse of his Peninsula Campaign in the Seven Days Battle just one month ago took McClellan from the list, although he left him in command of his troops. Lincoln appointed Maj. Gen. John Pope as the commander of the newly formed Army of Virginia, a mission to counteract the Northern Virginia Army of Gen. Robert E. Lee. Pope had achieved some success in the Western Theatre, and Lincoln wanted a more aggressive general than McClellan.

Pope had two basic objectives: protect Washington and the Shenandoah Valley; and draw Confederate forces away from McClellan troops by moving in the direction of Gordonsville. This action gave McClellan protection of Pope's flank, but no certainty that he'd release his men. Pope strategize that Lee saw McClellan as no further threat on the peninsula, and therefore had no compulsion for keeping all is forces in direct defense of Richmond. This gamble, he felt, required that Lee relocate Maj. Gen. Jackson to Gordonsville to block his Union troops, and protect the Virginia Central Railroad. If so, then he would ambush Jackson, perhaps capture this elusive icon of war.

Lee's plans were larger in scope.

Since the Union army was split between McClellan and Pope, and they were widely separated, he saw the opportunity for destroying Pope, before turning his attention to McClellan. Therefore he joined the 12,000 forces of General Longstreet with Jackson's men. A curious set of events had ensued when General-in-Chief Henry W. Halleck directed McClellan's withdrawal from the peninsula with orders that he joined Pope's regiment in Virginia. But Gen. Lee knew of McClellan's Achilles heel.

McClellan sat in his tent fuming over Halleck's decision to withdraw his army. He registered his protest to Pope, and did not redeploy until eleven days later. This blunder stuck in Lincoln's mind when he bypassed McClellan, but it was a death blow to the success of Pope.

Jackson met opposition at Cedar Mountain, but a Confederate counterattack led by A. P. Hill drove Union forces back across Cedar Creek. This action stopped Jackson's advance, and he learned that Pope's corps were all together in one fighting force. This foiled Lee's plan of defeating Pope's two wings separately. Jackson remained in his position for three days closely watching the troop movement like a chess player, and then he withdrew to Gordonsville. Lee sent Longstreet and reinforced Jackson.

Lee bided his time fighting skirmishes along the Rappahannock River, until Jackson was in place for deployment. Heavy rains swelled the river, mud ankle deep for his men, cannon wheels mired up to the axle. By this time reinforcement from the Union Potomac Army were arriving on the peninsula, but the mud played to Lee's advantage in the face of increased enemy forces. Lee designed a brilliant plan; cut the communication lines, and take the Orange & Alexandria Railroad. He sent Jeb Stuart with half the army to the railroad. Jackson departed and reached Salem that night.

The next evening, after passing around Pope's right flank through Thoroughfare Gap, Jackson's wing of the army struck the Bristoe Station of Orange & Alexandria Railroad. Before dawn Jackson destroyed the massive Union supply depot at Manassas Junction. This brilliant strike by Jackson forced Pope's abrupt retreat from his defensive lines along the Rappahannock River. That evening Jackson marched his divisions up the Bull Run River where he had fought the first battle of Manassas. A decisive victory escaped him due to impending darkness. But he had achieved General Lee's strategic intent, attracting the attention of Maj. Gen. John Pope. Pope wrongly assumed that he had "bagged" Jackson. This erroneous set of events prompted the issue of Pope's infamous "Joint Order," an enigma of military gibberish. Meanwhile Jackson hid his men in the thick woods with their backs to the Bull Run River. If Jeb Stuart didn't arrive with reinforcements, he'd retreat up the river.

The sun rose on the eastern horizon in a kaleidoscope of colors, shadows dancing on the awaking leaves of maple and oak trees. Down in the lush green Shenandoah Valley a lone eagle glided across a dawning sky. Suddenly cannons roared over the Bull Run River, piercing the grateful silence, as thousands of soldiers rushed toward certain death, screaming their battle cries.

Gen. Longstreet broke through light Union resistance at Thoroughfare Gap and marched through the gap to join Jackson. This little skirmish ensured the defeat of Pope during the coming battles; two wings of Lee's army were now united on the Manassas battlefield.

Jeb Stuart's cavalry encountered Union troops moving up the Manassas-Gainesville Road. A brief firefight halted the Union column, and it stalemated when a courier note was handed Maj. Gen. Irvin McDowell and Maj. Gen. John Porter, the infamous "Joint Order" from Gen. Pope. The loss of time used in unraveling the contradictory message allowed Stuart the opportunity of deception that added to the confusion.

Stuart's cavalry under Col. Thomas Rosser devised a plan that stabbed the Union Generals in the heart. Rosser ordered a regiment of horses with large branches tied to the saddle horns. The horses raced down the valley with great clouds of dust as if large columns of Confederates were marching toward the Union advance. At the same moment of Pope's ambiguous note, another currier reported 17 regiments of infantry, one battery of cannon, and 500 cavalry were moving thorough Gainesville that morning.

The next day Pope renewed his attack, unaware that Gen. Jackson had the reinforcement of Gen. Longstreet, and Jeb Stuart had stalled the Union column. Massive Confederate artillery devastated a final Union assault. Longstreet's wing of 25,000 men in five divisions counterattacked in the largest simultaneous mass assault of the war.

The Second Battle of Bull Run, or Manassas, the Indian name was a smashing tactical victory for the Confederates. What's more, it unleashed a rapid drop in Union morale. Lincoln relieved Pope of his command, and his army was merged into the Army of the Potomac, and subsequently marched into Maryland. Pope spent his last war days on the backside of the nation in the Department of the Northwest in Minnesota, dealing with the war of Dakota. His official days were wasted seeking scapegoats for his defeat.

General Lee smiled as he sat upon his horse with his telescope extended. He was vindicated after the diabolical sting of the Seven Days war. And he reasoned that by forcing the reassignment of Holmes and Magruder out of the Virginia Northern Army, the removal of their incompetent leadership gave him a better group of fighting men.

Chapter 30

Lee regrouped his Northern Virginia Army and crossed the Potomac River into Maryland. His army could rest, and it took the pressure off the Shenandoah Valley—the breadbasket to the Confederacy at harvest time. He believed the routed Union army required time for rebuilding. Therefore, he took the bold step of dividing his own army, and sent Gen. "Stonewall" Jackson to capture the union garrisons at Harpers Ferry. Likewise, he sent Lt. Gen. James Longstreet marching toward Sharpsburg. Lee informed his commanders of their routes and objectives in Order No. 191 on September 9.

A lone Lieutenant galloped along a dirt road his saddle bags bouncing with every rhythm of the horse's gate. Suddenly a package vaulted out of the saddlebags and floated on the wings of destiny to the earth. The rider pulled into the Best Farms to water his horse. As the mare stuck its muzzle in a trough of water, he wiped the sweat off his brow with the back of his hand, dismounted, and soaked his head in the trough of water. He wiped the bend of his elbow over his face, and placed his left foot in the stirrup. Suddenly he saw the un-strapped saddlebag. Quickly he shoved his hand into the bag.

Empty!

He mounted and retraced his tracks. One mile back he found the package on the trail. Excitingly he pulled back the reins and dismounted. He picked up the package and stuffed it back in his saddlebag. The Lieutenant galloped off toward the Union lines of Maj. Gen. George B. McClellan.

McClellan was recently recalled from the Virginia peninsula to take over the Army of the Potomac following the Seven Days Battle with orders to replace Gen. John Pope. Eager to reestablish his reputation after Lincoln had dropped him from the first Bull Run battle, Gen. McClellan had followed Gen. Robert E. Lee into Maryland.

The windfall of intelligence that Providence had placed in McClellan's hands came to naught. True to his former practice, McClellan moved at his familiar glacial pace. It took 17 hours before he got into position and finally faced Lee's rear guard of 12,000 Confederate troops that were staged clandestine in the gaps of the mountain. They fought until dusk when Union soldiers finally pushed the Confederates out the gaps at a cost of 2,500 Union casualties.

If cautious McClellan had moved decisively with his 75,000 troops, or even those atop South Mountain, the 18,000 troops Lee had at Sharpsburg would have been doomed. Instead, McClellan feared that Lee would outnumber him if Gen. Hill arrived. McClellan moved his men to the ridges east of Antietam Creek where he paused and let them rest.

By midday on the 16th, all three of Lee's nine divisions arrived. Two hundred artillery pieces supported the infantry that spread out in the woods and rolling fields in a bend of the Potomac River. Lee's army was fanned out crescent-like, its right flank on Antietam Creek, and its left flank on the Potomac. Lt. Gen. Jeb Stuart's cavalry guarded the gap between the Potomac and the infantry's left flank. He noticed his back was against the river, and there was no retreat, so he had to fight—that was too his liking. He snuggled his cap on his head with the red plume and straightened his red vest, and then withdrew his saber.

By the afternoon, McClellan sent Maj. Gen. Joseph Hooker across Antietam Creek which only resulted in a few minor skirmishes, nothing victorious. The sun finally set, and McClellan withdrew his men. At the rising of dawn on September 17, Hooker's corps arrived in support, and immediately mounted a bruising assault on Lee's left flank.

Miller's cornfield suffered one attack after another as fighting broke out around the Dunker Church. Combined forces of McClellan and Hooker chased Lee's defense along the Sunken Road and crushed the center of the Confederate line. But true to history of McClellan's hesitation, the advantage disappeared.

Late in the afternoon, Union Maj. Gen. Ambrose Burnside's corps entered the action and swelled the numbers of Union troops facing a faltering Confederate line. Burnside quickly captured a stone bridge over Antietam Creek and pushed his advance against the Confederate right flank.

Fortunately, Maj. Gen. A. P. Hill's Confederate division finally arrived from Harpers Ferry, launched a surprise counterattack, and drove Burnside back to Antietam Creek, ending the battle.

Although outnumbered two to one, Lee committed his entire force, while McClellan sent only a meager portion of his army. This mistake forced a fight to standstill, while Lee escaped in the night. Lee being more strategic-minded than his adversary moved his army south of the Potomac River to the safety of Virginia.

Lee rode his horse off to his tent behind the Confederate lines followed by Captain Bruce Taylor, his intelligence officer. The news he carried meant a court martial for someone, whether a General or a foot soldier. He was desperate to get to the bottom of it. When they arrived Captain Austin stood by the tent with a bag of evidence. All three men went inside the tent with two guards standing outside.

Lee poured a glass of wine and sat. "All right Bruce, give it to me straight."

Bruce breathed a deep sigh. "Well, sir. Last night a 2nd lieutenant caught up with me and told an unbelievable story. It seems that your Order 191 was found in the woods wrapped in a few cigars."

Lee's back stiffened, as he fingered his gray beard. "You're telling me that McClellan knew our marching orders?"

Bruce bowed his head. "Looks that way sir."

Captain Austin opened the bag. "Here is the evidence, sir," he said as he poured a few smelly cigars and a document on Lee's desk. "A sympathizer found this evidence in the woods south of McClellan's position," he added.

Lee slowly raised his head with a quandary of facts buzzing in the cortex of his brain as he saw the numerals 191. How had this order ended up on the ground and in the hands of the enemy? A light burned brightly in his mind. He suddenly leaped from his seat and burst through the tent flap. The guard stood at attention, startled for a moment of indiscretion.

"Guard, how long have you been on duty" he demanded.

"Ah, about two hours, I think," he stammered.

Lee turned to the other guard. "And you, how long?"

He cleared his throat. "I replaced a lieutenant at the change of guard at midnight, sir," he replied, standing stiffly at attention.

Lee gripped his bearded chin, and entered the tent. He sat down, his mind retracing his steps during the last two days. He couldn't imagine how this atrocity had happened, but it fit the pattern of last few days, one wrong move after another. Then his eyes lit up as the answer suddenly hit him.

"Lieutenant?" he screeched, "there are no officers on guard duty."

Bruce stood. "That must be it. The guard was a Union spy."

Austin disagreed. "It's thin, why would he drop the evidence on the ground?"

Bruce considered Austin's question. "Obviously McClellan had the order. Perhaps his adjutant was careless and it somehow fell to the ground—or your sympathizer may have stolen it."

Lee placed a hand on each side of his head as if to shield out the noise of incompetence, tears blurred his eyes. "This explains the massive causalities—the bloodiest single-day battle in American history."

The shame of a military standstill had amassed an astounding list of causalities. No matter how bloody and imperfect, Antietam gave Lincoln the victory he needed. On September 22 he declared that, ". . . as of January 1, 1863, slaves in all states still in rebellion would be thenceforward, and forever free."

In hindsight the battle discouraged the British and French governments from potential plans for recognition of the Confederacy.

McClellan had made a series of cautious mistakes, including the misuse of his larger forces, despite his knowledge of Lee's battle plans. He was embarrassed before his commanders by failing to destroy Lee's Army, even while the enemy escaped.

His caution had enabled Lee's counter by shifting forces and moving interior lines. In skirmish after skirmish Lee out-maneuvered McClellan with half the number of soldiers.

Lee had failed to win a significant victory, but proved McClellan's incompetence, and saved his army for another day.

Chapter 31

Following the Union battle of Shiloh, Maj. Gen. Henry Halleck waited for the arrival of three Union armies, the Army of the Tennessee Army, the Army of the Ohio, and the Army of the Mississippi. He planned for the Siege of Corinth, Mississippi. The Mississippi town of Corinth was a strategic point at the junction of two vital railroads lines, the Mobile and Ohio and the Memphis and Charleston Railroads. She was the last defense before Vicksburg. According to Gen. Lee's intelligence received by telegraphed from Captain Bruce Taylor, Grant waited for reinforcements as ordered by Lincoln. Halleck and Grant were not the best of friends, and Lincoln has his favorite.

Confederate commander Gen. P.G.T. Beauregard stage a hoax to save his army against 120,000 Union troops. Confederate morale was low and they were outnumbered two to one. The water was infested with typhoid, and dysentery placed thousands of his Rebel fighters on the sick list. In fact, sickness claimed the lives of almost as many men as the Confederacy had lost at Shiloh.

Beauregard cleverly instigated the hoax by giving some of his men three days ration and ordered them to prepare for an attack. As expected a couple of men went over to the Union camp with the news of attack; desertion had been common, and the enemy had to believe the false information they carried. The preliminary bombardment started, and Union forces dug in for position. During the night of May 29, Beauregard moved out his army to the Mobile and Ohio Railroad and loaded their sick and wounded, along with heavy artillery, and tons of supplies. As the train moved out, all the men yelled as if they had received reinforcements. He had staged dummy Quaker guns along the earthworks. Camp fires were kept burning, and buglers and drummers played loudly. Finally, the men that remained staging the last elements of the hoax slipped away undetected, withdrawing to Tupelo, Mississippi.

Halleck decided upon digging in for fortification. He knew the staggering losses at Shiloh meant he had a ragged army defense with no desire for offensive maneuvers. His orders were to take this vital railroad center. After moving five miles in three weeks, Halleck was finally in position to lay siege to the Corinth as he waited for the arrival of three Union armies. The old General was not cognizant of the poor condition of his adversary. When Union patrols entered Corinth on the morning of May 30, they found the Confederate troops had gone. The Union forces under Ulysses Grant took control and made Corinth the base for Union operations to grab control of the Mississippi River Valley, and his pursuit to the Confederate stronghold of Vicksburg. He used the hoax to his advantage, to upstage Halleck, the familiar trait of Grant.

Near the railroad center of Corinth at the edge of a dense forest, Bruce Taylor lay on his back wounded, his horse shot dead. All around him he'd heard the sound of Springfield rifles exploding with deadly mini balls zinging to their targets, soldiers screaming, moans of young lads calling for their mothers. Now it was so silent and peaceful a few birds were winging for their nests. He was unaware that Beauregard had moved out.

He lay unconscious.

Suddenly Bruce's eyes popped opened and rolled left to right. He saw his dead horse and the smoky mist settling over the railroad center. A scowl flushed his face as he raised his torso and leaned over his legs. They were not broken, but numbness in his left arm began to pain, life-threatening pain in his left upper arm. He shook his head as beads of sweat pooled in the wrinkles of his forehead. He gripped his left elbow and pulled his arm around; the shirt was bloody, a one-inch spot shone deep red where a mini-ball had ripped into his muscle. His mind told him that he'd bleed to death if he didn't stop the bleeding.

His eyes blurred as he ripped the sleeve off at the shoulder with his right hand. Then he unbuckled his belt and removed it, lay it aside. He pulled out the shirttail, and gripped one end in his teeth, the other in his right hand. He tore off a section of clean cloth. Somehow he folded the cloth and laid it over his extended upper arm, draping it around the wound several loops, holding it with his chin. Finally he tightened his belt above the wound as a tourniquet. He breathed an exhaustive breath, then snaked his body over to a near tree, and leaned against its trunk. He forced himself to stay awake; should he fall asleep, the tourniquet would shut down his heart. But he couldn't stay awake.

Two men rode nearby followed by a woman on a horse. She stopped, perked an ear thinking she heard a moan. She whistled to the two men ahead, and pulled her horse aside. Finally she dismounted, and walked slowly toward a tree were she judged the sound had emanated. Then she saw an arm lying limp, and heard a weak moan.

She rushed to the tree, her heart thumping wildly when she saw the familiar horse lying silently on the ground. Then she saw a man leaning against the tree trunk, and the sum of her fears crushed her heart. Tears blurred her eyes, clasping her hands over her mouth.

It was Bruce, her dahlin Bruce was wounded!

She dropped to her knees, and quickly surveyed his body. She spotted the belt tourniquet and quickly released it. His blue face began to regain color. She inspected the wound: a mini ball puncture, the ball still in his arm. He needed medical help soon. She took his right arm and pulled his body over her shoulder, stretched her strong legs and stood. Her horse obeyed her familiar called and trotted up to her side. She laid the body over her saddle, just as the two men arrived.

One man marveled at how Arabella had managed to put the six-foot-two man on her saddle as he shook his head.

She saw the frown on his face. "When a woman makes up her mind she can do most anything," she smiled.

"Yes ma'am."

She pointed to the railroad crossing. "See if you can find a cart or a wagon before the Yankees get here—see the dust rising over there?"

Both soldiers rode quickly to the crossing and indeed found a cart designed for one horse. One soldier jumped off his saddle and pulled the cart shafts up to his saddle, and wrapped a leather strap around both shafts and attached it to his saddle horn. The two soldiers rode back to the tree just before the squad of Yankee soldiers reached the railroad crossing.

Arabella motioned them to enter the forest for cover. She nodded for the two men to place Bruce's body on the cart, while she backed her horse into the shafts. Somehow she had to attach the shafts to her saddle without the proper hitching harness. Finally she used the leather straps to fasten each strap to the girth of her saddle behind the stirrups.

One of the soldiers suggested that they could wait for the Yankees to take their positions; their backs would face them and they could escape without notice. Arabella thought it good advice, but she inspected Bruce's wound and realized he needed a doctor soon or they'd amputate his arm. She wasn't about to let that happen.

Arabella mounted her horse and snaked through the bushes, dodging the trees until the forest bent away from the sight of the railroad crossing. She pulled out into the open with the two horses of the soldiers behind her. She dismounted and removed the vines caught in the cart wheel axels with a hunting knife given her by Nathan Forrest. Again, the two soldiers sat in their saddles steeped in amazement. The woman was self-sufficient. No wonder General Forrest like her so well.

Arabella headed the cart eastward toward Tennessee. She knew General Johnston was in that area and she might find a field hospital or somebody with medical training. Near dusk the threesome pulled in behind the lines where they saw the smoke of a distant campfire. Arabella dismounted when she heard a moan from the cart. She placed her hand on Bruce's forehead; he had a touch of fever. His head suddenly thrashed about and he muttered a few words. "Information . . . must get to Gen. Lee . . ."

Arabella mounted her house, Bruce's words on her mind. The camp was not far away and that was good, she thought. The distance was short in miles, but it seemed to her it took an eternity. Finally they neared the camp, and Arabella realized it was a Confederate field hospital. How could they be so lucky, but she'd take this gift from Providence. Her heart swelled with thanksgiving. She offered a silent prayer. *Oh God don't let Bruce die, I can't live without him.*

One soldier rode ahead and alerted a surgeon who had a field hospital set up in a covered wagon. When Arabella arrived the surgeon had a table sterilized with alcohol. The two soldiers took Bruce, one by the shoulders, the other by the feet, and laid him on the table. The surgeon quickly inspected the arm. He looked up at Arabella.

"Its infected—that ball has to come out or we'll have to amputate."

Arabella nodded. "Take the ball out, sir. There will be no amputation," she barked.

His eyes squinted. "You must realize that there is no guarantee that removal of the bullet will inhibit amputation."

Arabella handed him a set of forceps. "Remove the ball, doctor."

"If you insist," he said, and moved a kerosene lantern closer. He poked the probing end of the forceps into the bullet hole. As he twisted and probed, his eyes suddenly brightened. He'd located the slug wedged against the bone. Finally, he removed the forceps and dropped the ball in a tin basin, followed by the forceps.

He fingered a bottle of gin and flushed the wound; it was more concentrated with alcohol than the one bottle of wood alcohol he had in his bag. He wrapped the wound with gauze and sealed it with a knot of two torn ends of the gauze.

"That's all we can do for now. We will have to wait."

"How long will he be unconscious?" Arabella quizzed.

He gripped his chin. "He must be exhausted—he needs sleep, healing is faster when the body is inactive."

"That so?" she asked.

He wiped his hands after treating them with alcohol. "That's what the medical books say, but between you and me, I don't hold with bleeding a patient. The Bible says the life is in the blood."

"Doctor, I think you will rewrite some of those medical books during this war."

He smiled, but the wrinkles on his brow revealed how difficult it was to change tradition."

One of the soldiers poked his head into the back of the wagon. "Miss Arabella, ma'am if we hope to reach Richmond before the Yankees overrun us we must leave soon."

"Thank you soldier, I hope you see how important it is to allow Bruce to rest at least twelve hours. We'll depart early in the morning."

"Yes ma'am."

The doctor heard the soldier called this woman Arabella, his forehead wrinkled with a frown. "Excuse me for prying, but are you by chance Arabella Rhett?"

The first sign of surprise appeared on Arabella's tired face. "Yes, I am, doctor. Is there a question you wish to ask me?"

"Well, I'm a little embarrassed to ask this, but aren't you kin to Jeremiah Rhett."

Shock crossed her brow. "He is my uncle who lives in Washington."

"Yes, well Miss Arabella, your uncle rescued me from drowning in the Potomac, raised me, and paid for my education."

Shock transformed into amazement. "He never mentioned your name—what is your name, doctor?"

"Mudd, Doctor Robert Mudd."

Arabella's flashed back fifteen years. "Then you must be the son of Doctor Samuel Mudd of Maryland—my uncle did mention that he had an adopted son."

"I'm afraid the Mudd family never knew I was still alive. In fact, when they took me in as a ten year old orphan, I ran away. I was so distraught having known no family that I jumped off a bridge into the Potomac ready to end my life. Mr. Rhett rescued me." A tear clouded his left eye. "Far as I am concerned, I owe my life to him."

Arabella stood absorbed. "How is it you go by the Mudd name?"

He lowered his head. "Mr. Rhett found a paper in my pocket; it was the release document fostering me to the Mudd family. Mr. Rhett gave me the surname "Robert"—I think he did that out of respect for Robert E. Lee."

In the haven of a Richmond hospital, Arabella sat by the bedside of Bruce Taylor holding his hand. Doctor Winslow Mudd had asserted his rank and commandeered a train. He brought his patient to Richmond with Arabella nestled by his side all along the way. She brushed his hair from his eyes and planted a kiss on his forehead, frowning with concern about infection, the nemesis of a mini ball wound. This man must recover, she desperately prayed—God don't let him lose an arm, she whispered in a moment of providential hope. She wanted both his arms around her waist. On into the night she sat with him, until the dawning of the next morning.

Dr. Mudd gently shook Arabella's shoulder. "Wake up, young lady—wake up!"

She leaned back, shook her head, her eyes slowly focusing from a deep dark nightmare. "Wha . .

. what?" she stuttered, looking at Bruce soundly sleeping. "How is he doctor?"

"Good news. The fever broke overnight. He is healing just fine. Two days, and he'll be good as new," he smiled, feeling a kinship to this fascinating woman.

Tears streamed down Arabella's cheeks. She couldn't speak, just wanted to pray and offer thanksgiving for Bruce's recovery. Arabella snuggled up to Bruce on the bed and drifted off to sleep, a smile on her fatigued countenance.

Chapter 32

Two of Bedford Forrest's officers spurred their horses to a mountain top overlooking the Sequatchie Valley. Suddenly he heard the familiar voice of his captain calling out.

"What," he replied as he raised his torso?"

One office cupped his hands. "Two columns converging on Winchester, Manchester, and McMinnville," he screamed back to Forrest.

Forrest squeezed his fist. "We don't stand a chance against these overwhelming numbers."

He screamed a few orders, and the men were saddled and ready. They moved out following Forrest who always knew where he was going. He led his brigade down a hidden cove into a dry creek bed under high banks that jutted out. They presently heard hoof beats, and scurried under the high bank, sat in silence as marching hoards of bluecoats passed by their hiding place.

On the next day Forrest was officially promoted to acting Lt. General and ordered to join his group with the western army of Gen. Braxton Braggs. He moved into the state of Kentucky, his cavalry guarding the left flank of the army as they traveled northward. His horsemen badgered the flanks and rear of the Union army of Gen. Buell. The campaign for Kentucky was the target of Grant's army. But in its pathway flowed the Stones River and the city of Murfreesboro.

The Battle of Stones River dubbed the Second Battle of Murfreesboro but the Southerners called it simply the Battle of Murfreesboro, one of the major battles in the Western Theater with the highest causalities on both sides. Although the battle outcome was inconclusive, the Union repulsed two Confederate attacks.

Union Maj. Gen. William S. Rosecrans' Army of the Cumberland marched from Nashville, Tennessee, on December 26, and challenged Gen. Braxton Bragg's Army of Tennessee at Murfreesboro. Both general's planned a flank attack, but Bragg assaulted first. He sent Maj. Gen. William Hardee on a massive strike, followed by Brig. Gen. Leonidas Polk and they overran the wing commanded by Maj. Gen. Alexander McCook. A stout defense by the division of Brig. Gen. Philip Sheridan in the right center of the line prevented a total collapse. The Union assumed a tight defensive position like a wedge and backed up to the Nashville Turnpike. Repeated attacks by the Confederates were absorbed. Bragg continued the assault with the corps of Maj. Gen. John Breckenridge, but the troops were slow in arriving, and their piecemeal attacks failed.

Fighting resumed the next day, when Bragg ordered Breckinridge's assault on the well-fortified Union position on a hill to the east of the Stones River. Faced with massive artillery, the Confederates withdrew with heavy casualties. Aware that Rosecrans was receiving reinforcements, Bragg pulled back to Tullahoma, Tennessee.

Consequently, middle Tennessee was now wide open for Grant's march to Vicksburg.

Lt. Gen. Nathan Forrest was destined to play a part in the historic battle of Vicksburg. While bedded down on the outskirts of McMinnville, his men came from town with a coded wire from Arabella. Her message said that Grant was preparing to take Vicksburg, and Van Dorn was planning to go up against Grant to retake the vital town of Corinth. She wondered if Forrest might take his cavalry to the vicinity and assist, if at all possible.

As Forrest read the wire, his head shook from side to side, a reasonable request for a God of war, he thought. It was a long trip but his men were experienced in long marches. He lowered his head with a deep sigh, the message crushed in his fist. If Bruce Taylor doesn't marry that woman he was going to come down to Richmond and whip him. And then he smiled, the two men he'd sent her must have gotten her on a train to Richmond.

As they left, Nathan thought again of her message—a second chance to go up against Grant. His men were fairly good at stinging the tails of Yankees, although Forrest was still nursing a shoulder wound. Back in October he had trained a whole brigade for a march into Kentucky. But now he was rejoining four companies of his old regiment, boys who fought with him at Sacramento, Donelson, and Shiloh Church, and he'd take that loyal group anywhere. To go up against Grant again was a piece of pie for men who had not eaten a good meal in weeks since they left Murfreesboro after the first battle for that ragged town.

They gathered a fine battery of 6-pounder iron guns and a couple of 12-pounder bronze howitzers under Capt. Freeman. Nathan's men carefully prepared all the foodstuffs and armaments needed for a march to meet Van Dorn. At the end of a long marching day, Forrest laid his head on his saddle in the stillness of the evening dusk, his thought focused on Arabella. Jefferson Davis' message was clear. He needed this covert information before Grant stormed into Richmond. And he had confidence that Arabella would provide it. She was the bravest, most resourceful woman he'd ever met.

As Confederate Gen. Braxton Bragg moved northward from Tennessee into Kentucky in September 1862, Union Maj. Gen. Don Carlos Buell pursued him from Nashville with his Army of the Ohio. Confederate forces under Maj. Generals Van Dorn and Sterling Price were expected from middle Tennessee to support Bragg's effort, but the bulk of the arriving troops were required to keep Maj. Gen. Ulysses S. Grant's Army of the Tennessee from reinforcing Buell. Since the conclusion of the Siege of Corinth that summer, Grant's army had been engaged in protecting supply lines in Western Tennessee. Bragg had great respect for Grant's military prowess, and he thought it wise use of the reinforcing men.

    Van Dorn was senior officer and took command of the combined force numbering around 22,000 men. The Rebels marched toward Pocahontas on October 1, and then moved southeast toward Corinth. They hoped to recapture Corinth and then sweep into Middle Tennessee. During the earlier Siege of Corinth, Union forces had erected various fortifications described as an inner line for protecting the important transportation center in Corinth.

    With the Confederates approaching, the Federals numbering 23,000 were waiting in the outer line of fortifications and had men placed in front of them. Van Dorn arrived within three miles of Corinth at 10:00 am on October 3, and moved into the fieldworks that the Confederates had erected earlier during the Siege of Corinth.

    The fighting began almost at once, and the Confederates steadily pushed the Yankees rearward.

A gap occurred between two Union brigades, which the Confederates had manipulated around 1:00 pm. A lull so calm the silence was unnerving and the Union troops pushed back in a futile effort to close the gap. Price's brigades rushed in and attacked the Federals, handily driving them back into their inner line.

By evening Van Dorn was sure he'd finished off the Federals on the next day. His confidence weakened with the blazing heat, mosquitoes, and water shortages finally persuaded him otherwise.

Gen. Rosecrans regrouped his men in the fortifications for preparation of an attack the next morning. Van Dorn had planned his attack at dawn, but Brig. Gen. Louis Hébert came down with a sickness that postponed the confrontation until 9:00 am.

As the Confederates marched forward, their bayonets glittering in the morning sun, Union artillery swept the field like the Devil's scythe; soldier's dropping like flies on molasses, heavy casualties— 6,500 dead and dying in what seemed just a few minutes. But the Rebels fought on. They stormed Battery Powell, and closed on Battery Robinett, when desperate hand-to-hand fighting became the norm, a gladiator moment of historical proportions.

The Federal troops mounted a massive counterattack and forced Van Dorn into a general retreat. Rosecrans postponed any pursuit until the next day; no doubt, he saw the carnage and smelt the fumes of death. Van Dorn was defeated at Hatchie Bridge, Tennessee, on October 5, but his command would fight another day.

The culmination of the Stones River Campaign in the Western Theater essentially gave the Union forces a clear view to Vicksburg. The withdrawal of Rebel troops opened middle Tennessee control into the capable hands of Grant. Vicksburg was the last bastion of hope for the CSA with Grant at the helm and Sherman with his scorched earth policy.

Lt. General Nathan Forrest finally arrived in the vicinity of Hatchie Bridge in Tennessee just as Van Dorn withdrew. Forrest was one of the most successful officers who always seemed ready for assignment, one who had cut more telegraph lines, bent more railroad iron rails, one who gave the enemy a sting in the tail when lest expected, than any general in the Confederacy. He was finally giving his mean a well-deserved rest around campfires. His horsemen had covered over 1000 miles in the last three months, running the federals on wild goose chases, expending their ammunition, demoralizing their troops, and killing their officers. They had seized 800 head of cattle and 200 hogs, destroyed block house, and captured hundreds of Union prisoners. His men had weathered freezing rain, blowing storms, and soaked by wet snow, and steaming heat, but still they followed Bedford Forrest wherever he led. After marching three days over roads made impassable by frozen ruts and icy hills, Forrest cavalry caught up with the last of Van Dorn's men.

Chapter 33

Captain Austin stumbled into the Richmond office and slumped in a chair, exhausted and starving. Bruce Taylor arrived presently after just completing his recuperation, his arm in still in a sling. Dr. Mudd had released him from hospital and Bruce was up and feeling fine, except for occasion aches in his arm.

He stepped up to his friend and gazed at his unshaven face and dirty uniform. "What ran over you?"

Austin coughed. "The entire Union army, I think—you should have seen Stonewall Jackson—the guy is fearless."

"Well, you look exhausted, and perhaps hungry."

Austin stood. "Starving—let's find that place you spoke of—a tavern of some sort."

They left the office and walked across the street to a familiar tavern. The place was empty, probably everyone at home packing, in case Pope made it to Richmond. Austin ordered a huge plate of sausage and eggs with buckwheat cakes. It was a good time of uncommon relaxation with a good friend.

Austin downed a fork of potatoes. "Nathan Forrest tells me he has lost track of Arabella since his men left with her on a journey to Richmond. I don't know any more details. I got the feeling you would know."

"She found me wounded while they were on the way to Richmond. I'm told by Dr. Mudd that she sat by my side until I was out of danger from infection. I don't mind telling you I am worried about her."

Bruce left his covert office after talking with Doyle who had provided most of the leg work of late, and crossed the alley to Lee's office building. He dearly hoped that Arabella had contacted Lee; her absence was extremely painful since he desired her presence so much. The secretary waved Bruce by, and he opened the door.

Lee was reading a telegram when he entered. His belabored eyes lifted and he nodded at a chair. "How is the arm, Bruce?"

"Good as new, Sir," he replied not wanting to bother him with the aches.

"I expect your visit concerns this telegram."

"Sir?"

"Jefferson Davis has approved a plan from Lt. Gen. Forrest concerning you and Arabella."

"Yes, but I don't know the details, Sir," he stammered nakedly.

Lee inhaled as he laid the telegram on the desk. "Davis wants information on Grant and Sherman's conversation with Lincoln, the only meeting they had together. It's risky at best." He exhaled. "The President's secretary should have files on the discussions, "he proffered.

Bruce sighed in relief. "Then I take it you approve Sir."

"Guardedly so—you may not return—you or Arabella," he said in a voice so low that Bruce wasn't sure he heard him. "If you are captured disguised in an enemy's uniform it is punishable by death."

He sighed deeply. "It's your choice, Bruce."

Bruce inhaled. "I'll do it, Sir, but I don't know where Arabella is at the moment."

Lee rubbed his hand across his eyes, and then shook his head slowly as if to clear it. Finally he said, "That woman seems to be everywhere at once. I suspect your team can get you into the Capitol?"

Lee's secretary knocked on the door and cracked it ajar. "Captain Taylor there is a message for you," she remarked and handed him a wire.

With great anticipation, Bruce stood and took the wire, curiously scanning the words. His forehead wrinkled, and he dropped his good hand by his side, the wire crumpled in his hand. He slumped in a chair; a smile crossed his face as he absorbed the significance .

"Doyle says Arabella is arriving tonight by train," he said as if he disbelieved his words.

Lee nodded. "Remember, Bruce. The best laid plans can fail—I know from experience."

"It's not the plans, sir, it's the people," he saluted, and exited the office.

Lee bowed his head. Bruce had a point.

Bruce met the train about dusk at a crossing outside of Washington, and had brought a mount for Arabella. They met, arms surrounding each other. Another moment of ecstasy set apart from the turmoil of war. The stillness of the dusk, the muted sound of birds on the wing, enhanced the softness of the woman he loved embraced in his arm. Finally they released, and Arabella placed the bandaged arm against her cheek. She was at rest.

In the quietness of the blissful moment they discussed the mission, its dangers, and its success. As they looked into each other's eyes, they were each resolved in the mission. If they failed, then they would die together. They mounted the two horses Bruce had brought. He had also brought Doyle along, who stood with his back turned for their privacy. The threesome galloped into the darkness along a carefully planned route to Julie's home on the Potomac.

The air was fresh; the flowers that bloomed in May added a perfume that even masked the fragrance of cherry blossoms. Suddenly the clouds parted and opened up the star-studded heavens, a myriad of bright lights in the sky over the Shenandoah Valley, a lake of lush green that grew so magnificently in Virginia. In the presence of such heavenly glory, Bruce remembered Lee's words: 'God speed, son.' Presently they arrived at the house on the Potomac. Julie's new maid met them at the door. She ushered them inside, closed, and locked the door behind their entrance.

Josh sat on the bottom stair step and ran to Arabella's open arms. "Gosh, it's good to see you Miss Bella." She hugged the young lad. Bruce smiled; another sign had confirmed his heart's desire.

Julie opened a closet door in the hallway, and came back with a white gown and slippers.

"This gown belonged to my daughter who was killed in the war," she explained. "She was about the same size as you Arabella, though not as tall. But we can alter the hem."

Arabella smiled as she held the gown up to her tired body, but just being with Bruce again relaxed her muscles. It was beautiful complete with crinoline but no hoop.

"What do you think, Bruce . . . oh dear, almost forgot! Doyle, would you mind getting a package from my saddlebags?" she asked.

"Sure."

Finally, the couple came down the stairs dress for a ballroom dance. Arabella swayed in a stunning pink gown, Bruce in a handsome Union Captain's uniform, which Doyle had secured from Gen. Beauregard. Julie followed them with a needle and pin pincushion in her capable hands. She checked the hem length. The gown never looked so ravishing enclosed around Arabella's shapely body.

"Well my friends. Shall we have a bite to eat before this couple rides off?" Julie suggested, smiling warmly.

As they ate Doyle produced the package from Arabella's saddle. She wiped her mouth with a cloth napkin, as she took the package. She laid the package on the table in front of Bruce seated beside her.

"Gen. Nathan Forrest wanted you to have this for the occasion," she said smiling.

Bruce faced her with a curious frown. And then he tore open the paper wrapping. His eyes beamed at the sight of a metallic object. He stared mesmerized.

Doyle's eyes focused on a Colt revolver issued 1861 to the U.S. Army. "Where did that come from?"

Arabella looked into Bruce's surprised face, caressing his cheek. "Nathan took it off a Union Captain he killed in hand-to-hand battle."

Doyle's horse led the couple in a carriage up to the vicinity of the Capitol. Bruce and Arabella exited the carriage, and crossed the lawn to the Capitol steps. Doyle drove the carriage off into the night.

As Arabella mounted the steps she adjusted her shawl around her bare shoulders, and hooked her arm into Bruce's elbow. My, he was handsome, she thought. Bruce turned his head with a smile, she was 5 feet 7 inches tall, taller than most Southern girls, but he loved every inch. It promised a pleasurable evening together out on the town—if they weren't caught, nor his arm started to pain.

A Union lieutenant at the door saluted Captain Taylor and they went down the hall to the open ballroom. As they walked, the voice of Jenny Lind was obvious and the keyboard of her piano accompanist Julius Benedict. When they entered the ballroom they saw Jenny Lind talking with President Lincoln. Standing beside the President was General Grant and General Halleck.

They walked by the group toward the punchbowl just to enter the room unnoticed, while all eyes were on the famous performer and the President.

As they swilled a few swallows of punch, Arabella noticed that Grant gave Halleck one of his cigars. She nudged Bruce. "Watch Halleck, that cigar is loaded," she whispered.

Bruce covered his mouth camouflaging his giggle. And before he removed his hand, Halleck face looked nauseas, wild-eyed. But then he started picking something from the air as if he saw roses in his mother's garden.

Grant smelled the two cigars left in his pocket. He nodded to his adjutant. "Get rid of these things, and find me a new box," he whispered, concealing his smile behind his hand.

Lincoln craned his long neck hoping to see the hallucination Halleck apparently saw. "Halleck, maybe you had better sit down, and perhaps take a week off," his skeletal face smiled.

During the excitement, Arabella glided out into the hallway toward the offices. An orderly came by the punch bowl and gave Bruce a message: the President wanted a word with him. Bruce swallowed dryly and followed the orderly over to the President gathering confidence.

"Mr. President, Bruce Taylor at your service." Bruce replied with a slight bow.

The President stood taller than Bruce as he looked him up and down with his deep-seated eyes. "Aren't you the gentleman who talked with the War Department?"

Bruce gulped. "Yes sir. I want to strongly advise you to be careful in these treacherous times."

Lincoln bobbed his head of dark hair that matched his beard as shadows danced on the chiseled features of his cheekbone. "Does this have to do with the Booth man?"

He nodded, confirming that Lincoln had indeed talked with the men at the War Department. "Sir, the man is demented," rubbing his arm.

Grant's bushy eyebrow elevated.

Lincoln placed a finger aside his nose as his deep dark eyes blinked admiringly. "I appreciate your concern, Captain, I shall add your concerns to the growing list of my advisors," he said in a stoic stare, sizing the demeanor of the tall young man. "You appear to have wounded your arm—get hit in Corinth by chance."

"Just a flesh wound, sir—nothing of concern, many soldiers have paid a higher price."

"Well said, Captain," Lincoln replied admiringly.

Arabella finally found the chief of staff's office after a moment of searching. Fortunately, the door was ajar, and she tip-toed inside. She lit a candle with a match she found beside the candleholder. No files were on the desk, and she opened the side drawer. A few Matthew Bradey photographs of the war lay on top of a file. She slid the file out and spread it open. Under candlelight, she read the title: War Plan for the Western Theater.

"How can I be so lucky," she whispered.

She found some sheets of paper in a trashcan and poured India ink over the surface, then stuck them in the file folder. She took the papers from the file, folded them, and stuck then under her crinoline, secured them with a pin. And then she took bogus file folder and stuck it under the photos. She blew out the candle and waltzed to the door, and closed it behind her exit.

Then she strutted down the hall as before as if nothing had happened. Bruce saw her approach and met her at the entry to the ballroom. "Did you find anything?"

"Gold, Bruce, real Gold."

"Take my arm and follow me."

Suddenly a commanding voice sounded from the rear.

"Hold up, there!"

They turned and faced General Grant. "I'm sorry, but I didn't get to meet this charming young lady—noticed you at the punchbowl."

"Well, General Grant, sir. This is Arabella Rhett, just down from Fredericksburg," he lied.

Grant took her hand bowed and kissed it gingerly. "I hope you will visit us again, Miss Rhett."

"Why General Grant, sir, I'm sure we'll meet again," she smile alluringly.

"And Captain Taylor, I don't believe I've had the pleasure."

He clicked his heals to attention. "Just in from Texas, sir briefly attached to the War Office here in Washington."

"I see. Perhaps we will meet again, Captain Taylor, and please bring Arabella with you."

"If that will be all, Sir?" he saluted.

"Captain, I'm really concerned for the President in this upcoming election. Politics can be more dangerous than military action," he admitted unconsciously raising his empty cigar-fingers toward his mouth, then caught his digression and instead stretched out his arm and shook Bruce's hand. "If you should gain more information on this Booth man, I would deeply appreciate your contacting me."

"I shall be honored, sir."

"As you were, Captain," he said, "And you Arabella Rhett, it has been my distinct pleasure."

Arabella gripped the hem of her gown with both hands and slightly bowed. "I'm charmed, Sir."

Grant returned her bow with a finger on the brim of his hat, and walked back into the ballroom.

Bruce sighed in relief.

He quickly led Arabella down the hall as they gave each other startled looks. They finally stepped out on the portico. Fortunately, Doyle had the carriage parked below the steps. Bruce aided Arabella into the carriage, and stepped in beside her.

He tugged Doyle's tailcoat. "Get out of here, now," he whispered.

Chapter 34

President Lincoln and the Union Army and Navy were resolved to take control of the Mississippi River from the Confederacy, and the second phase was Vicksburg, a siege in that lasted two years. Lincoln had determined to break the stronghold of Vicksburg way back in 1862, but needed the right general. And the President now believed he had the right general in command, Maj. Gen. Ulysses S. Grant, whom he gave charge of the Mississippi Army.

Lincoln took notice of Grant's willingness to fight in 1861, when he discharged Fremont from active duty. This action gave Grant the initiative, and he took 3000 troops by boat and attacked the Confederate Army commanded by Gen. Gideon Pillow positioned at Camp Johnson. Grant finally won the approval of Maj. Gen. Henry Halleck, with permission to attack Fort Henry on the Tennessee River; from there he captured Fort Donaldson on the Cumberland River, and pushed his Army of the Tennessee overland steadily moving south.

After Grant's army had broken the line of defenses at Shiloh and Donaldson he gathered his entire Army of Tennessee for an attack on Vicksburg, the last stronghold of defense of the Confederate Line. By then his Army was cut down to 35,000 men. He commanded three corps to the battle; Maj. Gen. John A. McClernand, Maj. Gen. William T. Sherman, and Maj. Gen. James B. McPherson.

At the opening of the campaign, Grant attempted an overland approach to Vicksburg from the Northeast; however, Confederate Generals Nathan Forrest and Van Dorn thwarted the union Army advance by raiding Union supply lines. Sherman and McClernand combined their forces and finally defeated the Confederates at The Battle of Chickasaw Bayou. But Grant and most of his men remembered Gen. Forrest; the man was a maniac with a devil of a cavalry. Grant shifted his advance by water, but failed five times. News of these failures reached Washington with legislature demands for Grant's dismissal.

Grant dismissed the news and crossed the Mississippi River south of Vicksburg at Bruinsburg. He drove his army westward, and won quick battles at Port Gibson and Raymond, and captured Jackson, the state capital of Mississippi. The fighting finally stopped on a dark, gloomy hot night, and Grant went into his field tent.

There in uncommon solitude he thought of his lingering rivalry, and what must be done. Although Lincoln had told him to remove Gen. McClernand if he interfered with winning Vicksburg, Grant had waited six months for the right screw-up, since they first clashed at the Battle of Arkansas Post.

The moment came on May 30, 1863. McClernand wrote a self-adulatory note to his troops claiming the credit for the victories during the march to Vicksburg. With the note in his hand, Grant received permission to relieve McClernand. His army was turned over to Maj. Gen. Edward Ord now recovered from a wound he sustained at Hatchies Bridge.

General Sherman spoke to the soldiers on guard, opened the flap of Grant's tent, and stepped inside. Grant was smoking his 20th cigar of the day. He removed the butt between his two nicotine stained fingers. "Sit down Sherman."

Sherman sported a rare smile. "Scuttlebutt says you fired McClernand."

He swallowed a jigger of whiskey. "Just relieved him gently."

Sherman smirked. I'll give you odds that he'll be reinstated before we take Vicksburg."

"Don't think so, I hear that he's bound for the other rattlesnakes in remote Texas."

Sherman spread a smile.

The siege of Vicksburg would test the stubbornness of two opposing Generals in a long battle of flexibility and steady nerves. Grant faced a Northerner by birth General who was probably more influenced by fear of public condemnation if he abandoned Vicksburg—Confederate Lt. Gen. John C. Pemberton.

Pemberton's Army of Mississippi was station inside the Vicksburg line consisting of four divisions. This political general tried to balance the opinion of Davis—who insisted that Vicksburg must be held, and Joseph E. Johnston—who declared its military value worthless. He was caught in the middle of a convoluted command system and his own indecisiveness.

In addition to Pemberton at his front, Grant had more concern with Confederate forces in his rear under the command of Joseph E. Johnston, a man who had fought against McClellan, was severely wounded, and was replaced by none other than Gen. Robert E. Lee, a man that Grant deeply respected. Grant quickly stationed one division near Big Black River Bridge, and another patrolling north of Mechanicsburg, both covering any flanking operation.

A Union special task force arrived with the mission of stopping Johnston from interfering in the siege. Pemberton received a wire from Lee's intelligence man Capt. Bruce Taylor warning that Sherman was in flaking position, and used the opportunity to move his troops. He promptly withdrew his Army of 18,500 westward toward Champion Hill and Black River Bridge.

Fortunately he saw Grant's flanking forces and quickly realized that Maj. Gen. Sherman was indeed positioned to flank him from the north. He ordered his men across the Black River Bridge and burned it in retreat. He took everything edible in his path; pigs, chickens, and collard greens, and then retreated to the well-fortified city of Vicksburg where he had the advantage of terrain and almost impregnable fortifications.

There was a 6.5 mile line of elevations that included hills and knobs with steep angles that an attacker had to ascend under fire. The perimeter included many gun pits, forts, trenches, redoubts, and lunettes. It was a formidable defense.

Grant's strategy and his mounting victories had given him much notoriety to President Lincoln. He simply pointed his men to the target and marched forward. Similarly he wanted to overwhelm the Confederates before they could fully organize their defenses. He ordered an immediate assault against Stockade Redan.

Troops from Sherman's corps had difficulty against rifle fire and artillery as they ascended the open area up a steep ravine, and then faced a 6-foot deep and 8-foot wide ditch before attacking the 17-foot high walls. The first attempt was easily repulsed with horrible casualties. As a result, Grant ordered an artillery bombardment to soften the defense, and then Sherman's men tried again. The assault collapsed amidst rifle fire and hand grenades lobbing back and forth. The casualties were mounting, and Grant didn't favor such carnage, although his critics differed.

The failing dual attempts had injured Union morale and deflated confidence that they had felt while victoriously marching across Mississippi. The casualties were embarrassingly appalling. Grant did not regret having made the assaults, only that he'd failed—the attitude that endeared Lincoln's opinion of Grant's leadership, but it infuriated Grant's critics.

Undaunted, Grant immediately planned a third assault, and ordered artillery and naval gunfire to pound the offense objectives, a prelude to the bombardment of the city of Charleston later in September. Four hours before dawn the Union bombarded the entrenchments once more along a three-mile front. Sherman attacked again down the Graveyard Road leading the way with planks and ladders reminiscent of attacking a castle in ancient England. The strategy was to concentrate force in a narrow front. However, they were driven back again in the face of heavy gunfire.

The Confederates had held for forty days and now they were running out of ammunition. Over three quarters of Pemberton's forces were lost in the three preceding attacks. This daunting circumstance required reinforcements. Many officers in Vicksburg expected a relief force from Gen. Joseph E. Johnston. But unfortunately, Johnston never appeared. And now large Union forces were on the march to siege Vicksburg.

Johnston sent a stinging note to Pemberton. He asked him to give up the city and save the troops; apparently, his failure to send troops was based on his opinion that Vicksburg was not worth the price of human lives. Of course, Pemberton was politically minded and had no intention of giving up the city without a fight—not because he was brave—but because he feared public condemnation.

Grant's hidden compassion arose for a brief time during the battle as hundreds of Union and Confederate men fell by the wayside in heaps of dead bodies. He issued orders to his division commanders to reduce casualties. In fact, he wrote in his memoirs that he intended to incur no more loses. His troops dug in for protection, and constructed several elaborate entrenchments that surrounded the city.

With their backs against the Mississippi River, and gunboats firing bombs and canisters, the people of the city and the protecting troops were trapped. Yet to his credit, Pemberton decided he'd hold his few miles of the Mississippi River as long as possible, or die trying—at least he showed guts.

And soon the dead and dying lying in the blistering heat of Mississippi summer became a problem of hygiene and honor. The stench was atrocious; decaying bodies and bloated horses fouled the air, only buzzards stood in the disgusting odor. And even the wounded were wailing for mercy.

Grant at first refused a truce on the grounds of weakness, but recanted. The Confederates held their fire while the Union recovered their wounded and dead. Grant likewise held his fire until the Confederates recovered their men. The silence of no hostilities was deafening to their battled-scared hearing.

Finally reinforcements poured in from the west and increased Grant's force from 50,000 to 77,000. Pemberton was boxed in with deadly lack of food and munitions, and an enemy thrice his number of troops. By the end of June, half his meager forces were out sick with scurvy, malaria, dysentery, diarrhea, and other diseases of the searing summer. Yet, the constant shelling of an astounding 22,000 shells bothered him less than the lack of food and medicine.

War unveiled strange activity, sometimes inhuman. Over 500 caves were dung into the yellow clay hills of Vicksburg like groundhogs with massive claws. Construction was reinforced with rugs, furniture, and pictures. These dugouts gave the town the nickname of "Prairie Dog Village." Despite the viciousness of the Union fire against the town, fewer than a dozen civilians were known as casualties during the entire siege.

Pemberton sent a telegraph on May 9 to the Louisiana garrison requesting a movement against Grant's supply depot at Milliken's Bend. Lt. Gen. Edmond Kirby Smith received the request but failed to understand the importance of Pemberton's situation, perhaps because Johnston felt an explanation was unnecessary relative to the Vicksburg battle. Consequently, Smith sent a message to Maj. Gen. Richard Taylor who immediately realized his presence could provide an escape for Pemberton.

Grant quickly came to the same conclusion. But the presence of Maj. Gen. John G. Walker's Confederate division on the Louisiana side of the river was of grave concern. Grant hurriedly dispatched troops from the Vicksburg trenches in two brigades across the river to defend his supply depots. With the Confederate activity growing in the area, Grant decided he'd remove all his troops from the trenches and station them across the river. To accomplish this change, he ordered Sherman to the vicinity of Milliken's Bend.

On June 15, Grants brigades defeated Walker and destroyed the Confederate supply depots at Richmond, Louisiana. Vicksburg was in a pickle, stalemated on three sides with gunboats in the river.

On July 3, Pemberton sent a conference note to Grant. The grizzly General had demanded unconditional surrender at his victories, but he relented, logistics overruled valor; not wanting the task of feeding 30,000 hungry Confederates transferred to Union prison camps. He offered parole of all prisoners. His reasoning, as he smoked a cigar in his command post, was their destitute starving state would send a message of defeat into the Confederacy and bring the war to a close. This was his wish and that of President Lincoln, too. However, most of the men that were paroled on July 6 were exchanged and went back into the Confederate Army to fight another day, an issue of dispute until August 4, 1863, when Grant ended all prisoner exchanges during the war except for hardship cases.

Vicksburg stubbornly held on until July 1864. During that struggle the northern press went for the throat of the long campaign, charging Grant as a drunkard, and Sherman as a lunatic. Grant's drinking addiction was well-known. However, Lincoln never flinched; his eyes were on Grant's victories.

The surrender of Vicksburg gladly came.

Grant gave Sherman the rank of Brigadier general in the regular army, in addition to his rank as a major general of volunteers. Sherman's family came from Ohio and visited his camp near Vicksburg; his nine-year old son, Willie, the Little Sergeant, died from typhoid fever contracted during the trip. Perhaps Sherman had suitable reasons for his erratic behavior.

The Confederate surrender in the siege of Vicksburg is often seen as the turning point of the war, a campaign that lasted six months. In just a few months Meade will defeat Lee at Gettysburg, and the dye will be cast in the defeat of the CSA. Communications were severed with Confederate forces in the Trans-Mississippi Department for the remainder of the war.

Chapter 35

Over in the East Room of the White House a party brewed, while Ulysses S. Grant stood blushing and sweating briefly enduring a moment in his honor. President Lincoln watched him smiling, his deep seated eyes sparkling in the candlelight. At last he had found the general he wanted, the general he needed in this presidential year. It was a good night for celebrating, all except one, Gen. McClellan, who had let it be known that he was a Democratic candidate for the President, opponent against Lincoln.

Newspapers hailed Grant as a savior, the winning general from the West. This announcement publicly embarrassed the soldiers from the East. Yet Grant's arrival in Virginia underlined the differences between the armies of the East and the West. In the East, the soldiers titivated and paraded. The Western soldier was sloppy and looked messy when their generals let them get away with it.

Lee's soldiers were disciplined, more than the western forces. Yet they used their own drums, shoes, and pants. And the Rebel soldier knew the forces against them, what they were fighting for, not the slavery issue entirely in their minds, but their southern way of life. They took great refuge in their honor and religion.

The next day Lincoln gave Grant his commission as Lieutenant General—a rank previously held by George Washington and Winfield Scott. The obscure man from Galena became general-in-chief of all Union armies. Lincoln gave Grant the direct command of all the Union armies, for the specific purpose of breaking the Confederate line and pushing toward Richmond. He was a winning soldier among so many who had failed to capture the Confederate capital. Above all, northern bureaucrats wanted the Shenandoah Valley protected from bomb holes and muddy boots, but Maj. Gen. Lee was an elusive tactician, the very reason Lincoln originally had wanted Lee to command the Union Army.

Wiry Gen. Grant stood 5 feet 8 inches of 135 pounds of muscle and brawn, had no dashing gift of oratory at all, but his men obeyed—no officer under his command dared rile him. This quality of leadership was sorely missed in the ranks of the Union army. He started from obscurity and after the war became the President of the United States. He was calm as a cucumber, slow to anger, with nerves of steel. A story had survived that said the general was sitting on a fallen tree writing a dispatch when a shell burst in front of him; he glanced up, and kept on writing.

He had his faults, among them General Order No. 11, allegations of antisemitism, a blot on Grant's reputation. Lincoln had watched this man since his early days at Cairo, and sent Charles A. Dana to keep a watchful eye on the man who would be the next general of the Union Army.

The aftermath of Vicksburg was a turning point for the Union war effort. With Virginia open for the picking, Washington sat in a pretty fair position of ending the war. Yet, Lincoln had smelled that rotten egg before. Gen. Lee was a formidable adversary. And Lincoln vowed he'd not make that mistake again.

Only Gen. Grant was worthy of going up against Gen. Lee, was Lincoln's conviction.

The news of Vicksburg was disheartening for the Confederate Calvary under the leadership of Lt. Gen. Nathan Bedford Forrest. His men had fought skirmishes all over Tennessee, Georgia, Mississippi, and Alabama without leadership direction; bent more railroad track, destroyed more ammo dumps, and killed more Yankees than any regiment in the Confederacy. This they had done under the leadership of Bedford Forrest, until Jefferson Davis ordered Forrest to defend against Gen. Grant's march into Virginia. Federal troops were already pouring into the Deep South.

Forrest' army was bogged down in Gainesville, Tennessee, when he received the word, but his men quickly regrouped and marched day and night. They were in the vicinity of Grant's troops by nightfall on the third day.

Nathan Forrest was the only man who entered the war as a private and emerged a Lt. General. No general in the war had killed more enemies hand to hand, at least 30. A Tennessee native, he was fatherless at age 15, worked on the family farm with ten siblings and his mother. He taught himself to read, scraped up enough money, and started a business in land deals. Forrest finally amassed a fortune of $1,500,000 in 1860 dollars, one of the wealthiest men in Nashville. The Tennessee governor authorized Forrest to personally raise a battalion of mounted rangers. He relied on Colt revolvers and double-barreled shotguns until he was able to import Enfield's. His fast actions and lightning-quick decisions revealed his ferocious courage, a master of deception and bluff. Forrest was an innovating cavalry leader, a defiant *wizard of the saddle*, a nickname given by his men. Both Davis and Lee believed he was never fully utilized in the war effort outside of the Virginia Theater. Even Grant respected his tactics.

Chapter 36

Captain Bruce Taylor frantically worried about Arabella Rhett who had been reassigned by Beauregard to Lt. Gen. Forrest after such a difficult mission in Washington. She had ridden beside Forrest in many battles and had given him valuable troop information; where the Yankee's were camped, their numbers, and armaments. And now he heard that she had been wounded again in the Stones River battle, and was under care in Murfreesboro, Tennessee.

Somehow this woman was continually on his mind. Now that Julie was able to take Josh, Arabella had filled the void—the void in his thoughts, and now he was certain she had also filled the void in his heart.

Bruce recalled telling Josh about this woman who babysat him, when his mother was killed. Babysat, no, that wasn't exactly correct; this woman took him while under fire and kept him safe. Arabella had saved Josh's life, and he was eternally grateful.

General Forrest finally pulled out of Fort Pillow, and stayed in Jackson for a good three weeks. The much needed rest was used to roundup deserters. The problem was an issue for Commanders in the field just to keep up the moral of the troop. But time after time the deserters were mostly stealing just to stay alive. Their pants were a series of patches, the shirts a maze of blood spots.

Forrest ordered them out of Jackson on the dawn of the tenth day and they marched day and night. They had gathered about 3,000 men from the area, each man furnished with ten days rations and 100 rounds of ammunition. Trailing the men was a wagon train of foodstuffs and four batteries of twenty Napoleons.
    Finally they reached the outskirts of Tupelo, Mississippi. Forrest let the men stand down for a much needed rest until he received orders. It seemed that every time these horsemen found time to rest it poured rain—torrents of rain with thunder and lightning that scared the horses, and a few of the younger men. This part of Mississippi still look like the green South, the Yankees had not burned down all the buildings and the corn was still growing.
    Forrest grew weary of waiting and rode into Tupelo with two of his men. He found a telegraph key in a dry goods shop, and sent a wire to Gen. Beauregard. Presently the answer came: Beauregard wants Forrest to enter Middle Tennessee and cut the supply lines that feed and arm Sherman's army. He read the telegram a second time, calculating in his mind the length of the trip, and the time to get to Sherman's Army near Atlanta.
    Forrest and his men rode back out to his camp. He discussed the orders with his Captains and they decided to mount up and head out for Russelville in Alabama. The evening grew cold as the wagon train followed a line four-abreast into a star-lit night. After a ten-hour march, they finally pulled up beside a stream. Forrest ordered sentries on four sides with eight hour shifts before relief.
    While Forrest's mind was calculating the distance they'd traveled, his keen ears caught the rhythm of the familiar hoofs of a trotting mare. Much

to his surprise, Arabella strolled up to the campfire. Forrest holstered his Colt revolver, taking a deep breath. Beauregard had reassigned Arabella in the field, and he didn't like the decision at all.

"How are the wounds, Arabella?"

"You old warhorse, you've got more scars than me," she smile.

He gripped his chin, anger stirring in his mind. "It wasn't my idea to put you back in the field, Arabella," he barked, obvious that he was disappointed with Beauregard's decision.

"We are in a war, and we go where we are assigned," she shot back.

Forrest leaned against a counter. "Arabella, you've got the mind of a general—I knew it the day we first met in Washington, what's more you are more courageous than ten of my men."

"With all that flattery, don't you want to know why I'm here?"

"I thought you'd get around to that," he chuckled.

"General Lee urgently requests that you return to north Mississippi. It seems that Yankee General Sam Sturgis plans to run you and your men into the ground."

"Oh, and how much firepower does he have?"

"General Lee estimates about 3,000 cavalry, 4800 infantry, and maybe 20 cannon."

Forrest wagged his head. "Fairly exact numbers," he analyzed. "Still, it won't be enough to fret my army," he barked.

"Sturgis is marching into northern Mississippi as we speak," Arabella advised.

Forrest pinched his bottom lip. "Thanks for the intelligence, Arabella. And for what it's worth, I'm going to have a chat with Beauregard and get you back to Richmond."

Arabella winked. "Watch your back, Nathan."

He took her hand. "I'll take my men up to the crossroads at Brice's farm, about 18 miles south of here," he said, and looked into her tired eyes. "You head west toward the Virginia border and get back to that man of yours. Be careful. Yankees are pouring out of North Carolina for some kind of offensive in Tennessee."

Chapter 37

Late that afternoon a runner brought a telegram to Lee's office while Bruce and Lee were discussing the upcoming Chancellorsville campaign. Lee read the message, and faced Bruce.

"It's from Gen. Forrest—concerns Arabella," he said, with a raised eyebrow."

"Is she all right," he gasped.

"Let me read a line in the telegram. "Tell Bruce. Danville hospital. Arabella shot. Don't want no damn Yankee to arrest her."

Bruce managed a guarded smile, as he brushed a tear from his eye. "Sounds like General Forrest," Bruce replied sliding to the edge of his chair.

Bruce took the telegram from Lee's outstretched hand and scanned the message, his mind drifting to an earlier conversation with Lee. Forrest had released Arabella from duty when she was injured in Murfreesboro. Forrest had rescinded Beauregard's reassignment, and requested that Lee take her into his intelligence group based in Virginia. With the war moving into the Shenandoah Valley, she would be more valuable to General Lee. Truth known, Forrest wanted her out of conflict entirely. General Lee wasn't opposed, but warned Bruce that he couldn't guarantee her safe transportation.

Bruce immediately left Lee's office and walked across the alley to the office of his intelligence group.

Fortunately James Doyle was there, and Bruce poured two cups of coffee as he discussed the wire from Gen. Forrest.

"Any ideas, Doyle?"

"He sipped his coffee, and then slowly lowered his mug. "I might," he replied.

"Let's have it—we don't have much time, the railroads out of Richmond are closing down quickly"

"It's risky," he suggested.

"This is war Doyle; just walking out that door is risky."

"Hot-air balloon," he shot back.

Silence.

"Is that feasible?"

"Not only feasible, I know where we can secure one."

Dusk had swallowed the sun and the Virginian Mountains were outlined with an orange glow of twilight. The clouds blanketed out the stars as the sun disappeared over the peaks. A breeze floated in from the oceans and rustled the leaves on the trees. The sky was completely overcast, perfect for secretive air flight. Bruce and Doyle went to the armory of the Confederate Army, which was guarded by a squad of southern marksmen. As they walked along side by side, they discussed the dangers of this flight. It seemed that Doyle was trained in hot-air balloons before he was assigned to the Intelligence group. But somehow Bruce harbored a deep concern for the safety of his best friend, a friend who took responsibility for rescuing Arabella, when it was his obligation.

The Montgolfier brothers of Paris had invented the first un-tethered hot-air balloon in 1782. These monstrosities were propelled through the air rather than just being pushed along by the wind. A square wicker basket suspended by tethers beneath the balloon provided room for two people. The gas for propulsion that provided the lift was petroleum based, but was not refined to propane until early in the 20th century. However, benzene was discovered in 1825 by the English scientist Michael Faraday, who had isolated it from oil gas and gave it the name *bicarburet of hydrogen*. In 1833, the German chemist Elhaard Mitscherlich produced benzene via the distillation of benzoic acid from gum benzoin and lime. Mitscherlich gave the compound the name *benzin*. The toxic properties of "benzene" were not clearly understood until Charles Mansfield, an English chemist isolated benzene from coal tar in 1825, and still it was an explosive compound.

Fortunately Gen. Lee had the foresight to investigate the hot-air balloon concept for war purposes, and had purchased a hot air balloon system in the early years before the war. Lee was hesitant to use benzene because of its unknown explosive properties; therefore, the propulsion system received was modified by Army personnel to use coal oil piped through a line regulated by a hand-turn gate valve. The nozzle was supported in the opening of the balloon above the basket. The lift was achieved by heating atmospheric air within the balloon. The concept came from Montgolfier, who suspected he'd stumbled on a new gas, but actually he was only heating atmospheric gases of nitrogen, hydrogen, and oxygen.

The balloon had a 600-pound lifting weight. Bruce chuckled beneath his breath when he thought that Arabella may had gained too much weight while convalescing, but he dared not say a word if this imagery were true. But Doyle thought it not humorous; he was the pilot of the contraption, and didn't have that luxury.

The weight restrictions included the heavy coal oil generator and sand ballast for release in emergency altitude situations. Doyle voiced his disapproval of the coal-oil system; he thought benzene gave him faster response. Yet he didn't overrule Bruce, nor had they the time for conversion of the system. He checked his maps, carefully avoiding as many Union troops as possible and the mountain peaks. The armory cook made food for the trip, but Bruce provided several blankets. Take-off was scheduled for 9:00 o'clock that night. Bruce sent a coded message by telegraph to the Danville Army Station alerting them Doyle was coming.

The balloon cruised at 500 feet altitude, silent as death exposing no shadow under the overcast night sky. Down below Jason saw a bright flickering light looming in the distance—a campfire with six or seven Union soldiers warming their hands over the flames. Jason jerked on the tether tied to balloon pinnacle stem tilting its mass in the direction of his general flight path; crude, but effective at low altitudes. He checked his pocket watch and calculated his distance from the peaks up ahead.

Finally, Danville loomed just ahead in the distance as he guided the balloon through two mountain peaks. The air grew increasingly cold in the higher altitudes, and he pulled a blanket over his shoulders. He rotated the gate valve increasing coal-oil flow for more lift.

The gas lights of Danville appeared across the slope of a valley. Doyle rotated the valve counterclockwise, decreasing the flame feed. The balloon slowly lost it buoyancy and drifted downward into the valley.

The day was dawning when the wicker basket touched earth. Two soldiers were waiting for touchdown and grabbed the two tethers laced on the basket. They tied the tethers to a covered wagon laden with cast-iron cannon. Doyle douched the flame, leaped out of the basket as he checked his watch; he'd made good time, but needed to re-supply the coal oil. Doyle instructed the two Southern soldiers to replenish the coal oil. As he turned, a lieutenant stepped out of a door in a distant building and waved Doyle over.

The room was smoke-ridden with tobacco smell. Three soldiers were resting on cots as they cleaned their rifles. Doyle presented his credentials as being attached to Maj. Gen. Lee in Richmond and the lieutenant knew about Lt. Gen. Forrest's order that released Arabella Rhett. He provided a guide and a covered wagon for the trip to the hospital tent.

Doyle looked into the mesmerizing blue eyes of Arabella, and immediately felt her charismatic warmth. One arm was bandaged from the wrist to the elbow, a few scars on her face and the exposed arm.

"You are taking me to Richmond I understand," she smiled, a dimple in her smudged cheeks.

Doyle smiled. "Yes ma'am, we'll leave tonight about 9 pm."

She inhaled to full lung capacity. "Never flown in one of those hot-air balloons before."

Doyle cocked his head. "Well, this is only my second flight—so, are you hungry?"

Arabella threw back her head and laughed. "This will be fun—let's eat."

Somewhere over the open stretches of the Shenandoah Valley, Doyle sighted a glowing light. He brought a telescope to his eye and determined it was a Union campfire with several soldiers seated around the flames warming their hands. He necessarily released several ballast for fast ascension; how he wished he had used benzene, even if it were explosive.

He rotated the cold-oil valve full open the balloon slowly climbed as ballasts plunged into a stream near the campfire.

A lieutenant arose to his knees, focused his eyes toward the stream, and then he saw the moon's shadow of the balloon on the stream surface. He looked up, and pointed his Springfield toward the balloon, tapping the shoulder of his partner. Several shots from the other soldiers hit the balloon fabric, piercing several punctures. The holes began tearing, and finally the balloon lost buoyancy and plummeted to the ground several 100 yards from the campsite.

Doyle had made a fatal mistake.

When Union soldiers finally reached the crash site, they discovered one male body charred beyond recognition when the gas exploded on crash. They found no identification, no clue of any military importance. One soldier removed his cap and wiped his brow on his sleeve.

"This guy was stupid to take a joy ride over a battle zone."

Chapter 38

The Union cavalry under Maj. Gen. George Stoneman crossed the Rappahannock River on the morning of April 27, 1863. He began a long distance raid against Gen. Lee's supply lines, but the operation was completely ineffectual. The Federal infantry passed through Germanna and Ely's Fords, and crossed the Rapidan River. Stoneman concentrated his cavalry with Maj. Gen. Hooker near Chancellorsville in the late afternoon on the third day. Joseph Hooker's Army of the Potomac swelled to 133,868, and he faced Fredericksburg. He planned a double envelopment by attacking Lee from the front and rear.

To escape from Hooker's trap, and still guard the road to Richmond, Lee chose to send troops under Stonewall Jackson toward the advancing Federals and left only about 10,000 men to hold Fredericksburg. Jackson moved swiftly and entrenched along a cleared ridge facing an edge of the Wilderness.

On the next dawn Hooker advanced from Chancellorsville toward Lee's Army of Northern Virginia of just 60,892 troops. Greatly outnumbered, Lee's reduced force faced Hooker's charge in three columns.

Jackson rode from the rear against the Union headquarters stationed in the large house of Melzi Chancellor, once a tavern, now rumored a house of repute. Jackson's cavalry surprised Maj. Gen. O. O. Howard. There at the Chancellor family cemetery called Fairview Heights, Union artillery had waged a duel with Rebels on the grassy plateau called Hazel Grove. Hooker had made a fatal mistake when he yielded this plateau to Jeb Stuart, who brought up Confederate artillery.

Under protest by Stoneman, Hooker suddenly withdrew his defensive lines around Chancellorsville, which in effect gave the initiative to Lee. Stoneman rationalized that Hooker had enough troops to overwhelm Lee without exposing them to Gen. Jackson's onslaught. But Hooker probably damaged his competence in Stoneman's eyes, because the second bloodiest day of the war was about to explode upon his cavalry.

That night Jeb Stuart brought news from a scouting mission to the west of Chancellorsville: Hooker's right flank was wide open. Lee and Jackson planned the next move sitting on cracker boxes. Jackson's gloved finger traced a route to the west on a map where he'd strike Hooker's army from the rear.

Lee surveyed the route thinking of his thin number of soldiers. "What do purpose to make this movement with," he asked.

Jackson rubbed his finger under his nose. "With my whole corps," he replied. That meant taking 30,000 men away from Lee, leaving him with 14,000 troops against Hooker's main force of 73,000, he calculated.

Lee recited the manuals of war. "Never divide your forces in the presence of a superior enemy."

Jackson agreed with a disarming smile. "But Hooker doesn't know this."

Lee smiled. He had confidence in Jackson's judgment, loyalty, and bravery.

Jackson moved off the next morning, putting his men, wagons, and artillery onto a narrow road through the forest for a 12-mile march around Hooker's right flank. His column stretched 10 miles behind him as they quietly slipped past the Federal column. When he reached the point of attack, it would take about five hours for the rest of his corps to arrive.

Hooker, while standing at the front of his tent in the rear of his Army, saw the enemy column passing by. "Retreating without a fight," he whispered under his breath." He sent a warning to one-armed Maj. Gen. O. O. Howard, the corps commander on the right flank. The runner took the message, and gave it personally to Howard, who unfolded he paper. "Expect a flank attack."

The warning had no effect. Huddled in the thick woods, Jackson stood ready to attack. They moved quietly up behind Howard's position. The rustle of branches startled rabbits and deer stampeding before the column. Federal soldiers eating supper saw the animals and had a moment of curiosity before they heard the bugles and the heart-stopping Rebel yell, and saw the bayonets sparkling in the waning sunlight rushing toward them.

Howard saw an entire division vanish in minutes.

The fading sun eclipsed into a rising moon, full and eerie like a ghostly avenging demon ready to strike. "Push ahead," Jackson commanded. With his staff preparing for another attack, he went scouting beyond his pickets, close to the Federal position. Jackson kicked the flanks of Little Sorrel in a slow gate along the ridge between the battle lines. He looked down a slope into an open space of perhaps

200 yards, and his mind saw a bloody mass of soldiers, if they tried negotiating this killing field. Napoleon cannon were rolled to the ridge, its barrel plungers raised like a sea of chimney sweeps.

And then he heard the crack of a shot, then two. His left arm jerked, blood spouted from his upper arm and his right hand. He slumped forward, grabbed the reins and his horse, and galloped toward the Confederate lines. His own men of the 18th North Carolina brigade had opened fire. There was never a halt warning, just a nervous group of young troopers staring into the darkness among the biting mosquitoes.

"Cease Fire! Cease Fire!" screamed an officer in rapid cadence. "You're firing on your own men!"

Two bullets had smashed into Stonewall Jackson's left arm, and a third ball pierced the palm of his right hand. Sobbing aides lowered him from the saddle of *Little Sorrel*, and lay him under a tree. He was awake, spoke calmly of being wounded by his own men. Volunteer stretcher bearers carried Jackson under Federal artillery fire to a field hospital.

Lee received the news. He was greatly disturbed. He'd lost his "right arm." He placed Maj. Gen. Jeb Stuart as corps commander. It was a dark day, but a chance for Stuart's distinction as a cavalry genius with his patented saber hook which improved its attachment to the belt. Lee had lost his best general by a freak accident, yet Jackson still fought for his life, and stayed alive—how long, no one knew— he was in the hands of Providence.

The fiercest fighting of the battle occurred the next day. Lee launched multiple attacks against the Union position at Chancellorsville, resulting in heavy losses on both sides. That same day, Sedgwick advanced across the Rappahannock River and defeated the small Confederate force at Marye's

Heights, but Sedgwick had missed the major battle erupting in Chancellorsville: a decisive Union defeat.

A second battle of Fredericksburg erupted. Union Gen. Burnside had wintered his army in Fredericksburg, a key city on the shortest land route from Washington to Richmond. Only about 500 Confederates defended the town when Lee had started his campaign in mid-November, 1862.

Without rest, and on the same day, Lee fought a successful delaying action at the Battle of Salem Church. The next day they drove Sedgwick's men to Banks' Ford. During the delaying action, Lee had placed his men under Stuart's command in a position that surrounded Sedgwick's army on three sides.

Sedgwick withdrew his men across the ford in the dawning hours of the next morning. Hooker withdrew the remainder of his army over the next two nights. The campaign ended on May 7, 1863 when Stoneman's cavalry reached Union lines east of Richmond.

The blood-soaked earth revealed carnage of immense propositions. Lee lost 13,000 good men; Hooker lost 17,000 brave souls trained to follow orders, however misguided. The astounding numbers of casualties shocked both the Union and Confederacy. But no one was more shocked that Gen. Lee. He'd lost Jackson, a bitter moment of his military career.

Gen. Lee called a meeting in his Richmond office. Maj. Gen. Jeb Stuart, the last member of the old faithful guard sat in a rustic chair made of Virginia pine. Capt. Bruce Taylor, head of his intelligence group entered the office behind his friend, Captain Adrian Austin. No word was spoken, only somber faces staring into empty space. They sat solemnly around Lee's desk, a mask of somber resolve on each face.

Finally Bruce broke the silence. "Sir, Gen. Jackson is convalescing in a house at Guinea Station."

Lee raised his heavy head. "Can he be visited?" he whispered.

Bruce nodded. "He's suffering from pneumonia and is sleeping, sir." His head lowered. "I was there, sir when they amputated his left arm near the shoulder," he grimaced.

Heads turn, the same expressions exploding on each face. Gen. Stuart gripped the arms of his chair. "Well I say we ride over to Guinea right now."

Lee bobbed his magnificent head. "Agreed, but Jeb, I'd like you to stay and take command of the army," he spoke in a reverent whisper.

Stuart stood and saluted. "Your right, sir, I've seen enough death," he said and strutted out of the room, his perfume repugnant as he left.

Three men mounted their horses and rode over to Guinea. As they rode, Austin spotted the glitter of something in the trees. He immediately raised his hand, and they pull up on the reins. A buck with slick antlers bounced across the road into the lush wheat field. Austin wiped his forehead.

"Thought there was a sniper over there."

Lee smiled. "Sharp eye Captain, keep your eyes peeled."

Suddenly, two Union soldiers stepped from the brush behind the threesome with their rifles raised. Bruce heard the noise of squeaking saddles, gripped his Colt revolver and fired two shots. One soldier fell dead, the other ran. Austin galloped after the running soldier, plunging into the bush. Bruce stayed with Lee, his eyes examining every tree, every shrub. Then he dismounted and examined the dead soldier. He raised his head.

"Just one of Sedgwick's stranglers, Sir," he said as two sudden rapid shots rang out in the forest.

Austin appeared from the bush, his mount scratched below the neck by tangled briers, gripping his left shoulder. Lee's piercing eyes focused on his bleeding shoulder, as Austin dismounted.

"A rifle ball nicked my shoulder, Sir. It's nothing serious, but that bloat won't be hunting anymore."

The event pushed Lee's mind to the decisive moments of the Battle of Chancellorsville, the noise of the battle muted, and the action in slow-motion. In his mind's eye he saw Stonewall Jackson sitting on his favorite horse, *Little Sorrel*. It was a bitter moment, too bitter to contemplate.

Finally they rode up to the house and tied their reins to a hitching post. The two friends followed Gen. Lee to the porch. They stood behind their commander as Lee knocked on the door. A women with her sleeves rolled above her elbows opened the door, her face suddenly aglow.

"Why, General Lee, Jackson has been calling your name. Her hands suddenly covered her mouth. "It's so eerie that you are standing there as if angels had answered Jackson's call—oh excuse me, please come in."

Immediate glances exchanged between each of the three men as they followed the woman into the foyer. Mary Anna, Jackson's wife met them and stretched out her hand to Lee. He put his arm around her, but there were no tears, she knew her husband was on his last mission. The surgeon opened the door to Jackson's room, lit dimly by a kerosene lamp.

"Welcome, General Lee. Your presence is the best medicine I can offer," he whispered as he wiped his hands in a towel. Mary Anna moved to the back of the room. Little Julia was taken out earlier after talking with her father for the last time.

Lee knelt by the bedside of Jackson and tried not to look at his amputated left arm. His right hand was bandaged. Lee gently stretched his hand and touched Jackson's right wrist.

"Thomas, its Lee, I'm here," he whispered.

Jackson's eyes fluttered open as if he'd waited for this moment. "Sorry I let you down, General," he weakly replied.

A wrinkle creased Lee's forehead. "You have never let me down, Thomas, never."

Jackson's bearded face had the hint of a smile, an eyebrow arched. "Jeb is your man now, General—he's a good man."

A tear formed at the corners of Lee's eyes. "Oh my dear, dear friend—you both are the best men that a general could ever hope to command."

A slight smile blossomed on Jackson's tired face, he swallowed, his lips parched by the wind.

"Would you grant me one last request, sir?"

Lee gripped Jackson's hand with a squeeze. "It's my honor—anything."

Jackson sucked air into his gurgling lungs. "My little Julia, the only child I have who survived infancy, she was only four months old when I baptized her . . . would you see that she and Mary Anna are taken care of . . . and would you give Little Sorrel to Jeb—he's always admired that mare."

Lee closed his eyes blurred with tears as a breath of sorry gripped his heart. "It's done, my friend," he assured, as he gently patted his bandaged hand.

Lee lifted his head and glanced up at Mary Anna with a handkerchief pressed to her mouth.

Jackson's body relaxed. He'd given his last command. His head turn aside, his lungs clogged. The surgeon rushed to his side as Jackson stopped coughing. The surgeon placed his hand on his chest, leaned his ear to Jackson's nose. A moment of despair crossed his mind as he straightened his torso.

"Gentlemen: History has lost a brave warrior at mid-afternoon on this day of May 10, 1863."

Chapter 39

After Gen. Lee's success at Chancellorsville in Virginia the previous month at the high price of Gen. Jackson's death, Lee decided on a second invasion of the North, and led his army through the Shenandoah Valley preparing for what became known as the Gettysburg Campaign. He keenly remembered the Maryland Campaign, which had ended in the bloody battle of Antietam. Although unsuccessful because he left the field until the odds were more even, Lee's intention was to upset Federal plans for the summer campaigning season.

Lee bargained that the invasion would allow his army a life of sponging off the bounty of the rich Northern farms, while it gave his war-ravaged Virginia a much-needed rest. At the top of his plans, he thought his 72,000-man army could threaten Philadelphia, Baltimore, and Washington, and strengthen the growing peace movement in the North. Lee truly wanted peace, and he firmly believed Gen. Grant did also.

Lee had much thinking ahead of him. He'd lost Gen. Jackson to a battle with pneumonia, and he vowed that Gen. Stuart would take care of himself, although it was only a hope; yet he'd promised Jackson he'd protect the last of the twosome. He had a runner sent out on a call for Captain Bruce Taylor to come to his office in Richmond.

Bruce had received the call from Lee and dismounted his horse outside the Richmond office. As he entered the office door he saw Captain Adrian Austin standing in the foyer.

"Well, hello Austin, what brings you to Richmond?"

"I hear we'll be working together with General Lee."

"It's news to me, but I wouldn't be surprised. Grant is moving his men toward Richmond, and the general needs all the intelligence he can get."

"What's this I hear about some actor you've had under surveillance?"

"It's an incomplete story, I'm afraid; maybe you and I can look into it again."

The secretary stepped from the door to Lee's office. "The General's waiting gentlemen."

Lee stood when Bruce and Austin walked in his office. "Come in boys, I have a project where your expertise is greatly needed."

The secretary brought in cups of coffee for the two men; she knew the project was dangerous from them both.

"Thank you Janelle, your coffee is the best in Richmond," Bruce said, and was rewarded with her smile.

Lee rocked back in his chair, placed his hands in his lap. What he had to tell these two boys was necessary but extremely dangerous. Bruce was like a son and Austin now his best friend after the tragic loss of Doyle. He hated to offer them the task but he was short of good men.

"Gentlemen, you know we have lost General Jackson, and now Jeb Stuart needs your help."

Bruce sipped the coffee. Jackson had a fine cavalry. Jeb was a cavalier type, but not as trustworthy as Jackson.

"What's the mission, General Lee?" Austin queried.

Lee drew a long breath. "Grant and Sherman are bringing in troops spread around in the area for an overland campaign."

Bruce slumped in his chair. "And you want numbers and armament placements," he said lowering his cup.

"That's right, Bruce, especially the numbers and placements of those Napoléon cannon."

Bruce stirred in his chair, his coffee cup suspended in his hand, a finger tapping on its edge. "I suspect Grant has every soldier available ready to take Richmond, according to those plans we smuggled from the capitol."

"Those plans are what worry me."

"How is that, sir?"

"Grant is now the commander of the Union Army. He's no fool. He would never follow Halleck's plan if he sees another way."

"And you want our eyes to see that other way," Austin guessed.

"Exactly," he exclaimed! "Jackson was my right arm and you boys will be my eyes and feet," he said, slumping in his chair fondly recalling the bravery of his lost friend.

Austin cleared his throat. "Suppose Grant's generals do follow the plan," he suggested, measuring his words; he understood the general's loss.

Lee cleared his thoughts and forced a smile. "He'll replace them—he has before on a number of occasions."

Chapter 40

Bruce and Austin departed Lee's office with instructions to report to General Jeb Stuart. They task required as many troops as possible, and Jeb could muster up everything available in two days, according to Gen. Lee.

As the two friends mounted their horses, Austin spoke up. "The general seems a little cagey today."

"He's worried about protecting Richmond," Bruce replied staring forward with a frown on his face. "And so am I."

It was an important task and Bruce was glad Austin was with him, but they must find Gen. Stuart quickly. As they galloped toward a bridge across Bull Run River, the noise of cannon became louder. Suddenly Bruce spotted Gen. Stuart crossing the bridge about a hundred yards up ahead.

Jeb Stuart dismounted his horse with his light cavalry bivouacked in a set of trees about forty yards away. He noticed the dusk rising from two galloping horses approaching his camp. And then he saw the familiar smile of Captain Taylor. He removed his ostrich plume hat and leaned against a post, the yellow sash of his red-lined gray cape glistening in the afternoon sun.

"To what do I owe this visit, Bruce?" he exclaimed, expecting word from Lee.

"Just wanted to see your ugly faced again, General," he quipped. "You know Captain Austin."

"Yes, we met the day Andy was shot," he replied, soberly focusing his steely eyes on the Captains face, yet he saw the face of his lost friend Andrew Jackson.

A soldier took their horses and the threesome ventured to the edge of the bridge. Bruce tossed a stone into the water, tiny waves undulating from the impact, as he faced Stuart.

"General Lee wants you to gather every soldier possible up to an area near Gettysburg."

Jeb nodded. "I've seen Grant mustering an army over that way."

"Austin and I will try to get the numbers and placement of cannon back to Lee," Bruce said.

"Understand, we can meet back here early tomorrow morning; a brigade of North Carolina boys will be here by then."

Bruce rode to a covered wagon in the rear located near a telegraph pole. Two Confederate soldiers stood guard as he dismounted. A key operator wired the information to Lee's office, and then handed him a return message written on a piece of paper. Bruce took the paper and rode out to meet Austin. He and Austin rode off into the gathering twilight as Bruce disclosed that Lee expected them to continue to Manassas and report. The long hours without rest or food made the decision of taking an hour of relaxation before the trip out to Manassas. They pulled up under a tree and opened their knap sacks for a meal of hard tack and beans. As they leaned against their saddles, Austin glanced at Bruce with his finger pressed to his lips, his ears alert.

Over in the bushes two Yankee soldiers had noticed the Rebel horses tied to a tree. The leader, a second lieutenant gestured to the sergeant, and they separated while circling around the trees in a rather dense forest. As they approached the two Rebels, the private stepped in a rabbit hole, and his cocked Springfield fired!

Austin drew his colt, Bruce his Enfield, both staring into the forest. A second shot split the bark off the tree where they stood. They stooped and waddled behind a tree. Bruce saw the shadow of a man and drew down on it, firing. He heard a grunt, and the shadow slumped to the ground. A second shadow rose from behind a stump, and fired. Bruce grabbed his upper arm, blood oozing between his fingers. Suddenly Austin fired. The assailant fell dead. He rushed into the bush searching for other soldiers, but fortunately found none.

Austin immediately pulled Bruce's torso into his lap, tearing his sleeve away from the wound. It could have been worse; it wasn't a mini ball. He wiped the blood away with his sleeve, and wrapped his bandana around the arm over the wound.

"Better get back to Richmond, Bruce, if you can ride,—I'll stay and get the information for Lee."

Bruce placed his hand over the wound, nodding. "Thanks, Austin."

Austin helped Bruce mount his horse and gave him the reins. "Remember now; drink plenty of water from your canteen. Don't stop for anything. The night is starry enough to guide you."

He extended his good arm, and shook Austin's hand. "You are a good friend, Austin. Be careful."

There was no intention of fighting at Gettysburg. The first major action took place between cavalry forces at

Brandy Station, near Culpeper, Virginia. Jeb Stuart's cavalrymen were surprised by Maj. Gen. Alfred Pleasanton's two Union cavalry divisions. Stuart handily repulsed the Union attack, the largest cavalry engagement of the war. Although insignificant, it actually improved the moral of the Union cavalryman who greatly respected Jeb Stuart's flamboyant fighting style.

By mid-June Lee's army had marched to the shores of the Potomac River. He crossed over into Maryland, where he defeated the federal garrisons at Winchester and Martinsburg. Ewell's Second Corps crossed the river followed by Hill's and Longstreet's corps.

Although Lee's men took food, horses, and other supplies, the quartermaster reimbursed Northern farmers and merchants with Confederate money; though they were unhappy with the exchange, they had no choice. York and Pennsylvania townships paid indemnifies in lieu of supplies under threat of destruction. They also seized some 40 slaves, a few whom were escaped fugitives but most were freemen under Lincoln's proclamation. They were sent south under guard.

Major Adrian Austin had given Lee the numbers and artillery placement, and Jeb Stuart had alerted the forces. Although wounded, Captain Taylor had dispatched Lee that the Union Army had crossed the Potomac River. Hooker had pursued Longstreet and finally crossed on the 27th of June, and cautiously kept his army between the U.S. capital and Lee's army.

Lee sent Jeb Stuart with three brigades of cavalrymen riding around the east flank of the Union army for intelligence, since Captain Taylor was incapacitated; a decision that haunted him in days ahead, now left without adequate cavalry. And then he ordered forces around Cashtown, located at the eastern base of South Mountain about eight miles west of Gettysburg.

He never intended a battle in Gettysburg, nor had he heard that one of Hill's brigades under Brig. Gen. J. Johnston Pettigrew had ventured into Gettysburg in search of much needed shoes. While there, they noticed a Union cavalry arriving south of town, but didn't engage in accordance with Lee's orders. When Hill heard their report, he didn't believe there was a substantial force in Gettysburg, suspecting it was only the Pennsylvania militia. But it was accurately the Union cavalry under Gen. Buford. However, Hill mounted a significant reconnaissance on the following morning for determination of the size and strength of the enemy forces staged in front of them.

Captain Bruce Taylor, his arm still in a sling, caught up with Lee behind the lines and informed him that Hooker had been relieved from duty.

Lee's mind raced back raced back to West Point days. "Old Fighting Joe is gone, huh."

"Yes Sir, it seems a dispute developed over the use of the forces defending the Harpers Ferry garrison, Hooker became so enraged he offered his resignation. Lincoln accepted it," he chortled.

"I see—Lincoln was looking for an excuse to remove him," he predicted.

Bruce's head bobbed. "According to my northern contacts, Hooker has been replaced by Maj. Gen. Meade."

Lee massaged his gray beard. "George Meade. Well, Grant has chosen a good man, but this doesn't change our plans, but it will save lives."

He dropped his gaze and faced his intelligence officer. "Bruce, get back behind the lines, my boy. If that arm gets infected, you'll be no use to me."

Bruce nodded with a salute. "Yes Sir—I can use a telescope; I'll be at telegraph wagon."

Chapter 41

The new commanding general reviewed the layout of the Union forces as they were known when he took command by order of President Lincoln. He quickly recognized that Gen. Stuart was missing with two of the best brigades of Lee's cavalry, cognizant that Stonewall Jackson was deceased. At the time Gen. Meade wasn't aware of Stuart's mission, he only theorized he had a chance to flank Gen. Lee, if Union reinforcements arrived as expected. He bargained that his plan was sound.

The morning sun rose in the east and lit the Shenandoah Valley in green shadows, now brutally marred by marching feet, wagon wheel tracks, and hoof prints. Meade anticipated the Confederates would march on Gettysburg from the west, since Hill's army was stationed nearby, according to Gen. Buford. Meade laid out his defenses on three ridges west of the town. Although there was good terrain for a delaying action of a cavalry division against superior Confederate infantry, it was only meant to buy time for the arrival of Union infantry reinforcements. Meade planned for the these new troops to occupy the strong defensive positions south of the town on

Cemetery Hill, Cemetery Ridge, and Culp's Hill. Therefore, with Jeb Stuart missing, Meade reasoned that he'd wage his cavalry against the Confederate infantry until reinforcements arrived. He understood that if the Confederates gained control of these heights, the Army of the Potomac indeed had difficulty on its hands in digging them out.

The first shot of the battle was fired by Union Lt. Marcellus Ephraim Jones, Company E 8th Illinois Cavalry. Two brigades of Union infantry marched easterly in double-abreast columns along the Chambersburg Pike. In the dawning mist of that morning, three miles west of Gettysburg, they met light resistance. A dismounted group of Confederate cavalrymen were firing behind fence posts with breech-loading carbines. By midmorning the Confederates had surprisingly pushed the Union cavalrymen east to McPherson Ridge.

    North of the pike, federalists gained temporary success against Confederates but were repulsed with heavy losses in action around an unfinished railroad bed cut into the ridge. South of the pike, Gen. James Archer's Confederate lines met resistance from the Federal Iron Brigade assaulting through McPherson's Woods. Archer engaged for two hours resulting in the capture of several hundred of his men. His health deteriorating from long summer marches, he stood in dismay in a thicket. A Union private captured him, and marched him behind the Union lines. Archer became the first general captured from the Northern Virginia Army.

    Brig. Gen. James Johnston Pettigrew's brigade tangled with the Iron Brigade and all four of his regiments suffered devastating losses of over 40 percent, but he was successful in driving the Union forces off McPherson's Ridge. Pettigrew assumed command of the division after Gen. Heth was wounded. He reorganized the battered division for the next day's battle hidden behind Seminary Ridge.

The following day, Gen. Lee assigned Pettigrew's division on the left of Maj. Gen. George Pickett's infantry. The division charged forward under murderous fire. Pettigrew's horse was shot from under him, but he continued on foot reaching within 100 yards of the stone wall on Cemetery Ridge. Suddenly a canister exploded, and the shrapnel severely wounded Pettigrew in the left hand. Despite the great pain, he remained with his soldiers until it was obvious the attack had failed. Pettigrew walked toward the rear line on Seminary Ridge holding his bloody hand, when he saw Gen. Lee approaching.

Pettigrew attempted to salute but couldn't, nor could he speak. He stood facing Lee shaking his head.

"General, I am sorry to see you are wounded; go to the rear—but I commend your gallantry," Lee commanded.

Union Gen. Reynolds was shot and killed early in the fighting while directing troop and artillery placements east of the woods. Fighting in the Chambersburg Pike area lasted until high noon. It restarted after about two hours of peace in the stench of the dead and contorted casualties strewn over hills and ridges.

General Lee regrouped his divisions in a plan for defeatiing Meade's forces on this first day of battle against Virginia. He sent all of the armies converging into the center of the Union lines, with massive casualties; bloated horses, torn off arms, blood soaked earth. The Federal lines collapsed both north and west of town, and Meade ordered retreat to the high ground south of town at Cemetery Hill, straddling the Baltimore Pike. Fortunately for Meade the reinforcements he'd anticipated had finally arrived. Without these fresh troops, Meade surely would have lost the battle of Gettysburg.

Lee understood the defensive potential given to Meade if they held this high ground with the reinforcements. He sent orders to Gen. Ewell that Cemetery Hill must be taken "if practical." Ewell drew on his experience under Thomas "Stonewall" Jackson; "practical" meant a field decision. Therefore, he determined that such an assault was not practical.

However, Ewell's Second Corps marched west toward Cashtown in accordance with Lee's order, only intending to concentrate forces in that area. Ewell's troops turned south on the Carlisle and Harrisburg roads marching toward Gettysburg.

The Union XI Corp under Maj. Gen. Oliver O. Howard raced northward on the Baltimore Pike and Taneytown Road. By early afternoon the Union line ran in a haphazard semicircle northeast of Gettysburg, the men disorganized and battle worn.

Suddenly two large Confederate Corps assaulted Meade's army from the northwest, collapsing the hastily developed Union lines. Gen. O.O. Howard ordered a retreat to the high ground south of town at Cemetery Hill, sending the federalists retreating through the streets of Gettysburg into the hills just to the south. In the wake of the retreat, thousands of dead men and maimed bodies lay in the pong of death.

When Meade heard of Reynolds death, he sent Maj. Gen. Winfield Hancock, who took command of the battlefield. Meade instructed Hancock, his most trusted commander to determine whether Gettysburg was an appropriate place for a major battle. His eagerness to command this final blow on Maj. Gen. Lee prompted his answer: Yes.

The first day of the Gettysburg battle was more significant than simply a prelude to the bloody second and third days. Only about one quarter of

Meade's Army remained. And Lee had only had a few hundred more men engaged. The first day of the Gettysburg battle had been extremely bloody, seemingly victory snatched from jaws of defeat at each skirmish.

Throughout the remaining hours and into the next morning, most of the remaining infantry of both armies arrived on the field for the second day of battle. Longstreet's third division under Maj. Gen. George Pickett had marched from Chambersburg early in the morning, but didn't arrive until late on day of battle, the very day Lee had planned the assault.

Lee called for Longstreet's First Corps to position itself for a stealthily attack on the left flank straddling the Emmetsburg Road. In the interim he planned a diversionary action against Culp's and Cemetery Hills that would hopefully prevent the shifting of federal troops from the center to the left flank.

The battle sequence began with an attack on the left flank by the combination divisions of Maj. Gen. John Bell Hood with Lafayette McLaws corps, followed by Maj. Gen. Richard H. Anderson corps. Lee fully expected a full-scale attack when the favorable opportunity presented itself. The success of this complex plan was hampered by the absence of Jeb Stuart's full cavalry, and he had not returned.

Apparently no one told Maj. Gen. Daniel Sickles that Meade was buying time for reinforcements. He had been dissatisfied with his assigned position on the southern end of Cemetery Ridge. When he saw the higher ground just a half-mile away more favorable to his artillery, he advanced his corps, without higher command orders, to the superior ground along Emmetsburg Road.

In the absence of Stuart, Lee recalled his intelligent officer Captain Bruce Taylor to a slope on the side of Round Top overlooking Little Round Top. Taylor spotted troop movements of Gen. Sickles and Napoleon cannon arrayed on the Cemetery Ridge. Quickly he pulled the reins of his horse and rode down the slope, his stead squatting on all fours to prevent falling. When they reached the flat surface he galloped to Lee's position beyond Fairfield Road.

Lee was discussing a strategy with Longstreet, when Taylor dismounted. The gasping Captain stood at attention. Lee dropped his discussion and turned to Bruce.

"What is it, Captain?"

"Sir, Gen. Sickles has mounted twelve Napoleon cannon on the south end of Cemetery Ridge."

Longstreet's eyes bulged as he quickly turned to his aide. "Ride out now and tell Gen. Hood to expect a bombardment."

In the late afternoon Lee launched a heavy assault on the Union left flank. Fierce fighting raged. Unfortunately, the left flank remained intact, and the new battle line ran from Devil's Den, northwest to the Sherfy farm's Peach Orchard, into Emmetsburg Road, then south to Codori farm. The Confederate attack deviated from Lee's plan since Hood's division moved more easterly than intended, losing its alignment with the Emmetsburg Road, thereby assaulting Devil's Den and Little Round Top. Lee's positions were now untenable, subject to attacks from two sides, a longer battle line than his small corps could defend effectively. Stuart's absence surface in his mind again.

Captain Taylor was glad to get back into service and snatched the sling from his arm, tossed it on the ground. He galloped back with information that the Union's signal station on Little Round Top was not defended. Lee promptly stopped Longstreet's attack, and ordered him to wait for one of his brigades to investigate. Lee held back the second surge launching of Hood and McLaws attacks until about 4 p.m. and 5 p.m., respectively. This allowed the brigade's movement to within sight of the Round Tree facility. Longstreet advanced to his assigned position. Three Confederate corps slammed into the Union left flank. Fierce fighting broke out up and down the shaped line.

Meade's chief engineer realized the importance of the works facility and dispatched a brigade of infantry including an artillery battery to occupy Little Round Top, who arrived mere minutes before Hood's brigade reached the summit.

As fighting escalated in the Wheatfield and Devil's Den, the federalist infantry held a precarious hold on Little Round Top until inspired by the arrival of artillery just a few moments before the entry of Hood's troops. The defense of Little Round Top was a mighty artillery battle between bronze 12-pounder Napoleon cannon, standard issue of both sides. In the waning hours the fighting degraded to hand-to-hand bayonet fighting. It was one of the fabled episodes in the Civil War. Yet fables never really gave the gory details down on the fighting line, and over time then degraded into myths by repetition.

General Jeb Stuart and his three cavalry brigades finally arrived in Gettysburg around noon but had no role in the second day's battle because of his controversial absence.

However, under the cover of early evening darkness Pettigrew's division got off to a late start on the attack on Culp's Hill. Yet only one brigade of soldiers was left as defenders; most of the defenders were sent to reinforce the left flank against Longstreet's attack. Nonetheless the skimpy Union line held, although a portion of the abandoned Federal works on the lower part of Culp's Hill was captured by Pettigrew.

General Lee decided, against calculated odds to renew the attack on the next day using the same basic plan of the previous day. The orders were for Longstreet to attack the Federal left flank, while Ewell attacked Culp's Hill. The plans were laid, but Providence stabbed the launch in the back at the beginning third day of battle.

In the dawning hour, before Longstreet was ready, Union artillery bombarded the Confederates on Culp's Hill. The Confederates counterattacked, and the second fight for control of Culp's Hill ended just before high noon. Despite a bitter seven hour battle, the Union line was intact and held more strongly than anticipated.

Forced to change his plans, Lee placed Longstreet in command of Pickett's Virginia division of his first Corps, plus six brigades from Hill's Corps, with orders to attack the right center of the Union line on Cemetery Ridge. Before engagement, 150 to 170 Napoleon cannon had weakened the enemy's lines, probably the largest bombardment of the war.

To save ammunition for the infantry, the Army of the Potomac's artillery did not return fire under the order of Brig. Gen. Henry Hunt. After waiting 15 minutes, about 80 federal cannons added to the ruckus. Around mid-afternoon the cannon fire subsided, and 12,500 Confederates stepped from the ridge way and advanced three-quarters of a mile to Cemetery Ridge.

Waning darkness overshadowed two of Early's brigades as they attacked the enemy positions on East Cemetery Hill. As the Confederates approached, fierce flanking artillery fire exploded from Union position on Cemetery Hill and north of Little Round Top, including musket and canister fire from

Hancock's Corps. The barrage was a complete surprise, since Hill suspected the artillery had been knocked out. Union artillery opened fire on the Confederate infantry with devastating result; nearly half of attackers never returned to the line.

The Union line broke for a temporary moment; reinforcements rushed into the breach, and repelled the Confederate attack. Lee's Northern Virginian Army had reached the high-water mark, the closest the South ever came to achieving independence from the Union by military victory.

But Providence took the initiative; the CSA was destined to fail. In reality victory was outside the grasp of either battered army. History would remember this war as blight on the progress of America. But the South had lost its sovereignty, and so did America, which set the economic and political stage for its future failure, as the Federal government began its futile march to bureaucracy.

Chapter 42

The war lingered ominously like the angel of death, soldiers dying at every battle theater. Union forces under Maj. Gen. Quincy Gillmore moved a fleet off the shores of Charleston harbor with orders to retake Fort Sumter because of the military importance of the harbor. Meanwhile, General Lee sent word that Captain Austin must turn over his troops to Gen. P. G. T. Beauregard who had successfully captured Fort Sumter in the first battle, and would command the troops in the second battle of Fort Sumter.

Gillmore positioned his Union batteries on Morris Island out from the harbor. Gunners pounded the fort for agonizing hours. The fort was reduced to rubble, compromising the breech at the wall facing the island.

Confederates rushed to protect the wall. During the severe bombing, Beauregard replaced his battered artillerymen anticipating an attack at the breech. He sent Captain Adrian Austin to man the fort guns, all but one was still functioning, but he'd lost his artillery lieutenant. Austin took Captain Bruce Taylor with him and about 300 infantrymen. By the time the men were in place, the Union naval party had reached the breech. All the guns facing the breech fired at will, billows of gunpowder smoke curled into the southern sky, shrapnel filled the air ominously. A dozen naval soldiers fell like dominoes, but the blast had enlarged the breech opening, increasing the next wave of naval troops.

Rapid rifle fire from the breech zinged in the smoky air like missiles of jagged death. A lead bullet suddenly pierced the right arm of Major Austin as he gripped the bloody wound, his face gnarled with pain. Still he stood wobbly encouraging his soldiers with his sword drawn, slashing with his good hand. He staggered; his sword still waving his soldiers to the wall.

Bruce Taylor clumsily dropped his rifle and removed the sling on his arm. He grabbed Austin around the waist, and pulled him to safety. Quickly he wrapped the sling around the enormous wound from a dreadful mini ball that had even ripped open his sleeve upon entry. The bone was not shattered because the ball had fortunately exited with an enormous exit wound of muscle flesh.

It was fortunate that he would not face the cruel methods of current medical treatment; blood-letting, metal saws, and butcher knives. At the start of the war, the south had only two dozen medical men; the north perhaps a hundred medical officers, yet they were no better trained than the southern equivalents. Medicine was in the middle Ages.

Countless naval soldiers of the landing party rushed inside the breech. The artillerymen bravely defended their positions and finally repulsed the attack. Taylor wrestled Austin from the wall and haphazardly directed his staggering steps to the ground level. He removed his pocket knife, whispering, "This is going to hurt—here, bite down on this stick."

Austin grunted the stick clinched in his teeth. "Do it Bruce—do it," he gasped.

Bruce grimaced at his remark; he was a CSA officer who had relinquished his authority into his shaky hands. He dropped his gaze and ripped open the bloody shirt sleeve. He'd seen wounds like this while hunting with his cousins back in Fredericksburg. Then by chance he glimpsed a broken bottle of whiskey on the ground next to a crushed wooden case; part of the general's personal supply, he thought. Quickly he dipped the corner of the bandanna in the whisky and wiped the bloody area carefully, and then flooded the wound with the antiseptic. Bruce took Austin's clean bandanna from around his neck and gently wrapped the wound, securing it with a gingerly tied knot. He gripped the Captain by the waist and leaned him against a slanted post. The Major deeply signed.

"Thanks, Bruce—thanks a million," he said with a thin smile.

As Bruce looked for a less jagged base of the broken whiskey bottles, he finally selected one, and handed it to Austin. "Here, take a swig of this, it will ease the pain."

Austin supported Bruce's hand as he raised the broken base to his cracked lips, and took a guarded sip noticing the glass shivers floating on the bottom. He groaned at the pain and filled his lungs slowly. Then he looked into the muddy smudged face of his "surgeon" and cracked a weak smile.

"We must have a talk when this is over, Bruce."

A covered wagon was the regiment's surgeons' operating "room." Austin waited outside for the doctor's report after his operation. The physician washed his hands in a bloody basin of water and dried them with an equally bloody towel. "Well, Major. You owe your life to this young Captain. I'm losing every forth amputee that comes in—besides I have no more quinine but you did have whisky," he chuckled as he removed his cigar from his mouth and massaged his unshaven chin.

Austin gasped as he thought of losing an arm from a simple wound. But nothing was simple about the medical conditions existing in the Civil War. Quinine was overused; morphine was scarce, an ugly saw the most used instrument of certain infection. Yes, he owed Captain Bruce Taylor his life, he was a damn good soldier, and he was proud to serve with him.

Austin regained his confidence as he saw the Confederate flag still waving over the ruins of Fort Sumter. An important harbor would have peace for an uncertain time.

Charleston, South Carolina, was a hotbed of secession at the start of the war, and an important Atlantic Ocean port city for the fledgling Confederate States of America. The first shots of the war were fired at a Federal ship entering Charleston Harbor. Later, the bombardment of Fort Sumter on two occasions failed to yield a military takeover; however, it triggered a massive call for Federal troops to put down the rebellion. Although the city and its surrounding fortifications were repeatedly targeted by the Union Army and Navy, Charleston did not fall to Federal forces until the last months of the war—an unending assault from April 1863 until February 1865.

Still this southern port city was a thorn in the flesh of President Lincoln. He watched the overland battles closely, each day another General failed. When one particular general kept winning territory, he gained the President's attention. That man was Gen. Ulysses S. Grant. Lincoln promoted him to brigadier, then full general, and finally as commander of the Union Army. He was the man chosen for leadership of the Western Theater, but Charleston withstood every attempt as Grant ordered assault after assault; even blockades had failed.

Chapter 43

In the early spring of 1863, the Union began a two year offensive campaign against the defenses of Charleston Harbor, beginning with a combined sea-land engagement. The striking force, a fleet of nine ironclad warships of the Union Navy, including seven *monitors* that were improved versions of the original USS *Monitor*. However, a union Army contingent associated with the attack took no active part in the battle as ordered. The ships under command of Rear Admiral Samuel Francis Du Pont attacked the Confederate defenses near the entrance to Charleston Harbor.

Navy Department officials in Washington, including Lincoln, hoped for a stunning success that validated a new form of warfare, with armored warships mounting heavy guns reducing the effectiveness of traditional forts.

Lincoln placed great confidence in the ironclad concept. In fact, he diverted the resources from other naval projects for this attack on Charleston, and gave Du Pont the powerful *New Ironsides*, and the experimental ironclad *Keokuk*. After a long period of preparation, conditions of tide, and visibility made a naval attack possible. The slow moving ironclads got into position late in the afternoon, and when the tide turned, Du Pont suspended the operation because of shallow water.

After the ironclads finally got into position, lashing out with their powerful guns that lasted less than two hours; but the ships were unable to penetrate even the first line of harbor defense. The fleet retired with one ironclad in a sinking condition and several ships were damaged. In the aftermath, the ironclads sailed unceremoniously back to its Union harbor. Du Pont concluded that his fleet had little chance of success, and declined renewal of the battle the next morning.

After being repulsed twice using "ironclad" bombardments, which accomplished little, Maj. Gen. Quincy Adams Gillmore turned his attention to Fort Wagner on Morris Island. Two battles suffered heavy losses in a failed attempt upon the fort. The Union Army/Navy mounted a siege of Fort Wagner, and finally captured Morris Island. Union gunners used a new piece of artillery known as the Requa gun. It featured 25 rifle barrels mounted on a field carriage, the first Gatlin gun. They dug zigzag trenches and set up high-powered calcium floodlights that flashed bright light on the defenders. The light blinded them so badly they couldn't return accurate fire. Unnervingly during the digging of the trenches, they uncovered ghastly bodies left during previous battles.

With the development of newer, longer range artillery, and as Union forces were able to target batteries ever closer to the city, a bombardment began in late 1863 that continued off-and-on for more than a year. The accumulated effects of this never-ending cat-and-mouse bombardment finally humbled the devastated city of Charleston.

The grand ole southern city sat wide open.

As Sherman marched into the hopeless condition of the bewildered city, the situation for Charleston became ever more precarious. Gen.

Beauregard ordered the evacuation of the remaining Confederates. The mayor surrendered the city.

Lincoln gave Grant the mission to destroy the city, and Grant gave that task to Sherman. After all, Sherman had learned a valuable lesson as brigadier, and Grant admired the guy's guts. Like Grant, Sherman was convinced that the Confederacy's ability to wage further war, economy and psychological, must be definitively crushed, if the fighting were to end. Therefore, he believed that the Union had to conduct its campaign as a war of conquest and employ scorched-earth tactics to break the backbone of the rebellion. He called this strategy "hard war," historians called it the "scorched earth policy."

ARABELLA

ARABELLA

1864

Chapter 44

Bruce received a summons from Maj. Gen. Lee's office, left Julie's house, and rode his horse to the Richmond office. Janelle, the secretary told Bruce that Lee was out, but he'd left a telegraph message for him. She handed him the telegram. Bruce read the message; his mind seized by disbelief, and he suddenly slumped in the chair beside the desk. The hot-air balloon had crashed; only the charred male body of someone. No word of Arabella.

Bruce sat stunned, his mind dazedly computing nothing but mental static. He'd sent his best friend to his death, the reality crushed his spirit. Doyle told him how risky the trip was, but Bruce had not listened. He only wanted to be with Arabella again. His mind raced with incriminating thoughts, where was Arabella, was she even alive. His hands coursed through his hair, and then rubbed his unshaven face. Janelle suggested that he rest. But he just couldn't. He told her to inform General Lee that he was not available for a while, just how long he wasn't certain.

He walked aimlessly out of the room with the message crushed in his hand. Bruce ambled down the wooden sidewalk, not cognizant of where he was or where he was going. Somehow he found himself seated in a chair in the tavern across the street from the office.

Apparently he'd even ordered rum without his knowledge. After he'd consumed several mugs of rum, he felt dizzy and his mind was a whiling maze of indecision. Doyle was dead, and he couldn't stop thinking of the image of his suffering death. He downed another mug of rum. It was tasteless, ineffective. Sleep was the only anecdote, closing his mind from the world—an unrealistic world that had killed his best friend, and carried away the love of his life.

His mind snapped.

The proprietor came over to his stool. "Look buddy, you've had enough—could I call someone for you?"

Bruce thought he felt the eyes of the proprietor surveying his clammy face, but nothing else, only the agony in his mind. He looked speechless into the proprietor's blurry face, and dropped his head on the table, surrounded his arms around it, closing out the world. The images in his mind were the dead body of Doyle and a fuzzy picture of Arabella. "Oh where are you Arabella?" his mind screamed.

A troop train pulled into the railroad station in Washington. A woman in her late-twenties stepped to the exit door, the steam from the engine's boilers floating in her tired face, as she weakly surveyed the crowds at the station. She was dressed in plain clothes torn at the collar, her hair unkempt and no rouge to cover her scarred skin.

A young Union officer was careful not to disturb her wounded arm set in a sling as he escorted her to a covered wagon, and sat her by the driver. He didn't have the heart to put her with the other prisoners. She was a prisoner of war destined for the gallows. He patted her hand compassionately as he stepped down from the driver's seat.

He took the woman to the prison in Washington and placed her in a waiting area for assignment to sleeping quarters; whether with other woman, or with wounded prisoners of all gender, was not her concern. Her tormented thoughts reprimanded her for being caught.

Finally a soldier at his desk opened a file with the names of prisoners suspected of being spies. The number sewn on her collar matched a number in his book. She was found wandering in a daze on the outskirts of northern North Carolina. The sergeant stamped her file for execution by hanging, and sent for a runner.

Arabella sat stoic.

The total absence of light through her pale blue eyes took only a moment to shift the human mind into a state of confused disorder. She had the impression of falling from a vast height with her eyes closed on a moonless night; falling through an immense black void without the tinniest fragment of sensation.

An 18-year old first Lieutenant took the file and went to the holding area. He stopped at the post and handed over the file. The officer looked at the number and pointed to the woman on a bench at the rear. Finally, he was told the hangers were ready at the scaffolds. The Lieutenant sighed as he retrieved the file and marched toward the young woman sitting dazedly staring into space. He took her uninjured arm, and she stood as if he wasn't there. She walked mechanically beside him like a zombie.

When they exited the post, the sunlight lit the woman's smudged face. She was the spitting image of the Lieutenant's momma back in Maryland. Was it a coincidence, or was it a nightmare. He looked at her file—no, she hailed from Charleston, had fought with

Gen. Nathan Forrest, and was reassigned to Captain Bruce Taylor of the CSA—that name, Taylor; he'd met this man.

He stood in sudden silence, his mind whirring with indecision. Everything he'd heard was that war was winding down at Gettysburg. Grant's army outnumbered the Lee's defenses two to one. There was enough pain in this war to last a lifetime, he thought. A decision seized he mind. He would not sanction the death of a young woman who still had life to give to a wounded nation.

Instead, he placed her in a covered wagon and drove down the street to a telegraph office. He stepped out of the wagon, carefully assisted the woman out to the ground, and went into the office.

The telegraph operator read the message and saw the note pinned to her collar. He looked up at the Lieutenant with a quizzical gaze.

"What are you doing Lieutenant?"

The young soldier stared into his eyes. "Well, what would you do if they were hanging *your* momma," he barked.

The telegraph operator ran his fingers through his balding hair. "I see nothing—I hear nothing," he whispered, gazing into the young officer's eyes.

The soldier threw a silver dollar on the desk. "Will this pay for it?"

The operator looked into the woman's spacey eyes, dropped his gaze. "Keep your money, son. We ain't all barbarians."

The officer nodded his head. "Thank God somebody has some sense."

The telegraph operator pushed up his sleeves, rubbed the tips of his fingers as if he were opening a safe, and gripped the key. He read the note and tapped out Morse code signals that were received in the Confederate headquarters in Richmond. Finally he closed the key. "It's done, soldier—you get that woman somewhere to stay the night."

He winked at the sergeant. "Thank you—this woman has said not a word, but I believe she thanks you, too."

He took the woman's arm and led her to the wagon. As they rode away, he touched her hand and she moved for the first time.

"Ma'am, my name is Jeremy Hostetler from Philadelphia. I'm repaying a debt I owe to a nice southern man who saved my life when I was seriously wounded at Fort Sumter."

She vaguely smiled; the mention of Fort Sumter awakened her mind.

"Did you say Fort Sumter?" whispered weakly.

"Yes ma'am. A man by the name Bruce Taylor—I'll never forget that name."

Arabella swallowed, it was the news that lifted her out of a deep dark hole of guilt for being caught. She now had a reason to live.

"Young man," she paused for breath, "I think I know this Bruce Taylor, and I'll never forget him either," she feebly whispered.

Finally they stopped in front of a tavern, and hitched the horse to a rail. Again, he helped the woman from the wagon. As she stepped down, he knew he'd never see the lady again, and he snatched the sign off her collar, wadded it tightly, threw it on the ground, and twisted his booted foot on it until torn into ragged pieces—the boot of justice, he thought.

She deeply sighed and slowly laid her hand against his face. He understood and was glad he'd kept her from a hanging. They walked into the tavern and he sat her at a table. He gave the proprietor two silver dollars.

"Someone would call for her, ma'am."

Arabella gently took his hand, all the strength she could muster. "Jeremy, when this war is over, America will need young men like you. Don't harbor guilt or hate. This land belongs to everyone. Freedom has been bought at a great cost. Thank you for your kindness and compassion," she said almost out of breath, and kissed him on his cheek.

A tear gathered in the corner of Jeremy's eye. "Yes ma'am. I won't forgit America, and surely I won't forgit you."

As he looked into the woman's eyes, the ageing proprietor grinned, and brought the woman a sandwich and a mug of rum.

Chapter 45

Suddenly, the door to the tavern across the street from the Confederate headquarters in Richmond burst open, and Janelle, rushed in waving a telegram. She spotted Bruce seated with his head collapsed on a table against the wall, and ran over with a telegraph messages squeezed in her fingers.

"Wake up, Bruce, wake up," she screamed as she jerked his shoulder.

His arms dropped by his side, and a hand rubbed his darkly shadowed eyes. Finally he was cognizant of his circumstances.

"Yes . . . wha . . . what is it?" he stuttered.

She shoved a telegraph message in his face. "This—Arabella is alive! Two soldiers are taking her to hospital in Richmond!"

Bruce shook his head, desperately attempting to clear the cobwebs as his hazy eyes squinted dimly at the message. When his eyes finally focused, he read an unbelievable message from a Union Lieutenant. "You will find a woman named Arabella Rhett in a tavern on Franklin Street in Washington. Come quickly."

Bruce looked up into Janelle's frantic face; tear's welling in his eyes. "Maybe you could get me some black coffee, please."

The proprietary stood wringing his hands in his apron, and smiled, a pendant tear in his left eye. "Yes sir, right away."

The hospital bed in Richmond had been adjusted so that Arabella sat nearly upright. Her color had returned and her eyes seemed brighter. Only the bandage on her arm showed any sign of injury except the right hand was wrapped in gauze. Some thoughtful nurse had primped her face with rouge, and combed her hair. Although she felt alive emotionally, her body ached from head to foot. Her frazzled mind could still remember that Bruce and Austin had taken her from the tavern in Washington.

"I'm sorry, but she is under sedation—the last morphine we have—and I cannot allow any visitors at this time," said an aristocratic Virginia voice, quiet and courteous, but there was no hiding the anger that clouded the doctor's gray eyes.

"Is she able to talk?" Bruce frantically asked.

"For a woman who regained consciousness only minutes ago, who has not eaten a decent meal for a week, and had a bullet in her arm for at least four days, her mental faculties are remarkably alert." The cloud remained behind his eyes. "But don't let that fool you for a moment. She won't be riding any horse for a long while."

"Just how serious is her condition?" Bruce prodded.

"Just that: serious. The infection in her arm is septic—lucky gangrene has not set in."

"What does that mean," Bruce barked.

"Bacterial poisoning leading to putrefaction."

"Speak English, doctor."

"It means I'll have to amputate the arm if I can't find some sulfur."

"You want sulfur, I'll get it, now let me into that room."

"I think we are clear on that issue," he muttered.

Bruce took a step forward so that he was eye-to- eye with the doctor. "Get this into your head, Doctor. I am going into that room whether you like it or not. If you try to stop me, I'll put you on one of your operating tables—I can use a hacksaw rather well, get my drift. Now then, Doctor, the choice is yours."

Arabella lay flat on the bed, her skin surprisingly olive colored as he remembered. And her pale blue eyes were astonishingly bright. And then she quietly whispered.

"Bruce, dahlin'..."

Bruce stood frozen in time, like some unspeakable apparition that had risen from the watery depths of the Potomac. He reached out and gently touched her hand.

"Don't talk darling, the doctor wants you to lie quiet. Let me talk and you listen." He smiled and gently patted her hand, thinking, "I can't hold my feelings inside much longer." Again he touched her hand and felt the urge to lift it to his lips and kiss it. Instead he leaned forward and touched his lips to hers. "You sleep quietly, I'll see you tomorrow."

Tears welled in her eyes; her heart ached to hold him again, to kiss him, to be with him. It was a sign that she loved him, and she loved him even more for coming to her bedside, for bringing her to Richmond. Oh how she wished he could hold her, caresses her aching back, sooth her longing heart. But she was at rest just knowing he was there.

"Don't leave just yet, dahlin'," she weakly whispered.

Bruce nodded that he understood and sat in a chair by the bed. He gently took her hand and held it against his cheek until she was fast asleep.

In the next room, the doctor peered through the open door, moisture welling in his eyes. He saw medicine at work that he could not give, medicine unavailable in the apothecary.

He sniffed.

Chapter 46

Harp-strings of moonlight glittered from a dew-gleam silver sky overlooking the injured Shenandoah Valley. Bruce sat on a bench outside of the hospital enclosing Arabella in his arms, the woman who had saved his son, the woman who rescued him from the deep doldrums of despair. He sat holding her for what seemed an eternity, his heart wanting never to let go. His mind stuck in the past, but somehow he knew this woman was his future. Finally he pushed her back to the full length of his outstretched arms. Tears flooded her deep blue eyes; she struggled to speak, after weeks of saying nothing.

The understanding doctor stood at the door, his hands stuck in the pockets of his white smock. Finally he quietly stepped up to the bench and touched Bruce's shoulder.

"Thank you for the sulfur," the doctor said, "it saved her life." And then he turned and left the couple alone.

Arabella sucked in a breath of life-giving air, her lungs desperate for oxygen, facing Bruce. "When we parted back in Washington, I thought we'd never see each other again," she breathed, her voice raspy, clogged with emotion, and her heart aching to kiss him.

A smile creased Bruce's unshaven face. "When word came that you were injured, I knew then we had to bring you here, Arabella—Lt. Gen. Forrest agreed. He wants you to retire."

She looped her arm under his, and revealed her best convalescent smile, though the pain in her other arm felt it might explode.

"I'm so sorry about Doyle."

"Yes, I know. But he paid a dear price for your safety. Let's remember him for that way," he replied, swallowing a gulp of emotion.

It was a decision he'd made while in a drunkard nightmare, and he'd never forget his best friend, not while Arabella rested in his arms to remind him.

Tears flooded her eyes anew. She couldn't speak. The stilled silence—no guns exploding, cannon blasts spreading death, no nights alone ever again—healed a multitude of war-torn wounds. Now that her physical wounds were healing, her romantic emotions for Bruce rang true again. It was a blessing in disguise, a miracle in the midst of war.

The doctor who cared for Arabella sent a note to Lee's office stating that the best medicine for her was for Bruce to take her out somewhere alone. She was able to walk, now and although it was against his best advice, the woman was dying from loneliness.

Bruce sprang into Lee's office like a giddy teen when he received word from Janelle. He bounded up to her desk with a broad smile on his face. Janelle returned his smile harboring the joy of Arabella's recovery as she handed him the note. She remembered how desperate Bruce reacted when he first received the note of Arabella's disappearance. It was wonderful to see him alive again. There was no envy in her heart, only delight that one couple in this horrible destruction of life had found the reward of peace granted by mutual love.

Bruce met the doctor in the hallway of the hospital, took his arm, and shook his hand. Racing though his mind was the way he'd treated this man when he first came into the hospital. His conscious nagged him.

"Doctor, I want to apologize for the way I spoke to you, I should be on my knees thanking you for getting Arabella through this crisis."

The doctor was taken aback by his comments as he gripped his chin with thumb and index finger.

"Captain Taylor, if that woman were my girl, I'd have punched *me* in the nose," he smiled, revealing a full set of white teeth.

A nurse rolled Arabella down the hall in a wheelchair. As they approached Bruce and the Doctor, she extended her hand to her physician.

"Thank you, Doctor Gentry," she said weakly, but confident with a smile.

"The pleasure was mine, Arabella," he bowed.

The nurse rolled her toward the door, Bruce following. Dr. Gentry watched them exit the door, and finally rushed off to his next case. It was his practice not to get too close to his patients, but this case was his nemesis.

As the nurse assisted Arabella into the carriage seat, Bruce tucked a wool blanket over her lap. The nurse patted Arabella's hand, and gave Bruce a few instructions.

"She needs a quiet place—you understand," she said peering over her spectacles.

Bruce nodded as he gently touched Arabella bandaged hand. "How about the tavern, you remember." Her eyes blinked, her head slightly dipped.

Bruce understood, gripped the reins, and looked down at the nurse.

"Thank you for all you help, you've been so kind."

She smiled, yet in her heart she fantasized that it was she in the carriage seat. He was a handsome man, and somehow she envied Arabella, how every woman in Richmond envied that she had a man to come back to, a whole man.

"Be gentle with her, Bruce," she replied adjusting her spectacles on the bridge of her Roman nose.

He winked, and drove the carriage slowly along at a walking gate, the clip-pity-clop of the mare's hooves tapping out a rhythm in C-minor. Arabella took Bruce's hand and pulled his arm into her lap, her long fingers clasped tightly around his hand. The morning breeze caressed her face, and rustled the leaves on the trees lining the road. The sound of birds tweeting in the trees dwarfed the noises of the war ringing in her ears.

She was at peace.

Bruce pulled the carriage alongside the tavern located across the street from Lee's office, a familiar place they had frequented in what seemed a million years ago. Bruce carefully assisted her descent from the carriage seat, and draped the blanket around her shoulders.

The proprietor met Bruce and the woman as they walked in the tavern; he was a familiar customer.

"Welcome Captain Taylor—and this is the lovely lady I've heard so much about, I presume."

His jolly greeting, his robust shape, and the dirty apron clinging to his beer stomach were a joyful, unencumbered reception. He had a graying beard, freckled face, and rings in his ears like Black Beard, and yes, a wart on his nose, too.

He looked into Arabella's blue eyes. "Would it be too presumptuous, dear lady if I might speak?"

Her eyes brightened. "Speak you mind, dear sir."

"I have seen your man in my tavern on many occasions, but I have never seen a man so distraught until he heard you were alive. My dear, the world outside is a lonely place. Don't let this man slip away."

Bruce stood stunned.

Arabella only smiled, as if the waiter was an angel in disguise.

The waiter escorted them to the best table in a secluded corner. The table was lit by a single candle, lest it attracted unnecessary attention from snipers, and it was a nice setting for Bruce to admit what was in his heart. He took her hand across the table.

"What are you thinking Arabella—can you imagine how often I've thought of you?"

Her pale blue eyes gleamed with visions of the dinner Hattie had prepared when she first had Bruce alone on the porch of her plantation. How long ago was that, she thought?

"I'm thinking how much I love you, Bruce, how much my heart has longed to hold you in my arms," her heart replied nakedly.

He swallowed. The music from her lips was tantalizing, the gleam from her face irresistible as the candle flickered dancing shadows over her olive face.

By irresistible impulse, he took both her hands. "My heart is empty without you, Arabella. I have felt your presence wherever I wandered. I admit that sometimes I have been evasive—I can't explain that—"

A tear formed at the edge of her tired eyes as she touched his lips with her index finger. She had finally found him again as she had promised herself that she would. Even in a war, it was a peaceful thought now that she was with him again, never again to wander alone, she silently prayed.

Suddenly he overwhelmingly scooted his chair around beside her, placed his arm around her shoulders, and kissed her on the cheek just above a bandage. "I owe you everything—anything."

It was the statement she had waited to hear from his lips during those tormenting months alone in the turmoil of danger and desperate hope—he was her last hope, she had often imagined.

"Bruce dahlin', I want all of you—can you find it in your heart to release Marceline?"

The question stung his ego, his chivalry, his manhood, or was it cowardice, he thought? How blind he'd been, choked by tradition.

And suddenly a mist appeared in the room over the table, a white cloud in which the image of Marceline appeared in shimmering ghostly light, her long black hair swirling in a distant wind. Her Creole head tilted, staring down upon the couple. The mystic light shrouded Bruce, and the torment of withholding his true feelings somehow vanished, the agony of holding Arabella afar, all seemingly was absorbed in the light. He looked at the image of Marceline—the face was blank, no features, and no life—she was at rest, and so was Bruce, at last.

A distant audible voice echoed words from a deep place beyond authenticity.

"Bruce . . . Josh needs a mother . . . I release yooooouuuu . . ."

The vision imploded into nothingness.

The silence loomed deafening, the stares static. Finally the rustle of a tiny noise worthy of a field mouse broke the eeriness; a figure rustled near the kitchen.

The middle-aged proprietor nervously sneaked a peek from behind the counter, his eyes the shape of his rum mugs. The black female cook opened the kitchen door just a crack, her body trembling, ogling eyeballs roving left and right.

Bruce swallowed, felt his throat raspy. He wasn't sure who saw the vision, but he did, and his heart was finally released. He gazed across the table at Arabella, who sat with a smile on her face, Marceline finally had closure, she thought. Bruce moved the center candle aside; there was a glow around her head, words in his lonely heart that must be spoken.

"Arabella, I do love you with all my heart, everything I am is yours,—will you have me?"

Her face came alive. The cloaking shadows in her heart that had concealed her pain faded. Only his memory during the torment of days alone had kept her existing. Many times he'd appeared in her dreams when dozing in her saddle. And now he was hers at last. She pulled him into her arms and pressed him against her chest.

"Yes, yes, I will dear Bruce."

Chapter 47

The ride to Julie's house was a journey of quiet relief from the world swirling around Arabella, the death and dying. Yet now she and Bruce could hold on to each other—there was a future ahead if the war ever ended.

Arabella wanted only to hug and kiss Bruce, and tell him how much she loved him, how much she'd missed him every day in the turmoil of war. Bruce felt a wondrous emancipation of his heart; the thought suddenly triggered the Lincoln question, but was it too soon to abandon Arabella. That was on his mind.

They finally reached the Potomac about 5 o'clock in the early evening, and led their horses down a dirt road to Julie's house. Bruce hitched their horses to an iron hitching post, and helped her out of the saddle, careful with the tenderness of her wounds. They walked hand-in-hand to the door, two people wrapped in a single coat. He gripped the brass ring attached to the center of the wide door, smiling at Arabella as he gently wrapped it. He held his gaze into her lovely face until the door knob turned.

A maid opened the door, new maid, he realized. She bowed at the knees when Bruce asked for Julie.

Julie heard his voice and rushed to the door, her eyes brightened when she saw him. "Well, Bruce my old friend, how good of you to call—and who do we have here?"

His face lit up like a jack-o-lantern, mostly because Julie had noticed Arabella, but a decision was churning in his mind. "It's so good to see you again, Julie. This is my good friend Arabella Rhett."

Julie stretched out her arms and took Arabella's hands. "Well, my dear, aren't we a little bruised up. Why don't we go upstairs and I'll show you to your room, and see what we can do about those cuts—perhaps I've got an old remedy to help that arm, too," she beamed.

Bruce watched them walk up the stairs thinking that things had worked out better than he'd expected, yet he'd forgotten how cordial Julie was, never at a loss for words or cordiality. Somehow Bruce was relieved. And then it occurred to him how oblivious he was of the details of Arabella's rescue. Why, he ought to find that Lieutenant who telegraphed him and give him a medal—oh, that's foolish, his mind chastised. Suddenly his mind indicted him, writing mental notes on the retina of his eyes: Words like stupid, drumhead, obstinate, weakling, indecisive, idiot. Yes, how obstinate he'd been with Arabella's emotions. You are an idiot Bruce Taylor! The screen of his retina cleared, but Bruce had received the message.

Finally Arabella and Julie came down, chattering like old schoolmates. The two women were instant friends. They sat on a pair of adjacent sofas arranged before the blazing fireplace discussing memories, mostly about the teenage years of Bruce. Little Josh was upstairs asleep, and the maid was preparing dinner. Bruce watched the women from his opposing seat closest to the fireplace. Quietly, as if by some magical power, it occurred to him that he'd not noticed how beautifully Julie had dressed Arabella. She wore a clean lavender gown with lace around the fringes, a warm appearance just as he'd remembered her when they first met back in Charleston; Julie had done wonders. The two women sat engrossed in women talk, as Bruce sat absorbed in the softness of his seat and the sound of the crackling fire, smoke curling up the chimney.

The restful moment seized his thoughts; his tired, aching muscles uncommonly relaxed. He had been a lonely man, just as Arabella had predicted. And it occurred to him over and over again how much he loved her, adored her, and wanted to always hold her by his side. As he sat watching the fingers of flames leaping out of the fireplace, the smoke curling up the stack, the restful interlude created a tranquil atmosphere that rocked him to sleep. Deep in the shadows of his mind, the Lincoln matter surfaced again.

Bruce was awakened by the touch of Arabella's soft hand on his shoulder. "Oh . . . sorry, I must've dozed off," he whispered as he looked up into a smiling face, a face no longer a dream. Unconsciously his hand stretched out and lay on her cheek; harbored emotions stimulated his vocal chords. "Forgive me, Arabella, if you can. I love you more than you'll ever know, more than I've been willing to admit until now."

An applauding smile blazed over her face. "Oh, my darling Bruce, how long I have waited to hear you speak those words," she whispered, tears cascading down her olive face.

Bruce stood and took her into his arms, rubbing his hand up and down her back. Arabella relished the fulfilled moment of her dreams. Bruce finally released her from his grasp, and recognized that the sling was missing.

"Your injured arm—is it healed?"

Julie cast a glance at Arabella. "I applied a tonic that my mother gave me way back in Fredericksburg days—you may remember that tonic—your mother used it on cuts and bruises when you boys were so rowdy."

Arabella threw back her head suddenly laughing, a comforting release of tension. "Bet you were your mother's pride and joy, Bruce," she beamed.

His only reaction was a broad smile. Yes, he had fond memories, but now he clearly understood how much he needed this woman. Arabella was so caring and kind. Finally he was released from his puritan upbringing.

His thoughts vanished when he heard the maid as she brought in a tray with cups of tea. The discussion was much about the war and Bruce's plans, mostly questions from Julie. Arabella and Bruce sat serene in the warmth of the crackling fireplace. Bruce had place another log on the fire while the ladies were chattering.

The night lingered, an evening of fond moments, and finally Bruce stood. "Well, I guess I'd better get some sleep, tomorrow promises to be a busy day."

Arabella arose from her seat. "Why don't you take me to my room, Bruce," she suggested as she glanced at Julie.

Julie's wrinkled face unveiled the long years of her life with her deceased husband. It was a joy to see such a young couple enjoying their youth—and Bruce really needed Arabella, she discerned. And then her mature mind was transported to her days as a teenager back in Fredericksburg, and she cast her eyes on the glowing embers of the fireplace.

Bruce followed Arabella to the stairwell, and they climbed the winding steps together. Near the top of the staircase Bruce paused, his hand on the baluster. He focused his eyes on Julie who sat gazing into the fireplace. A deep sigh collapsed his chest as he exhaled. A prayer crossed his mind. *"Lord protect Julie, she's a good woman."*

Arabella reached the second floor, glanced back at Bruce standing tall and handsome, a glow in his eyes created by the flickering flames from the fireplace, its shadow dancing on the walls in shimmering dark shapes. She took his extended hand as he stepped on the floor, gripping the railing of the balcony stretching to the far wall. She said nothing, hoping he'd make the first move. Arabella just couldn't wait any longer; her heart was at the point of explosion. She loved him even more than she'd realized.

Bruce gazed into her face; the clarity of his thoughts now released to share his emotions longing for expression, the memory of Nathan Forrest's words cawed from his memory banks. *"She is a helluva woman."*

"Arabella, I can't let you go again," he said sternly. He pulled her into his arms, and held her closely against his thumping chest. He felt her lips on his neck, the warmth of her body. They stood at the top of the stairs; indeed, at the top of heaven, a moment of rhapsody enclosed them from the rest of the world, the torment of war, in a pleasant moment of peace and rest. He gently pushed her back in his arms and kissed her on the forehead. "Rest comfortably, Arabella, my darling.'"

She inhaled and took his hand. "I can't do that without you," she whispered, as she took his hand and led him into her room, and closed the door.

Chapter 48

It was the eve of spring in the Shenandoah Valley when Ulysses S. Grant first met Robert E. Lee in a series of battles known as the Overland Campaign. Grant's Army of the Potomac crossed the Rapidan River and marched into an area of secondary growth of trees and shrubs known as the Wilderness. Lee skillfully used the protective undergrowth to counter Grant's superior troop strength by masterfully using insurgent tactics.

Union Maj. Gen. Winfield Hancock's corps inflicted heavy causalities and drove back Confederate Gen. A. P. Hill's corps a distance of two miles. However, Lee pushed back Hancock's advance using Gen. James Longstreet's reserves. The difficult, bloody, and costly battles lasted two days, resulting in a standstill. But unlike other generals who retreated after similar battles with Lee, Grant ignored any setbacks and continued to flank Lee's right, moving southward. The tremendous causalities for the Wilderness battles were astounding. Disregarding the costly standstill, Grant moved ever southward and continued the fight with Lee. As the Army of the Potomac marched from the blood-soaked Wilderness, Grant was forced into a 14-day battle at Spotsylvania. Lee had anticipated Grant's move toward his right flank, and had positioned his Northern Virginia Army in an exposed rough known as the "Mule Shoe," at Spotsylvania Court House, before Grant and his army arrived.

Lee successfully resisted multiple attacks from Grants army for the first six days of the battle. The fiercest fighting in the two-week battle took place on a ridge known as "Bloody Angle."

A summer shower doused the battlefield and soaked the green landscape in sparkling light. Rifles refused to fire wet gunpowder, and forced the assault into a hand-to-hand struggle. Dead bodies were piled up on top of each other, forming a point of struggle similar to battles fought in ancient Roman days.

The bloody struggle finally ended; Grant lost almost twice as many as his adversary. Many talented Confederate officers were killed. Union Maj. Gen. John Sedgwick was killed by a sharpshooter and was replaced by Maj. Gen. Horatio G. Wright.

Gen. Grant sat in his field tent smoking his 16th cigar of the day, blew a puff of smoke, and took a bottle of whisky by the neck and downed a gulp. He wiped the back of his hand across his bearded mouth and looked up at Gen. Wright.

"Hell, I will fight it on this line if it takes all summer," Grant declared.

When Grant found that he couldn't break Lee's line of defense at Spotsylvania, he turned southward again, and moved his army to the North Ana River, a dozen miles closer to Richmond. This was exactly why Lee he'd told Captain Bruce Taylor a war plan was useless with Grant in command. Grant knew that he must coax Lee out in the open to break the stalemate. He sent a small group to the west bank of Mattatopi River hoping a diversion would bring Lee into the open.

Lee was too smart for such an obvious trick and never took the bait. Instead Lee anticipated a second right flank movement by Grant and retreated to the North Anna River in response to the Union corps withdrawing from Spotsylvania. Lee knew many of his generals were incapacitated by dysentery or injury, including himself, and how he longed for Gen. Jackson at his side. But, alas, his "right arm" had paid his final debt to the military.

Because of his own illness Lee failed in taking advantage of defeating parts of Grant's army. After a series of inconclusive minor battles at North Anna, Grant's Army of the Potomac withdrew 20 miles southeast to an important crossroads at Cold Harbor. Grant and Lee fought each other at Cold Harbor for three gruesome days, with the heaviest casualties on the final day. Grant had ordered the final assault, and it was disastrous and lopsided with tremendous Union causalities. Grant's audacity finally unveiled the brilliance of his adversary, and he sulked with respect.

After 12 bloody days of fighting in the Overland Campaign and costly Union causalities, Grant's Army of the Potomac broke away completely from Robert E. Lee, and secretly crossed the James River on a pontoon bridge. But the large Union casualties could not replace the loss of Jeb Stuart in the final days of the overland campaign. Stuart was mortally wounded at the Battle of Yellow Tavern. His wife wore black for the rest of her life in remembrance of her perished husband. Lee lost his "right arm" with the passing of Stonewall Jackson, and now he'd lost his "left arm" with the death of Jeb Stuart.

Lee immediately sent for Captain Bruce Taylor, his intelligence man, the last and only man he trusted. But his orderly said he was on a mission and due back soon. Lee pondered the situation; he had to know were Grant was heading, his intentions, and his troop numbers. Suddenly a commotion outside the tent caught his attention, as Taylor dismounted his horse, and walked into Lee's tent. He was out of breath, his uniform filthy.

Taylor stood and saluted. "General Lee, sir. Grant has sent Gen. Smith to capture Petersburg—he's due there by midday. I spoke with Gen. Beauregard and warned of Smith's advance."

Lee slumped on a folded stool. "That railway juncture is our supply line!"

"Yes, and it looks like Grant will make his new headquarters at City Point."

Lee sucked in a breath of air. "Grant knows that the public is against his slaughter of men and waste of his soldiers. He'll sit it out there and meet with Lincoln. We've got to consolidate our forces," his tired, but still keen mind predicted. He suddenly slammed his fist on the map table. "I'd like to march on Washington tonight!"

Taylor saw Lee's exhausted condition and adjusted his reply. "But sir, I think we had best protect our supply lines."

Lee sighed, slid his fist from the table, and rubbed both hands over his face, swelling his chest with air. "Of course you are right, Bruce," he exhaled.

"There is more information I gathered on this mission, sir," Bruce replied.

Lee rotated his head and faced Bruce expectantly.

Bruce realized that Lee had lost Jeb Stuart—he saw it in his eyes. "It seems that Gen. Joseph E. Johnston has repeatedly retreated from Sherman all along the railroad line from Chattanooga to Marietta, Georgia. It leaves Atlanta wide open for attack."

Lee leaned back in his chair, weary from generals who had no guts, only misplaced caution, but Johnston was no patsy; he was greatly outnumber by Grant's forces.

"Yes, Bruce, that's a problem the staff addressed recently. Jefferson Davis will remove

Johnston and placed him with Lt. Gen. John Bell Hood."

Bruce hadn't heard of Johnston's impending removal. "Jumping Jehoshaphat," he barked! "I hear Hood has a few skeletons in his leadership, too."

Lee wiped his brow. "You're right, Hood is a real risk, daring, but lacking in military discernment."

Chapter 49

Sherman's march to the sea kept gaining ground as he continued his summer campaign, pushing from Chattanooga toward Atlanta, always seizing the important rail and supply centers. Gen. Joseph E. Johnson had done much preparation for an assault on the city. Atlanta's outskirts bristled with palisades, rifle pits, and rows of spiked logs called *chevaux-defrise*, part of a 12-mile defensive ring that Confederate engineers began in 1863, and had strengthened in 1864, anticipating Sherman's advancing armies. Stormy command changes in the Confederate leadership erupted in the early days of Sherman's march, which he watched closely.

It was after the two armies clashed at Kennesaw Mountain that Jefferson Davis finally had stepped in and dismissed Johnston, a controversy of immense propositions.

In fact, Grant remarked that Johnston had conducted a masterly fighting retreat. "Nobody could have done it better," he said. Sherman's army overmatched Johnson, but he had his men ready and the city uncommonly protected with defensive barricades.

Gen. John Bell Hood found himself at the helm of the Confederate Army of Tennessee commissioned temporarily as a full general by Jefferson Davis. The job was dumped in his lap in a controversial appointment because of the Texan's relative youth and inexperience in leadership of an army. And his physical disabilities were an issue as well. However, Hood performed well in the field, riding as much as 20 miles a day without apparent difficulty strapped to his horse with his useless arm pinned to his jacket, his artificial leg hanging stiffly, and an orderly following closely behind with extra legs and crutches. The leg, made of cork, was donated by members of his Texas Brigade. They were imported from Europe through the Union blockade at Wilmington.

Hood had a reputation of bravery and aggressiveness that sometimes bordered on recklessness. Arguably he was one of the best brigade and division commanders in the Confederacy. Yet Hood became increasingly ineffective as he was promoted to lead large, independent commands late in the war. And this precursor assignment marked the first attempt at leading a large army.

He was a veteran of the Civil War severing admirable as a brigadier commander under Robert E. Lee during the Seven Days Battles, and was promoted to division commander under James Longstreet. He was wounded severely at the Battle of Gettysburg, having permanently lost the use of his left arm. Hood recuperated in Richmond, where he befriended Jefferson Davis. He was transferred to the Western Theater, and led a massive assault into a gap in the Union line at the Battle of Chickamauga, was wounded again, requiring the amputation of his right leg.

And now Hood faced his first major battle as full commander. His first order was to withdraw; hoping that he'd entice the engaging Union troop to come forward. Union Gen. McPherson's army closed in from Decatur, Georgia, to the east side of Atlanta.

This maneuver, though subtle to Hood, creased a smile across Sherman's unshaven face. He had just seen his adverse as he made a fatal mistake. Hood needed to defend the city of Atlanta, an important rail hub, and industrial center for the Confederacy, but his strategy drew his protective army out of the city into the suburbs.

Hood had previously ordered Lt. Gen. William J. Hardee's corps on a march around the Union left flank, sent Maj. Gen. Joseph Wheeler's cavalry on a march near Sherman's supply line, and had placed Maj. Gen. Benjamin Cheatham's corps up front ready for attack.

Hardee failed in getting into his position. McPherson saw the forming threat to his left flank, and sent his own corps to strengthen the line. Hardee met the McPherson's corps, and the battle began on the left flank rather than down the middle where Cheatham's corps was placed. The Confederate line was repulsed, but the Federal men of the left flank suddenly turned in retreat. McPherson rode to the front for observation of the retreat, and was killed by the Rebel infantry.

Wheeler took the Fayetteville Road while Hardee's column took the Flat Shoals Road toward McPherson's position. Near Decatur, Brig. Gen. John Sprague was attacked by Wheeler's cavalry. The Federals fled the town in a stampede but saved the ordnance and supply trains. The failure of Hardee's assault placed Wheeler in no position for holding Decatur, and the town fell back into Union hands late that night.

The main lines of battle formed an "L" and Cheatham's attack on the union front stood at the top of the line. Hood planned his attack from both east and west, the fighting centered on a hill east of the city known as Bald Hill. Sherman had anticipated the situation and had already placed artillery on the hill two days earlier. Shelling began on the city proper and killed several Atlanta citizens. Finally a vicious struggle, savage, brutal, hand-to-hand developed around the hill that lasted until dark. The Federals held the hill while the Confederates retired to their lines.

Just before dark, two miles to the north, Cheatham's troops broke through the Union lines at the Georgia railroad. Sherman smiled again, seated in his headquarters at Copen Hill, and ordered the shelling of the Confederates, while Gen. Logan's Corps regrouped and corralled the remaining Confederate troops.

With resistance nullified, Sherman shelled Atlanta, sending in raids west and south of the city, and cut the supply lines from Macon. Sherman's cavalry raids were defeated by superior southern horsemen.

Sherman fumed.

His diabolical thoughts raced back to his discussions with Grant: the only way to win the war was the total destruction of the will to fight—that was Grant and Lincoln's decision and Sherman's obliged task.

He swung his entire army of about 34,000 men in a broad flanking maneuver toward the west. Finally, Sherman's army captured the railroad track from Macon at Jonesborough. And then the Federalists pushed the Confederates to Lovejoy's Station. With its supply lines severed, Hood abandoned the city of Atlanta the next day on September 1, destroying its supply depot in the wake of their withdrawal.

The following day Mayor James Calhoun, along with a committee of Union-leaning citizens met a Captain on the staff of Maj. Gen. Henry Slocum, and surrendered the city, asking for protection of citizens and property.

Sherman was in Jonesborough at the time of surrender, another smile on his hairy face. He'd give the citizens protection, all right, if they'd get out of the city, he thought. He was ready for razing Atlanta, burning it to the bloody ground, a diabolical event that sealed Sherman's epitaph.

Two months later Sherman ordered evacuation of the city. On November 14, his army of 60,000 men burned all but about 400 buildings, including homes and factories, anything else that served the war. Sherman's men drove away with herds of cattle and sheep, stole goats and hogs, and left dead beasts rotting. A hundred men went into homes with bayonets, slashing paintings, sticking holes into tapestry, and swept everything off the tables, plates, cutlery, even stole from the slaves they purported to set free. They tore up fences and camped in front yards, raided smokehouses for bacon and hams, chopped through walls where slaves had hidden wheat and grain, pillaging with unrestricted licenses to plunder and burn.

Southern lifestyle was at an end; the city of Atlanta blazing wildly amidst crumbled debris. Like a scythe that had sheared 60 miles wide, Sherman's armies stripped the land once green and fertile. And then with the ravings of a lunatic, he decided that he'd maintain his headquarters in Atlanta and gloat over his victory. In the interim he prepared his army for moving east toward Savannah in his march to the sea with a policy of scorched earth.

The capture of Atlanta and Hood's withdrawal revealed that a conclusion of the war was now in sight, weakening any support for a truce. Lincoln felt at ease for a fleeting moment awaiting the political race against his Democrat opponent, Union General George B. McClellan in 1865.

Chapter 50

The battle of Franklin, Tennessee was fought on two occasions as part of the Franklin-Nashville Campaign; the first battle fought in 1863, was a minor action associated with a reconnaissance led by Maj. Gen Earl Van Dorn on April 10. This second battle in 1864 was one of the worst disasters of the war for the CSA, conducted by Maj. John Bell Hood's Army of the Tennessee against Maj. Gen. John M. Schofield's Army of Ohio.

After Hood had withdrawn from Atlanta he marched until he crossed the last major water barrier, the Chattahoochee River. At this point, Hood and Jefferson Davis met to devise a strategy that would defeat Sherman. There plans included attacking Sherman's lines of communications between Chattanooga and Atlanta, where Sherman kept his headquarters for some two months. Then Hood would move north through Alabama and into central Tennessee, assuming that Sherman felt threatened and would follow. Hood's rather ambitious hope was that somehow he'd maneuver Sherman into a decisive battle, defeat him, recruit additional forces in Tennessee and Kentucky, and then pass through the Cumberland Gap and join Robert E. Lee.

Sherman did not cooperate.

Instead of pursuing Hood with his army, he sent Maj. Gen. George H. Thomas with a portion of the troops for the expressed purpose of assuming control of the Union forces already in Tennessee, where he would coordinate the defense against Hood. Instead, Sherman marched the bulk of the army toward Savannah.

Davis spent a day in conference with Lt. Gen. Hood, expressing his disappointment in his defense of Atlanta, losing almost 20,000 men with no gains, and implied that he was considering Hood's removal. Yet, Davis took off to Montgomery, and telegraphed Hood that he'd decided on retaining him in command. He also transferred Gen. Hardee out of the Army of Tennessee. Davis created a new theater commander with Gen. P.G.T. Beauregard in charge. Lee informed Davis not to expect any real operational control of the armies in the field; Beauregard was needed in the Northern Virginia Army.

Hood's Tennessee Campaign lasted from September into December of 1864. He engaged seven battles and hundreds of miles of marching, many days in heavy rains and mucky mud. He was unsuccessful in trapping the Union Army of Ohio at Spring Hill, poorly commanded failures and military misunderstandings. Maj. Gen. John Schofield escaped in the night as he passed Hood's men, cloaked in the blankness.

Lt. Gen. Nathan Forrest's cavalry finally caught up with Hood's army near Franklin. His valiant horseman pushed the Yankees northward till they finally took their position behind the solid breastworks outside Franklin. With the Union line anchored firmly between two rivers, the only approach to their fortifications was over about two miles of open ground.

Hood's next mistake that almost equaled to his withdrawal from Atlanta was already forming in his active mind. Hood was about to issue an order that would go down in military history and moral abhorrence: a frontal assault, a reckless charge at sundown into the face of enemy muskets and Napoleon cannon.

Forrest pleaded with Hood, his cavalry experience knew there was another choice; he was ready for flanking action with his horsemen, and his experience said that he'd succeed. But Hood held on to his decision, despite Forrest's clear advice. He ordered the headlong charge even before Forrest's artillery had arrived in a three-day march toward Nashville. Up and down the line the signal was made, the bugles blared and the drums sounded. The battle flags of every corps, brigade, and regiment fluttering in the chilly air, the South's bravest sons marched forward as if on the parade ground, unaware of instant death.

Forrest's cavalry arrived just in time and covered both the right and left flanks, because Hood had no information on the fire power of the enemy. Nathan sat on his horse overlooking his men, sarcastically smirking. Hood needs someone like Arabella, he thought—wondering if Bruce Taylor had gotten her out of the hospital. He snorted, knowing it was the boys in the center walking over that two-mile stretch of open ground—they had it the roughest.

Then Forrest spotted the Union artillery on the hill, and knew the men had no chance. And then the cold sun dipped behind the mountain, the sudden dimness cast shadows on the field. The artillery opened up, muskets, Enfield, six-shooters, every weapon the Yankees had positioned. The men on the open field ran toward the fortification. A few dozen men made it through the bloody field. It was a slaughter. Hood strapped in his saddle, his cork leg stiff, and his one arm holding his saber. History had another Pickett's Charge reenacted in its memoirs.

Hood's exhausted men were wasted, yet he lived.

Despite his fatal efforts, the Union forces marched into Nashville anyway. Lt. Gen. Nathan Forrest advised Hood a second time to wait for his artillery, due within a few days. Unwilling to abandon his original plan, Hood stumbled toward the heavily fortified capital of Tennessee, with inferior forces, which barely had endured the beginning of a severe winter.

Two weeks later, Union Gen. George Thomas attacked and defeated Hood at the Battle of Nashville. Nathan Forrest saw the handwriting on the wall, and pulled his cavalry out the day they spotted Thomas' men in the distance. Leaving the Army of Tennessee was a good decision; his cavalry functioned better alone, not with these incompetent generals, he decided.

Forrest pulled out his entire army and headed for Kentucky, hoping to find a few Yankees on the road. He slowed his horse's gate with a gentle tug on the reins and gave his men time to rest during the long trip. He reminded himself how fortunate that he was being ordered into Kentucky, or he might have killed that stupid General Hood. He still had nightmares about his only defeat in a standup hand-to-hand fight during the war at the First Battle of Franklin. Perhaps his men were burned out, he reasoned. Deep in his mind he realized that Sherman was about to do a lot of burning in Savannah. But this Union firebug was to consume Atlanta with a horrible blaze.

Chapter 51

As a result of the battle of Nashville, and the subsequent relentless pursuit to the south, the Army of Tennessee ceased as an effective fighting force; the campaign had cost the Confederate army about half of its initial strength of 38,000. Hood and the rest of his ragged remnant retreated as far as Tupelo, Mississippi. Some survivors eventually joined Joseph E. Johnston in the Carolina Campaign against Sherman. Lt. Gen. Beauregard sought permission to replace Hood with Lt. Gen. Richard Taylor, and the change of command occurred about two weeks later.

The mounting Union victories presented President Lincoln with a landslide reelection victory in November 1864.

Lincoln's reelection inauguration was nearing and Bruce had remembered that at his last meeting with the Union general, he had requested that he and Arabella attend as his guests. He dare not refuse, lest he blow his cover. They were dressed in Yankee attire as before, hopeful to discover useful information for Gen. Lee. The evening grew long and somewhat boring. Sometime after the event, Grant called Bruce aside.

"Taylor, I want you to pursue your leads on this John Wilkes Booth fellow. Report directly to me at the War Office. I will expect candor in your investigation. Tomorrow the President is expecting your visit—do you understand?"

Bruce shook his hand. "Precisely, sir."

Grant led him to a side door where Arabella waited. He took her hand and kissed it. "My dear, you do look splendid today."

She cocked an eyebrow. "That's sweet, General Grant, give my best to your wife."

It seemed that Grant was fascinated by Arabella, and Bruce began to realize how urgent Grant needed his help. General Lee had given him permission to follow this Booth investigation to the end. And that was exactly what he planned to undertake. Only one thing concerned him: how long would this masquerade as a Yankee Captain hold before Grant realized he was using a Confederate intelligence officer to protect the Union President.

Bruce assisted Arabella into the carriage seat. "Looks as if Grant wants us to continue to investigate Booth," he said as he stepped into the seat beside her, and gripped the reins. Deep in his mind he wondered if he should involve Arabella in her guarded physical condition. It was a decision he had to make, soon.

Arabella sat quietly staring into the distance as Bruce snapped the reins across the horse's backside. The breeze rustled her hair and she turned up the collar of her cape. Her mind was imbued with questions concerning Hattie and Danny Boy. She had not heard from them since she had placed them on a train to Richmond. Even more unnerving, she had known the tracks were torn up by the Yankees just over the border in North Carolina, but she trusted Danny Boy implicitly.

"What's on your mind, Arabella?" Bruce asked.

"Hattie and Danny Boy—where are they, are they safe."

A smile stretched Bruce's tanned face, with a hint of embarrassment as he pondered the information he'd forgotten to deliver.

"I must confess. It simply slipped my mind. They both arrived in Richmond yesterday, seems they were lodging with Danny Boy's uncle in Raleigh, and rode to Richmond when it was safe to travel."

Arabella's head turned as she swallowed her guilt. "That's wonderful, Bruce," she replied and buried her face in his shoulder.

"I instructed Captain Austin to take them both to Julie's house," he added.

Her head raised and she kissed him on the neck, and then on the lips, and fell into his arms. The moment was beyond any resistance, any shame, now that Marceline had found release.

As Bruce and Arabella rolled along on the cobble streets, the words of Grant buzzed in Bruce's mind. Apparently Grant assumed that he had contacts unfamiliar to the Washington police. Finally, they arrived at a tavern just outside Richmond, and Bruce tied the reins to an iron post. He assisted Arabella into the front door.

"Thought we'd get a bite to eat—I'm starved."

She only smiled as she nestled her head against his shoulder.

Bruce and Arabella sat at a table in the early evening, mist hovering over the Shenandoah Valley. General Grant's statements were annoyingly unshakable, and answers were cloaked in the incredulity that the President may be assassinated. It made no sense. The war made no sense. Only Arabella drew him into reality.

Arabella sipped on coffee, her eyes sparkling brightly because the war was grinding to an end, and Hattie and Danny Boy were safe; how she longed to see them again. Most women understood the pain and horror of war, but men loved the honor and glory.

The war had taken many sons and husbands, even attempted to take her man. She cast her eyes upon Bruce, and thought of the years they had together, the times of joy and sorry—but never again the sorry of war, it was her fervent prayer.

Finally Bruce focused his eyes upon Arabella. She looked vibrant, alive. It was so pleasant sitting alone with her that he hated to even mention the scope of the mission facing them. But as usual, Arabella read his mind.

"Where do we start," she said, a radiating smile embellishing her face."

Bruce released his mug. "I suppose we should start with Doyle's old friend, Walter in Maryland who steered him to an agency that knew about Booth."

Arabella's pale blue eyes squinted as if a bee had stung her. Dear, dear Doyle, the man who gave his life to bring her back to Bruce, she fondly thought. He was a good man like all the men who had died in this war.

"Yes, let's get going," she replied with the urgency she had learned while working with Nathan Forrest.

"We will go to Julie's house first; I know how anxious you are to see Hattie and Danny Boy."

Finally, they parked in front of the Potomac home, and Bruce assisted Arabella from her seat. "If you don't mind, I have a meeting with Captain Austin. I should be back in the morning."

She nodded. "See that you don't do this Booth thing alone. I want to be with you."

He bobbed his head, but in his heart he wondered if she was strong enough.

A group of five deserters walked into the front yard of a house located on the Potomac. Deserters were frequent, and many became robbers, thieves, and murders. Some were simply separated from their command in the chaos of battle; others left their command post on purpose—traitors with a hatred of the war. They needed an outlet for their bitterness.

Candlelight flicked in the front window. A scrawny unkempt former private stared through the glass. He saw a big Irishman, and two—no three—women seated around a fireplace. The warm flames were inviting, the prospects of food even more so.

A big burly former Union sergeant twisted the front door knob.

Locked!

He motioned the four men around to the back. The moonlight lit the yard that was concealed behind a rock fence. The shadow of a door at the corner signaled a basement, and the sergeant again twisted a knob. It, too, was locked. He signaled two soldiers to bear against the door.

They pushed.

The doorjamb splintered, and the door swung open into eerily darkness that concealed the basement area. A dim light shone beneath a door at the head of a stairway. Four Yankees followed the sergeant up the stairs. As they stood on the top step, the sergeant gently twisted the knob, and the door creaked open. Het looked at his men with surprise written on his unshaven, dirty face as he stepped into an open space. The glow of a sconce with three lit candles on the wall dimly lit a hallway. In the stillness he heard the crackle of the fireplace through a set of double sliding doors.

Five men stealth toward the sliding doors. Warily the sergeant slowly pushed back the oak door entrance. Flaming logs lit a large room with opposing sofas and cushioned chairs. Two female heads sat on one sofa facing the fireplace; a black and an older woman. Easy prey, he thought.

He stepped inside.

Something suddenly crashed on his head; he fell unconscious. Two men walked into the room, two others ran toward the basement. Danny Boy grabbed the collars of both men and crashed their heads together. The two men in the hall rushed down the basement steps directly into a white mist.

A huge Creole woman stood in the mist quivering like a spirit from the pits of hell; her eyes were two black buttons, fire streaming through the thread holes like lightning bolts, staring directly at the two men. Both men crashed to the floor, holding their hands in the air, eyes goggling, and jaws dropped wide open, only unintelligible sounds emanated from their vocal chords.

Arabella descended the basement steps and saw Marceline's spirit at the foot of the stairs, a ghastly sight even though she'd seen it many times, but never so grateful as now. A smile crossed her face. Marceline had to protect Josh. Arabella waved.

"Thank you, Marceline. Your son is safe."

The mist vanished.

Two soldiers dropped their weapons, rushed out of the basement door, and ran down the dirt road screaming as if insane.

Seized by the event, a bit disheveled, Julie placed her hand on the big Irishman's shoulder. "Thank you, Danny Boy. What would I have done without you?"

He cocked his bushy eyebrow. "My dear lass, 'twas indeed my pleasure. Tis not often a handsome lady as ye needs a burly man like me, but I remain at your service," he smiled.

Julie returned his smile, somewhat taken aback by his remark. He was a fine specimen of an Irishman, and she kept her romantic thoughts to herself for the present. Instead of replying, she turned her head searching for Hattie.

"Where is Hattie?" Julie wondered, her eyes traversing the kitchen. And then she spotted her hiding behind the kitchen door, her big eyes surveying the situation.

"Are you all right, Hattie?"

She poked her head from behind the door. "Lord, Miss Julie, I don't mess wid no Yankees."

Chapter 52

The chief of staff for Lincoln's newly reelected administration, an older man in his late fifties with the grandiloquent name of Walter Washington, swiftly answered a lady's question. He adroitly shuffled papers from one pile to another obviously disregarding the single visitor seated against the wall with other chairs empty. Finally he condescended to look in Captain Bruce Taylor's direction.

"I want you to freely be aware, Captain Taylor that this meeting is highly irregular. If General Grant had not made the request and replied it was urgent, you would have not gotten past the front gate."

Bruce only smiled, whispering under his breath, "If you knew I was a Rebel, you'd be exactly right."

At that decisive moment the President's secretary came out of the office.

"Captain Taylor, the President will see you now."

The chief of staff stared indifferently, and may have peed in his pants. He embarrassingly checked to be sure. He had.

Bruce followed the secretary into the presidential office. The President stood and courteously held out his long hand. "Captain Taylor,

Grant tells me you have important news about this Booth fellow."

Bruce swallowed, gathering his thoughts. "Thank you, Mr. President. General Grant is concerned about your safety, sir," he articulated, releasing his ethereal leather-like hand.

"And you, Captain Taylor tend to agree, I take it."

"I do, sir," Bruce retorted.

The President pulled out a pocket knife and began pealing an apple. "All right, my boy, let's hear the evidence," the President said, his lengthy body folded in his chair.

Bruce took a deep breath when the President offered him to sit. He gathered his wits, wits that were diminishing with each harrowing moment.

"Booth has an older brother, Edwin who kicked him out of the family house."

Lincoln's leathery body leaned over the desk, his hand gripping the knife in a pointing motion. "Hold on, Captain, are we talking about a family squabble here?"

"No Sir, Booth intended to kidnap you," Bruce said flatly.

A bushy eyebrow arched above a deep-seated socket. "That's fatuous, young man," he said with the force of a lawyer, returning the knife to its pealing operation.

Bruce rustled in his seat. "Indeed, who can know the deceptions of a demented mind?"

Lincoln's skeletal head bobbed, considering the consequence if this intelligent man were correct.

Bruce pushed his point. "Booth intends to exchange you for the release of Confederate Army prisoners of war held captive in northern prisons."

Lincoln breathed a deep breath, his loose tie dangling. "Deception at its highest pinnacle," he said, chewing on a slice of apple.

Bruce persisted. "Booth reasoned it would bring the war to an end by embolden opposition to the war in the North or forcing Union recognition of the Confederate government."

Lincoln sat with his long hands folded in his lap munching on the last slice of apple, the news of interest only because of the drama presented by this articulate man.

"So, when is this dastardly exploit to take place?" he puzzled.

"I don't know at this time, sir. After your reelection Booth reasoned he no longer had bargaining power."

The candlelight enhanced the ridges of his chiseled face. "And what does this Booth plan to do now?"

Bruce leaned forward in his chair his forearms on the desk. "He plans to assassinate you, sir!"

The air went out of the room and a sort of chill filled the empty space. Lincoln sat with his mind contemplating the statement. He'd been warned before, but he could not let a demented mind determine his destiny.

"My good Captain. You have given me much to ponder. I deeply appreciate your concern, and I value your candor. We must talk of this matter later."

The secretary cracked open the door and Bruce knew his time had ended.

1865

Chapter 53

The first week in April, 1865 marked the end of the War Between the States. The final campaign for Richmond, Virginia, the capital of the Confederate States of America, began when the Federal Army of the Potomac under Grant crossed the James River in June 1864, and built up a series of victories stretching from September 1864 through March 1865. He marched steadily toward Richmond after the decisively victory at Vicksburg, the overland battles, and the screw up by incompetent generals; Sherman took Atlanta, Thomas took Nashville, middle Tennessee was wide open.

The battle of Appomattox began at Petersburg, the supply center for Gen. Lee's Northern Virginia Army with five railroads meeting at one junction. Its capture meant the immediate downfall of Richmond. Lee left Petersburg with minimal protection under the leadership of Gen. P.G.T. Beauregard after fighting Grant at the Wilderness, Spotsylvania, and Cold Harbor.

The Union forces attacked Petersburg for three days, and Lee realized Washington was left unprotected with Grant's entire army in the field. Lee devised two options if he detached a corps under Lt. Gen. Jubal Early; Grant might pursue leaving time from reinforcements from North Carolina, or Gen. Early may capture Washington and embarrass the Union and deeply wound moral.

The order was given.

Gen. Early marched 15,000 men through the Shenandoah Valley, defeated Maj. Gen. Lew Wallace at Monocracy, and reached the outskirts of Washington, inciting great alarm at the Union capital. Lincoln quickly urged Grant's action that dispatched Maj. Gen. Horatio Wright's corps to the capital. Just the presence of Gen. Early's troops so close for effective artillery sent an embarrassing scare through the capitol city.

Grant blew up a section of Lee's trenches at Petersburg with gunpowder that his men had planted inside a huge mine tunnel, which had been dug by Pennsylvanian coal miners. The explosion blew out a gigantic crater and opened a gap in the Confederate line. The Union attack was spoiled when Grant's troops milled aimlessly around in the crater, allowing time for Lee's counterattack, which drove the federals out of the gap.

Ironically the crater incident produced a Congressional investigation. During the lull that Grant had established his new headquarters at City Point for the rest of the war. It was from these headquarters that Grant had earlier ordered Sherman's attack on Atlanta. This interim period allowed the only three-way meeting between Lincoln, Grant, and Sherman.

Lincoln sat behind his desk, his long arm wrapped around a report from General Grant. He raised his skeletal head, and faced Grant with his deep-socket eyes.

"So this is how you plan to take Richmond, General Grant?"

Grant removed a cigar from his mouth. "Yes, Mr. President. I will give you Richmond in six days."

"Well and good, Grant, but don't forget to protect Washington from Lee's counterattacks."

Sherman leaned forward. "Mr. President, I assure you that General Lee will be sufficiently occupied with his zeal to protect his beloved Richmond."

Lincoln crossed his long legs, brought the report into his lap. He squeezed his bottom lip with thumb and index finger.

"Six days you predict—the same time God took to create the earth," he replied as he uncrossed his legs. "Well gentlemen, let's hope that General Lee does exactly as you propose."

Lee's withdrawal from Petersburg opened the last chapter of the Army of Northern Virginia. Grant pushed Lee onto Lynchburg Road. Meanwhile, Jefferson Davis avoided the advancing army and moved his capital into the Deep South through North Carolina. Sherman's cavalry repeatedly attacked Lee's rearguard from the rear as he retreated toward the small village of Appomattox.

On April 4, Lee wired the quartermaster's at Lynchburg to send four trains of supplies desperately needed at Appomattox. Yet unknown by Lee, Sherman's scouts had intercepted the message.

On April 5, Sherman's men watched the trains advance slowly along the Lynchburg railroad. He ordered Gen. George A. Custer's advance and he secured the Appomattox depot, and destroyed the tracks between the cars. Lee's forward artillery units were surprised in an attack by Custer, and the Confederates were forced in retreat, capturing 25 pieces of cannon. The majority of Lee's 28,000 men were positioned north of Clover Hill near the village of Appomattox. His men were hungry and depleted after a rapid march to their defensive position.

On April 7, Grant and Lee were in communication while the battle pursued at Saylor's Creek. Lee faced the futility of continuing. Yet his "never quit" attitude told his military mind that if he had the supplies at Lynchburg, he had a chance of a small victory. At a council of war, he learned that Custer had moved the Confederate supplies into Union territory. Lee saw the futility of continuing, still, Longstreet and Gordon urged attack. However, both corps retreated in the face of unlimited federalists, and Lee was convinced that the hour he dreaded had come.

Just before 11:00 am, Lee was surrounded on three sides by the entire Union army. Lee ordered raising a white truce flag by Longstreet and Gordon, while he attempted a ceasefire with Gen. George Meade.

Chapter 54

In the late afternoon of April 8, the sun cast long dreamy shadows near the Hillsman house that overlooked the assault at Sailor's Creek. Still seeking food and rest, Lee led the remnants of his army toward Appomattox Station relentlessly pursued by Grant. Lee's forward troops crossed on High Bridge.

Lee quickly ordered the railroad span burned, but his action failed to dissuade Union soldiers, who readily extinguished the blaze. Instead, Grant had already chosen a detour route and had crossed on a wagon bridge, pushing his army across the span at record pace.

Lee stopped near the Appomattox Courthouse, and met with his staff, stating there was nothing left to do by meet with Gen. Grant. Lee bowed his head and lethargically said, "I would rather die a thousand deaths."

He ordered a breakout at dawn the next morning, Palm Sunday, April 9. With the sun just rising over the hills of the Shenandoah Valley, and the shadows on the grass faded in a band of cosmic light; it reminded Lee that his army was also fading unable to fight. He dispatched an orderly under a white flag to Gen. Gordon's camp, requesting a meeting with Grant. Lee finally arranged a meeting, and Grant met with him at the nearby brick home of Wilmer McLean.

The signing of the surrender documents occurred in the parlor on that afternoon. Lee appeared resplendent in a new uniform and gleaming sword, wearing freshly polished boots and golden spurs. Grant rode up wearing muddy boots, his slouch hat without cord, his enlisted man's blouse wrinkled, and unbuttoned. He did not carry a sword, and he did not ask for Lee's sword—he decided on a simple agreement between respected soldiers, the war was over, time to rebuild.

A formal ceremony marked the disbandment of the Army of North Virginia, and the parole of its officers and men, effectively ending the war in Virginia. The event signaled the surrender of forces across the South.

Grant sent 25,000 Federal rations to Lee's starving men. Grant set the terms: Lee's men would lay down their arms, sign paroles, and head for home. Anyone claiming a mule or horse would take one. He promised that officers and men would obey the laws where they reside, no harassment from the Federal government. Lee's men lay down arms, sign paroles, and headed for home claiming their mules or horses as instructed.

Chapter 55

On April 12, after hearing the news that Robert E. Lee had surrendered at Appomattox Court House, Booth told his friend, John Surratt that he was done with the stage. The previous day Booth was in the crowd outside the White House when Lincoln gave an impromptu speech from his window. When Lincoln stated that he was in favor of granting suffrage to the former slaves, Booth declared that it would be the last speech Lincoln would ever make.

The morning of Good Friday, April 14, Booth went to Ford's Theatre to get his mail. While there he was told by John Ford's brother that President and Mrs. Lincoln accompanied by Gen. and Mrs. Ulysses S. Grant would be attending the play, *Our American Cousin* at Ford's Theater that evening. He immediately set about making plans for the assassination of Lincoln.

Bruce spent an hour with Arabella at the Potomac home where they could sort out the details of the trip to find Booth. He wanted to be sure that she knew the dangers and whether she was physically able for a trip into Maryland. He quickly learned that when a woman's mind was made up, it's the best advice to accept it without argument or analysis. After talking with Josh, and having tea, Julie turned to Arabella.

"My dear, I wonder if you could use a bath." It was a rhetorical question. But she knew every woman relished a bath, and this woman most of all, she had bathed in the cold waters of rivers and creeks.

Arabella's face swooned. "Really!"

"Yes, my dear, my husband purchased one from England some years ago. It's out on an enclosed porch—come with me."

They stepped out on a porch overlooking the Potomac, a room at one end with a door. Julie opened the door and stepped inside ahead of Arabella. There against the wall was an iron enameled tube with claw foot legs—she'd never seen such a devise, galvanized tubs, perhaps, but this tub was a luxury of the wealthy. In the corner was an iron tank with a stove beneath, a door for wood that burned and heated the water; no need to heat buckets on a wood-burning stove and pour them into the tub. It was too marvelous for her to critique the technology.

"My dear, there are towels on the rack over there, and a cotton bath coat. Enjoy yourself. We while dine when you are dressed."

Arabella reached out and hugged Julie. They stood enclosed in each other's arms for a moment of sweet silence. Julie now all alone without her husband could relive her life through this young couple and their dear little child, a child she never had. She felt cheated until Bruce came and brought this dear woman into her house, now a home. And now, like all women of this war, she worried for their safety on this dangerous trip into Maryland.

Bruce hired a boat at a Potomac wharf for a journey over into Maryland. He discussed the landing site with Arabella at his side, taxing his brain for something Doyle had casually mentioned. After an agitated search in the doldrums of his mind, a message suddenly flashed on his retina: Ford's Theatre. Yes, Doyle said he landed at a shore near the theatre, he thought.

An early afternoon gust transformed into a steady wind out of the northeast, cold air jam-packed with frozen needles that jabbed exposed skin into stinging numbness. It was obvious that the temperature was dropping, but to Bruce, as he stood looking over the churning waters of the Potomac, Arabella sensed nothing. Apparently her years in the field of battle had desensitized her nerves, but he was certain it had not affected her emotions, her passion, and her tenderness. A warming smile crossed his face.

They rode their horses along the jagged shoreline looking for a passage, a bridge, or some way they might crossover. Suddenly Bruce inhaled the smells of the docks jutting into the little inlet a few miles from a bridge where Doyle must have crossed.

It was dusk when Bruce and Arabella stopped their mounts at a small turn in the path, and he elevated his collar up around his neck. He glanced at Arabella who had only buttoned the collar of her coat, her mind flashing back to the sign that once pinned to this very coat: She shivered not from the cold but the distant memory. Somehow she wondered if things were different, would she have been a spy after all. She only did it because she loved Bruce so much. She knew his wife had first bid, but what a horrible woman she was. And because Bruce stood beside her, it gave her courage to wait. Wait for what, she wondered. Of course, it was worth it all just to be in his arms at last. She raised her head and her skin soaked the last of the radiant energy of the western sky with alternating orange to blue-purple haze.

Dusk slowly became night.

ARABELLA

The docks no longer cast a shadow. Bruce thought he saw something jutting in the murky distance. He knelt on his haunches, eyes squinting. Two solid piers rose like forlorn sentinels from the watery depths of the Potomac. The bridge had been repaired since the Maryland Battle. They mounted their horses and trotted across the bridge, hoof beats echoing over the river.

The overland battle had sucked the life out of Maryland activity, the streets empty, doors locked, candlelight snuffed in the front windows. Bruce noticed a side street that resembled Doyle's description of where he had met Walter. Suddenly a door opened and lit an alleyway. A tall man strolled up the alley toward Bruce and Arabella. Bruce gripped the handle of his Colt. The man walked out into the moonlight, and smiled.

"Captain Bruce Taylor, I presume?"

Bruce relaxed his trigger finger. "Why yes, ah . . . is that you Walter?"

"That's me," he said with a sour face.

"So, you got my wire?"

"Yep! What can I do for you?"

Bruce dismounted. "Is there some place we can talk?"

"Follow me."

Walter led them back down the alley. Arabella slid from her saddle and Bruce tied both mounts to a small stump as Walter opened the same door he exited a few minutes before. The candlelight revealed a small room with a kitchen adjoined. Two men were in the kitchen area nursing coffee cups. The man leaning against a counter appeared as the leader.

He was an elephant of a man, broad-shouldered, and had a thrusting, square-jawed face, unshaven. His sparse sandy hair was down to his collar, and the beard masking the great jaw was uncut, fuzzy, and ragged. He stretched out his hamlike hands.

"Henry Woodson, good to make your acquaintance."

Bruce clasped the strong hand.

"Bruce Taylor and this is Arabella Rhett," he said, gesturing his head toward the shivering woman.

Walter poured Arabella a hot cup of coffee, smiling as he handed it to her. "Forgive my stupidity," he smiled.

Henry pulled back a chair around a beat-up table, and the foursome sat. Eyes circled the table, and Bruce broke the monotony.

"Walter, you remember Doyle, who came by here a few months ago, inquiring on a John Wilkes Booth—what can you tell me about his whereabouts?"

Henry rustled in his chair. "The last we heard of him was in October '64, Booth made an unexplained trip to Montreal, which then was a well-known center of clandestine Confederate activity."

Walter entered the conversation. "We did get a report after Lincoln's reelection. It seems that Booth changed his mind about kidnapping Lincoln, and decided he would assassinate him. This radical turn of events caused us to cut our relation with this lunatic."

Bruce filed the assassination information in his mind. "Any idea where he's holding up now?"

Walter nodded. "After his brother kicked him out of the family house, he lived at Ford's Theatre."

After another round of coffee, they all agreed the meeting was offer, Lee was on the brink of surrender, and there were many loose ends to tie together. As they all stood, Henry added a last comment.

"Booth intends to decapitate the Union government and throw it into a state of panic and confusion, allowing the Confederacy to reorganize. The man is truly demented."

Arabella had listened and said nothing, but she drew her experience from Nathan Forrest's dealings with wimpy generals as she leaned over the table.

"Gentlemen, if Booth assassinates the President, the people will end in chaos, not those bureaucratic representatives in Washington. We had best find this man before he commits this dastardly act."

Walter had taxed his mind during the entire conversation. "You know, Booth spent a lot of time at the old soldier's home in Pikesville."

Chapter 56

Dawn lit the sky of the next morning as lances of sunlight splashed the tattered forest's floor. Bruce led Arabella's horse to a small tavern located on the Brandywine Pike. They dismounted and Bruce suggested they go inside for breakfast where they might discuss the trip to Pikesville, or at least decide if there may be a better starting place. He helped her from the saddle, and somehow wondered if she felt well. She slid down from the saddle, placed her arms around him. The stood in each other's arms for a moment and Bruce placed his hand under her chin.

"Is anything wrong, Arabella?"

She looked into his dreamy eyes a second, and kissed him gently on the lips. "Nothing a night over in this tavern wouldn't cure," she said reminding herself of that wonderful bath she enjoyed back at Julie's house.

He took her hand and they strolled toward the tavern. As they approached Bruce read the sign over the door: Surratt Tavern. The door swung open and immediately they heard the noise of a rowdy group drinking rum. The proprietor met them, wiping his hands in the dirty apron around his robust waist.

They sat at a table near the window. "We've got wheat cakes, eggs, bacon, and coffee. What'll you have?"

Arabella piped up. "It all sounds wonderful," she remarked gazing into Bruce's face.

"We'll take two orders—everything you mentioned, we are hungry," Bruce said.

The man turned and walked behind the counter. Presently he came back with two large platters, and sat them on the table with a pot of coffee.

"Enjoy the food folks."

Bruce raised a finger. "Wait up, ah, could point us in the direction to Pikesville?"

He wiped his hands in an apron strung around a well-fed stomach, his face a porcupine of whiskers. "Up near Baltimore—what are you looking for?"

"The Old Soldiers home."

He sat down at the table, placing his elbows on the table, his mind willing to educate a couple of strangers.

"Perhaps you need a little history. Maryland is a slave state; the people are not too keen on Lincoln's policies. That house was once an arsenal, converted in 1888 into a residence for soldiers who served the Confederacy," he said, rocking back in his seat.

Bruce sensed that he must lay his cards on the table. "We are looking for John Wilkes Booth, the actor out of Ford's Theatre. Can you help us find him?"

He released his feet that held back the chair as it settled on all four legs, and stared at Bruce as though he was a Yankee spy, an eyebrow arched and his piercing eyes deviously glaring.

"You two ain't Yankees by any chance?"

Bruce immediately disarmed the stare. "I'm Captain Bruce Taylor, General Lee's intelligence officer. We have reason to believe that Booth is dangerous to the nation: Union or Confederate."

The man stood, placed both hands on the table, leaned low and whispered. "Listen carefully, John Surratt owns this tavern, and he is involved with Booth. It's mighty fortunate that he's not here tonight—I'd start at Ford's Theatre about 10 miles north of here, if I were you."

Arabella rolled a glance at Bruce as she gulped down the last wheat cake. "Well, that's about where we were heading this morning."

Bruce and Arabella reached the Washington area in early daylight, and found Ford's Theatre near an inlet from the Potomac. Bruce had no idea whom he might speak with, and they tied their horses, and ventured to the front door of the theatre.

The door swung open, but there was no one nearby, although they heard distance noises. They entered and slowly walked down a long hallway. Arabella spotted a poster, and the information nearly startled her out of her wits.

"Look!"

Bruce read the poster: **President and Mrs. Lincoln accompanied by Gen. and Mrs. Ulysses S. Grant to attend a play entitled,** *Our American Cousin,* **Evening of April 14.**

"Great Scott," he thought. "That's tonight. Come with me, Arabella," he said, the urgency of wiring Grant pressing on his mine, but Arabella was nowhere in sight. Then he heard her voice.

"Bruce, come here quickly."

Arabella was around the corner. "What is it? We've got to go." "Here is the door to the presidential box—look there, it's a spy hole bored through the door."

Bruce stepped up and placed his eye near the hole. He could see every seat in the box. Why? Then it hit him like a ton of bricks. Booth must have bored the hole, planning his assassination tonight.

"Come Arabella we've got to wire Grant."

They crossed the street, looked up and down, east and west, north and south—nothing. Then Arabella saw a man leave a building one street up.

"Let's see where that man came out," she said, holding her arm out stopping Bruce's progress.

They walked, skipped to a hop, and then ran to the same door, and stepped inside. It was a side door to a hotel or apartment, Bruce decided as they walked up the hallway, turned left to a front desk. Presently, a clerk came to the front desk, saw them standing.

"Sorry we are all out of rooms, the President's election and the end of the war, you know."

Bruce stared in his face. "Listen to me carefully, I must send a wire to General Grant immediately. Can you help?"

The tension in his face, the insistence of his request seized the man's empathy. "If it's that important, we have a key operator behind this counter, would you care to come with me?"

Bruce and Arabella rounded the counter to the place where the man opened a hinged gate, and followed him around a corner. A young man, about mid-twenties, sandy hair, nicely dressed sat on a stool, listening to his supervisor. He placed his fingers a Morse code key, and looked up at the tall stranger.

"Son, shall I dictate or write it out."

"Dictate, where to?

"General Grant, the War Department."

He gazed up at the clerk standing behind his stool, who nodded affirmatively.

He elevated an eyebrow. "Shoot."

Bruce fingered his chin, what an ironic choice of words, he thought as he rubbed his chin. "Here goes: Booth plans his caper tonight, April 14, at Ford's Theatre [STOP] Keep Lincoln from attending play [STOP] President must not attend [STOP].

The young man swallowed. "Who shall I say sends this telegram?" he said with his voice stammering.

"Bruce Taylor."

The clerk and young man stared shockingly at each other, what a curious message, they each thought, but neither dared ask for clarification.

Chapter 57

Bruce and Arabella rode their horses back toward the bridge where they had crossed over into Maryland. Somehow Bruce thought it best if he left Arabella with Julie. The risk was too great, he had no idea what might happen in this crazy search for Booth. The bridge finally appeared in the distance, once a gruesome sight, but now a welcomed repose.

When they crossed over to the Virginia side, their horses trotting along side-by-side, Bruce rotated his head toward the woman he loved.

"I think it best if we go by Julie's place first." He paused. "Truthfully, Arabella I'm concerned for your safety."

Her hands fashioned a tighter grip on the reins. "I thought you may say that, and I understand—really I do, and besides, I could use another bath," she smiled broadly.

He pulled the reins, and his horse moved close to her mare, leaned over, and kissed her on the cheek.

"Why did I wait so long to realize how much I love you?"

She focused straight ahead. His question wasn't rhetorical. He really didn't know. She knew.

It was a woman's prerogative to know. No matter. He was hers now, but she never intended to relax until wedding bells chimed.

All along the trail, Arabella reminded herself that she must settle down, now that she had the one she wanted to settle down with. Her wounds needed healing, her heart needed examination. Had she overplayed her hand? Would Josh consider her as his mother? And what of this ghost of Marceline? Would she really set him free, or would she haunt them both?

Too many questions, she thought. Tomorrow was another day, she visualized; it was her way of hope, her way of existing.

Julie's house appeared on the horizon, its complex roof a misty black. It reminded Arabella that she felt dirty, her hair skuzzy, and she had a nasty headache. Both horses were tired, and slowly moved along at a walking speed. A new day was dawning, stars had lost their brightness, and the sun peaked over the horizon in orange and yellow colors, as shafts of light spilled into the lush green valley.

Bruce tied the horses at the familiar iron tie-post, and helped Arabella from her saddle. Julie's maid heard them arrive and opened the door as the stepped on the porch. The grand foyer was like home to Arabella, and she relished another bath in that wonderful iron tub. The sliding doors to the living areas opened and Julie walked out to meet them.

"Well you two, I didn't expect you back so soon, but mercy me, I'm glad to see you safe," she announced. "You must come into the living room by the fireplace. There is news of great importance."

They followed her into the living room and each took the seat she directed. Julie brought her hand together in a prayerful position.

"Lee has surrendered at Appomattox!"

Bruce was not surprised. "Is there any news of Lincoln," he injected.

"Only that he sat down in Davis's chair at his desk in the presidential mansion."

"Are you sure Lincoln is okay?" Arabella inquired.

"I've heard nothing to the contrary," Julie replied.

Bruce stood. "Julie, I think Arabella may want to use your bathtub again. I must leave and check on something important."

"Why don't we have a bite to eat before you go," Julie suggested.

Arabella took Bruce's arm and whispered, "You will be careful, dahlin'. I want very much for us to marry."

He smiled. "Me, too—really I do, Arabella," he replied, apologizing to Julie.

An eyebrow arched over Arabella's left eye as Julie took fresh towels into the enclosed porch.

Bruce left Julie's house and rode south along the Potomac back to the bridge across the Potomac. An armada of covered wagons lined the road in a sea of forest green when he crossed over. Must be people celebrating the war's end he guessed. He galloped his horse, not knowing if Grant had gotten the message or if the President actually went to the play. But he'd be there soon. The sky became cloudy, perhaps a rainstorm approaching. The dreary sky reminded him what the nation would face if Booth were successful with his diabolical plan. He whipped his horse into a blinding gallop.

Finally he saw the lights along the street of the Theatre, and pulled his horse into the alley behind the stage entrance. He dismounted and rushed into the rear door. He heard the voices of the play in progress. He ran down the hall, pushing aside two guards.

Suddenly he heard a shot ring out, then a medley of screams.

He snatched open the presidential box door, saw Lincoln's body sprawled in his chair blood streaming from his head. Booth stood on the rail, waving a .44 caliber Derringer in his hand shouting, "Sic *semper tyrannies.*"

As he leaped from the rail, Bruce grabbed the knife that stabbed Maj. Rathbone, screaming to the Major, "I'm an agent for Gen. Grant—get word to him if at all possible."

He leaped from the rail behind Booth, and ran down the aisle between the theater chairs amidst screaming women, some thinking it was part of the play. Bruce crashed out the rear door, a host of men following him.

Booth had already reached the back stage door, and had mounted a waiting horse. Bruce raced outside; saw Booth galloping down the alley. He threw his leg over his horse's saddle, and dashed down the alley, as Booth turned the corner up ahead.

He followed the dust rising from the hoof beats of Booth's horse, and then he realized there were two horses, probably the man who waited outside with Booth's horse. Suddenly he saw the two horsemen; one rider was beating his horse's backside mercilessly with a whip. Bruce thought he recognized one man. It was Booth all right; he remembered that day in the tavern when Booth spoke Shakespeare so eloquently.

It began to rain, slowly at first, then a downpour. Bruce pulled off the road and sat on his horse under a thickly branched tree. A fearful thought entered his mind. Suppose Booth got away, then he'd doubly failed his mission. Now it was vitally important that he follow Booth. In about an hour, the rain stopped, and Bruce rode back on the trail.

Up ahead he saw the roof of Surratt Tavern. As he neared the establishment, he saw in the distance two horsemen ride out onto the trail ahead of him. Bruce decided to stop at the tavern, and slowed to a trot. Finally, he pulled into the tavern and dismounted.

He entered the door, hoping he'd find the same waiter that he and Arabella had met yesterday. He sat at the same table by the window, and presently the waiter approached him.

"Well, good to see you again, where's your wife?"

"Ah, she's with my . . . aunt—how about a cup of coffee?"

"I've got some fresh hotcakes, made them myself."

"I'll take a stack with the coffee."

"Be right back." He paused. "Listen, I might have some news for you."

While Bruce waited he taxed his mind on the subject of the news. He looked around at the few customers, but Booth was not among them. Presently he caught a whiff of steaming hotcakes and coffee.

The waiter leaned in and whispered. "John Wilkes Booth and David Herold just left here heading for the woods and the Zekiah swamp—Herold knows these parts well. I expect he'll try crossing the Potomac into rural Virginia."

Bruce pushed the plate of hotcakes aside. He had lost his appetite. He stood, walked over to the counter and paid, and then walked out into the cloudy morning stillness. The eerie darkness of another storm gripped his heart as he walked to the rail where he'd tied his horse. He straddled his horse and rode back to the bridge. He was tired and disappointed—no need to continue without knowing where he was going. Lincoln was dead, and his death could have been prevented. The thought stuck in his craw.

Bruce could not have known at that moment that Grant had declined the theatre invitation at his wife's insistence. The Grants had departed Washington by train that evening for a visit to relatives in New Jersey.

Grant never got the wire Bruce had sent.

Chapter 58

General Forrest made the announcement to his men of Lee's surrender on May 6, and it was not taken well by his proud troops. Many of these men had been fighting steadily somewhere over the southeast for several years. They didn't give up so easily, sorry because they lost, and swore to hate Yankees till they died. But everyone was happy to be going home, although the more reckless men who couldn't stop fighting wanted to ride to Texas or Mexico and continue the fight.

This was the same decision of Jefferson Davis, but he had to face reality. Davis had moved his government three times, hoping for a restart of the war out west. From Richmond he settled in Danville, Virginia, then to Greensboro, North Carolina, then to Shreveport, Louisiana. He sent a telegram from Greensboro, activating the Trans-Mississippi meeting. Lee thought Davis should surrender least he be killed by Union hunters, but Davis kept moving the Confederate capital when the CSA was effectively disbanded on May 5. In the Shreveport meeting, a decision was made that moved Davis' government to Havana, Cuba. From there the government planned regrouping, and heading for the Confederate-controlled Trans-Mississippi area by way of the Rio Grande, and hoped to revitalize the CSA.

Despite the strong case for surrender, Davis balked. Somehow Davis continued with the Havana plan, the human need for survival pushing him to the brink of insanity. A boat arrived in New Orleans, and transported the Confederate government to Havana.

Havana rejected a lengthy stay of Davis and his government. Consequentially, the Trans-Mississippi arrangement fell through.

Davis fled to Georgia.

Union Colonel Benjamin D. Pritchett was hot on his trail, and followed leads to Iwindale near Abbeville, Georgia. He learned from local residents about a military camp just north of town.

Pritchett charged into camp and captured Davis.

He left him with an adjutant until Major James H. Wilson arrived. Davis' wife persuaded the adjutant to allow her old mother to fetch some water. Davis's wife and the old mother left the tent. One of the ranking offices noticed the mother was wearing riding boots with spurs, and snatched off an overcoat, revealing Davis masquerading as a woman.

On May 10, Mayor Wilson announced Davis' capture. Davis was held in prison for two years at Fort Monroe, Virginia.

ARABELLA

1866

Chapter 59

Sometime during the late afternoon at Professor Robert E. Lee's office at Washington College, Grant sat in a chair and lit one of his 20 cigars a day. Lee finally walked into his office after a student told him he had a visitor. Grant obviously had many things on his mind and sought the confidence of his old adversary in war. He had a worrisome secret he wanted to get off his chest; liquor and caffeine had not relieved his guilt.

Grant gathered his nerves for a confession. "Robert, about this Captain Bruce Taylor, I suspected that he was one of your men, since we met with Lincoln in the White House," he gloated without the usual pomp.

Lee's eyes squinted, rubbing his magnificent beard giving Ulysses his full attention.

Grant squirmed in his seat. "You see, Bruce had far more information than the Washington authorities on this man Booth," he said gazing into space.

General Lee raised an eyebrow. Grant's uncommon posture, told him that he had more to say.

Finally Grant regained his posture. "I thought you should know that I sent Bruce and Arabella on a mission to find Booth." He failed to relight the cigar as he gained the courage to say what must be said.

"Robert, this is hard for me to say." He fiddled with his cigar. "Bruce wired me, told me to keep Lincoln away from Ford's Theatre. Booth was waiting to kill the President." He paused. "With God as my witness, I didn't get that wire." He coughed, clearing his dry throat. "The Misses declined the invitation to be with the President. I was on a train to New Jersey." He sighed. "Your man did his job. I failed him," he said and threw the unlit cigar into a trashcan.

The silence was earsplitting.

Lee poured a glass of whiskey that he kept in the bottom drawer of his desk, and slid the glass over to Grant. The tired old General breathed a sigh of relief, graciously lifted the glass to his dry lips. He swilled the whiskey, gripped his bottom lip with thumb and index finger, feeling the tension subside into a tolerable numbness.

Lee knew how Grant felt, and he had to change the subject, change the mood. As they stared silently at each other, Lee's face suddenly stretched into a smile, accented by a manicured gray beard, and his lean stomach began to shake. And then he rocked back in his chair, suddenly laughing.

Grant's bushy eyebrow elevated. "What?"

Lee regained his composure. "Did you know that Arabella was a spy for Nathan Forrest?"

There came a silence of several moments as Grant thrashed the statement over in his mind. He rubbed his fuzzy chin, his thoughts rushing back to Gen. Halleck smoking one of his cigars. Visions of deception dance in the synapses of his mind.

"I'll be damned," he said in a voice so low that Lee wasn't sure that he heard him, but he twisted the knife.

"She injected mushroom poison into your cigars," Lee added.

Grant suddenly gripped his stomach, and roared a long laugh, releasing a mountain of tension and guilt.

"So that's what happened to Halleck," he shrieked, unable to constrain his laughter.

Finally Grant wiped his eyes with the back of hand, looked up at Lee. "Anyone that elegant needs a pardon."

Lee raised his empty glass. "Let's drink on that, we both understand each other, Ulysses."

"That was my intention. We've got a lot of work ahead of us to rebuild this nation."

Lee's secretary cracked open the door. "Sir, your appointment has arrived."

Lee glanced at Grant as he snapped his fingers. "Almost forgot. Bruce and Arabella have announced their marriage," he said. "Excuse me, Ulysses."

As Lee left the office, Grant sat his glass on the table and the secretary's message suddenly hit him.

"Marriage! I will be damned."

Lee closed the door behind his exit. Bruce was so excited that he could hardly get the words out of his mouth.

"Professor Lee, I would consider it an honor if you would stand by me at our wedding next month."

Lee smiled admiringly shifting his stance. "It is my pleasure, Bruce," he said and faced the prettiest person in the room. "Arabella, my dear, I hope you will invite Nathan Forrest—that's one man I'd like to thank for his service," he said clasping his hand over Arabella's bruised hand.

"It's already done," she replied. "He and his wife both plan to attend. Nathan will stand in as my father and give away the bride. The reception will be at Julie's house," she announced with her arm linked through Bruce's elbow, giddy as a future bride might act. But she had waited a lifetime for this event, it seemed. Somehow she wondered if it was all worth the cost, and then she reminded herself how much she loved Bruce, how much she'd suffered just to be by his side. It was worth it, darn right—one of Nathan's favorite idioms, she thought.

Lee released Arabella's hand as he noticed Grant standing outside the door to his office; he'd seen that stare before. "If I may, General Grant has something to say."

Grant stepped over beside Lee without a cigar clenched between his hairy fingers. He was now commandant of the U.S. Army, dressed in full General's uniform; the vest buttoned smartly, compete with highly polished boots, but no hat. He focused his deep brown eyes upon Bruce.

"Bruce, my boy, I've been asked to run for President," he announced forthrightly.

A hushed rumble of ooh's floated over the group as Grant fumbled for the match to light his cigar. Arabella stepped forward and lit the fag with a match she had taken from a nest on the desk.

"You know General; you'd look nice with a pipe."

He kissed her hand. "My dear, I will smoke a pipe, if you and Bruce will accept my proposal."

Arabella stepped back beside Bruce, wondering what Grant hand in mind.

Grant drew a deep draw of smoke into his lungs and breathed it out slowly, casting his intense eyes on the couple, reinforced with a rare smile.

"Bruce, I'd like you to establish a sort of secret service to protect the future presidents. We can't allow the assassination of Lincoln to stand without reforms."

Bruce winked at Arabella. "Well, I'm flattered, Sir, but I think Arabella should have a voice in this decision," he admitted, gazing into her radiant face.

Grant turned to Lee with a nod of his head. "See, Robert, I told you he's a smart boy."

Lee only smiled, enjoying the exchange.

Grant took Bruce's hand in a double-handshake, the cigar gripped firmly between his teeth. "After the election, assuming that I'll win, of course, I want you and Arabella to move into the White House. I think perhaps Arabella will make a grand assistant for my wife—she certainly will light up dignitary events—I'm no good at diplomacy."

Bruce seized the moment. "You know, Sir. The purpose of diplomacy is to prolong a crisis. We need a leader who can lead."

Grant removed his cigar. "Son, I'm a general, not a politician—but I will call the shots as I see them."

Lee could not resist. "We know Ulysses, you just charge straight ahead," he said. "Take it from me, old friend. Bruce will be your anchor in the trouble sea ahead, and Arabella will keep you supplied with cigars," he beamed, glancing at the charming young lady.

But Arabella had the last word. "Why General Grant, I will make sure that my Bruce stands by you," she replied with a wink.

Chapter 60

The war was indeed over. Arabella sat on a sofa facing the fireplace in Julie's Potomac home. Hattie was in the kitchen with Julie's maid preparing a wedding reception dinner for tomorrow. Danny Boy and Bruce had gone to Washington College to converse with Professor Lee. Julie nestled beside Arabella, who sat with her legs drawn under her skirt, her arms clasped around her knees gazing into the burning embers.

Julie spoke in a whisper her mind reviewing the episode of Yankees in her home. "I never realized what danger you must have faced, Arabella. But it's so nice to have you here in this house."

Arabella touched Julie's hand, gently patting it. "Thank you for taking us in, I mean Hattie and Danny Boy—I've loved them both for as long as I can remember. They are my family, all that I have after my mother and father passed."

Julie's recollection of the past reminisced. "You must cherish those fond memories, my dear. Memories are all I've have since my husband was killed."

Arabella gazed into the curly flames leaping up the chimney. "I know what it is to love someone and cannot hold him in your arms," she replied, gazing into the crackling flames.

Julie understood. "There has been a marvelous change in Bruce since you first came here. For that I thank you from the bottom of my heart. My husband and I never had children, it's marvelous having Josh here, and he's such a charming boy."

Suddenly a knock sounded at the front door. Out of habit Hattie wiped her hands in her apron, and opened the door, while the maid was indisposed in the pantry.

A young Yankee lieutenant stood with his hat in his hand fingering the brim nervously. "Excuse me, please. I understand a Miss Arabella Rhett lives here, may I speak with her. if you please?"

Hattie tilted her head, measuring the young lad from foot to head. "Step inside young fella," she said, and rotated her head. "Miss Bella, somebody tah sees ye," she screamed.

Arabella walked out into the foyer, sudden surprise written on her olive face. It couldn't be, but it was! She rushed to the door and took the young lads hand. "Jeremy. Dear Jeremy. Please come with me."

They walked into the parlor and Julie stood, met them at the door. "And who might this be, Arabella?"

"This is Jeremy Hostetler, the young man who saved my life," she replied, hugging him with blurring tears in her eyes. A sudden knock on the door caught her ear, and she released Jeremy with a long gaze, memories flashing in brain. She kissed him on the cheek. "Would you introduce Jeremy, and I'll get the door."

She turned and opened the door. Bruce and Danny Boy stood in the doorway like two sycamore trees, both tall and handsome like Arabella remembered them. She brushed a tear from her eyes with an index finger and a sniff.

"Well hello King Arthur and Sir Lancelot," she grinned.

Bruce chortled. "Thank you, darling," he replied and kissed her on the cheek, pulled her into his arms.

Julie heard Bruce's voice and met them in the foyer. "Come in boys, we were just speaking of you two."

Bruce and Danny Boy glanced at each other with opposing smirks. As they entered the parlor, Bruce noticed young lieutenant standing by the fireplace. Moving closer he suddenly recognized his face: it was the young lieutenant—Jeremy Hostetler! The young lad gazed intently at the entrance, left the fireplace in a brisk and surged toward Bruce with his hand extended.

"Mr. Taylor, I'm so glad to find you; look, the leg is just fine, no infection, no limp."

"Well Jeremy that's just great," he said gently slapping his hand on the lad's back.

Jeremy's youthful face beamed. "When I described your work to the regiment doctor, he felt sure you must have been a physician." A sudden inquisitive frown creased his forehead. "Do you by any chance know Arabella?"

Bruce grabbed his arm and placed his hand on back of his neck, "Jeremy, it's a small world."

They hugged.

Arabella rushed over to Bruce, her mind astonishingly mystified. "How is it that *you* know Jeremy, too?"

Jeremy answered her question. "Miss Arabella, this gentleman saved my life; he found me dying with a broken leg."

ARABELLA

Arabella admiringly gazed into Bruce's eyes as she hugged Jeremy. "This man saved my life, too, Jeremy," she smiled with moisture in her eyes.

Arabella hooked each arm into the bend of the two men's elbows as they waltzed over to the fireplace like the three Musketeers. She laid her head on Bruce's shoulder, an arm around the waist of Jeremy with their backsides to the warmth of the fire. As they stood smiling, Julie interrupted the bond of mutual acquaintance.

"What did the Professor have to say?" Julie asked Bruce.

Bruce's hand stroked Arabella's hair. "He says Grant is delighted to attend the wedding with his wife. Nathan Forrest and his wife are due in on the afternoon train." He glanced at the host. "Julie, do you think you can room and board the Forrest's during the wedding?"

Her fingers clasped together and supported her chin. "Why certainly. This old house will come alive again," her aging face gleamed.

Wedding day arrived sooner than anyone expected, and the Potomac house was indeed alive. The entire household of the Potomac house gave Arabella free access to the bathroom for Hattie to get her dressed. Nathan Forrest and his wife were resting in their bedroom, Hattie and Danny Boy were in the kitchen with Julie, and Bruce and Austin were out on the back pouch seated in rocking chairs sipping on tankers of rum.

Hattie left the kitchen and ascended the stair steps. She pleasantly knocked on Arabella's door. Presently the door opened. Arabella stood with dreamy eyes. "What is it, Hattie."

"Miss Bella, dat General Forrest, he wants a word wid ye in dah parlor."

ARABELLA

Confusion melted her thoughts. "Tell him I'll be down in a minute, would you Hattie."

Arabella pinched her cheeks, fussed with her hair, and walked out on the balcony. She leaned over and saw Nathan Forrest entering the parlor. Quickly she descended the steps and strolled to the parlor door, her gown swishing as she walked, the crinolines rustling. Nathan stood by the fireplace his elbow leaning on the mantle, when she entered, a rare grin on his face.

Arabella took his hand. "Thank you for coming, Nathan. I know how busy you must be."

He looked into her familiar face, a woman with an analytical mind and excellent horsemanship, who traveled always in danger gathering valuable information that kept his cavalry in the right place at the right time. She should be decorated as a General, he thought.

He kissed her hand. "My dear Arabella—I see you took my advice and will marry that man."

She pressed his hand against her face. "You are a sweet man, Nathan," she smiled, suddenly realizing he was the father figure she had missed growing up without her father.

He sighed deeply. "I've brought a wedding gift, but I wanted to give it to you personally."

Her pale blue eyes blinked. "How thoughtful, Nathan!"

Nathan gripped a package that sat by his feet, and placed it into her open hands.

"What could it be," she whispered as she laid the package on the sofa, and rapidly ripped off the paper like a kid on her 10th birthday. The contents lay open. Her face was aglow.

"Why Nathan, it's beautiful," replied a startled sigh.

"Hattie spent all night altering the size to fit you," he explained.

She stood stunned, totally taken aback.

A complete Cavalry Confederate uniform lay on the sofa, the pant legs were light blue with a yellow strip rising from the bottom leg to the top, complete with the two rows of evenly spaced seven buttons grouped in pairs lining the chest, leather brads draped on the front, metal CSA belt bucket, riding gloves, and boots, with a French Kepi hat topped with a fussy ostrich feather.

"The hat is patterned after Jeb Stewart's fancy hat, the gloves were donated by Stonewall Jackson's daughter," he announced proudly, pride not for himself, but for Arabella whose admiration had spread from Richmond to Tennessee.

She stood with tears in her eyes as she hugged Nathan. A long moment of memories coursed through both their minds.

He pulled a sword from its scabbard. "Kneel, Arabella Rhett."

She sniffed, gathered her gown, and kneeled. Nathan laid the sword blade on the head of her chestnut hair.

"Arabella Rhett, by the authority granted to me by the Governor of Tennessee, I dub you *aide de camp*. Rise, you are the honorary guest of the Southern States."

She stood and Nathan handed her the sword, the blade in one hand the handle in the other.

They saluted

Arabella cried on his shoulder.

Arabella sat on the window seat upstairs in her bedroom, one leg bent in the seat and her hands resting on her knee supporting her face. Her wedding gift from Nathan Forrest lay on the end of her bed. Distant thoughts drifted to the war.

The winds of war had swept away the family-oriented lifestyle of the South. No more days fishing in the creek barefoot, no watermelons placed in the bubbling stream cooling until the evening meal. No more aunts, uncles, and cousins of three generations eating barbecue on the holidays at the Rhett Estate. Her mind wandered to the wrecked home where she was born, and the day she first met Hattie and Danny Boy. Those days were gone. And then she thought of all that had happened since the day she first met Robert Bruce Taylor. The fond memories stretched a smile on her tired face, and she released her folded hands under her head, and then tilted her gaze out the window.

Outside the window, birds were busily making their nests; in fact, a Robin sat on a forked branch near the window sill. It occurred to her that she might see the birth of newborn birds in the spring. The thought thrust her mind into the future. Suppose she and Bruce had a child, what would they name it? Would it grow up in a world of peace and tranquility, or in a horrible war of brother against brother? She took a deep breath, and raised her head. "For heaven's sake, I hope not," she said aloud, her warm breath fogging the pane. She wondered if she'd live another day, another hour. Then she reflected on Gen. Grant's proposal. Perhaps this new position at the White House would allow them to participate somehow in keeping the peace.

"Oh well," she finally whispered, releasing a deep sigh. "Tomorrow is another day."

Made in the USA
Columbia, SC
16 August 2022